HIGH STAKES EDUCATION

The *Critical Social Thought* Series
edited by Michael W. Apple, University of Wisconsin—Madison

Contradictions of Control: School Structure and School Knowledge
Linda M. McNeil

Working Class without Work: High School Students in a De-industrializing Society
Lois Weis

Social Analysis of Education: After the New Sociology
Philip Wexler

Capitalist Schools: Explanation and Ethics in Radical Studies of Schooling
Daniel P. Liston

Getting Smart: Feminist Research and Pedagogy with/in the Postmodern
Patti Lather

Teacher Education and the Social Conditions of Schooling
Daniel P. Liston and Kenneth M. Zeichner

Race, Identity, and Representation in Education
Warren Crichlow and Cameron McCarthy, editors

Public Schools that Work: Creating Community
Gregory A. Smith, editor

Power and Method: Political Activism and Educational Research
Andrew Gitlin, editor

Critical Ethnography in Educational Research: A Theoretical and Practical Guide
Phil Francis Carspecken

The Uses of Culture: Education and the Limits of Ethnic Affiliation
Cameron McCarthy

Education, Power, and Personal Biography: Dialogues with Critical Educators
Carlos Alberto Torres, editor

Contradictions of School Reform: Educational Costs of Standardized Testing
Linda M. McNeil

Act Your Age! A Cultural Construction of Adolescence
Nancy Lesko

Tough Fronts: The Impact of Street Culture on Schooling
L. Janelle Dance

The State and the Politics of Knowledge
Michael w. Apple with Peter Aasen, Misook Kim Cho, Luis Armando Gandin, Anita Oliver, Youl-Kwan Sung, Hannah Tavares, and Ting-Hong Wong

Political Spectacle and the Fate of American Schools
Mary Lee Smith with Walter Heinecke, Linda Miller-Kahn, and Patricia F. Jarvis

Rethinking Scientific Literacy
Wolff-Michael Roth and Angela Calabrese Barton

High Stakes Education: Inequality, Globalization, and Urban School Reform
Pauline Lipman

Learning to Labor in New Times
Nadine Dolby and Greg Dimitriadis

HIGH STAKES EDUCATION

Inequality, Globalization, and Urban School Reform

Pauline Lipman

ROUTLEDGEFALMER

NEW YORK AND LONDON

Published in 2004 by
RoutledgeFalmer
29 West 35th Street
New York, NY 10001
www.routledge-ny.com

Published in Great Britain by
RoutledgeFalmer
11 New Fetter Lane
London EC4P 4EE
www.routledge.co.uk

RoutledgeFalmer is an imprint of the Taylor and Francis Group.

Printed in the United Stated of America on acid-free paper.

10 9 8 7 6 5 4 3 2 1

Cataloging-in-Publication data is available from the Library of Congress upon request.
Hardback—0-415-93507-5
Paperback—0-415-93508-3

CONTENTS

Acknowledgments   vii

Series Editor's Preface   ix

Chapter 1   Globalization, Economic Restructuring,   1
             and Urban Education

Chapter 2   Chicago School Reform and Its Political,   23
             Economic, and Cultural Context

Chapter 3   Accountability, Social Differentiation,   41
             and Racialized Social Control

Chapter 4   "Like a Hammer Just Knocking Them Down"   71
             Regulating African American Schools

Chapter 5   The Policies and Politics of Cultural Assimilation   105
             Coauthored with Eric Gutstein

Chapter 6   "It's Us versus the Board—The Enemy"   139
             Race, Class, and the Power to Oppose

Chapter 7   Beyond Accountability   169
             Toward Schools that Create New People
             for a New Way of Life

Methodological Appendix   193

Notes   197

References   203

Index   215

ACKNOWLEDGMENTS

This book owes much to the insights, critiques, and advice of many people over the past several years. My biggest debt of gratitude is to Eric (Rico) Gutstein, my partner, intellectual collaborator, comrade, and principal supporter. The work we did on chapter four—from conceptualizing and carrying out the research to analyzing the data and writing and revising was completely joint. But much more, he read the entire manuscript several times and, as usual, zeroed in with uncanny accuracy on my "fuzzy thinking" and missing data and gave me plenty of good advice. (Most of which I followed even when I stubbornly wished I hadn't heard it.) The book is obviously stronger because of his contributions. He also cooked delicious dinners, shared my righteous anger at the injustices we are surrounded by, and otherwise made life hopeful, comforting, and fun.

The teachers in Chicago Teachers for Social Justice have been a source of insight and inspiration as well as solidarity and collective action. Our regular conversations have been a window on the reality of teaching in Chicago public schools: its pressures, tensions, joys, abominations, and triumphs-in-spite-of-everything. I especially want to thank the long-term TSJ core: Jesse Senechal, Lori Huebner, Peg Dunn, Cecily Langford, and Rico Gutstein. Their ideas and experiences echo through this book. A number of other people helped me to understand various aspects of Chicago public school policy. I especially want to acknowledge Julie Woestehoff, Laurence Hadjas, Rebeca de los Reyes, Sonia Soltero, Angela Perez Miller, Carmen Aguilar, Karla Kelly Daye and the many teachers, administrators, and students whose ideas and collaboration were essential.

I began to conceptualize this project as a Senior Fellow in Urban Education at the Annenberg Institute for School Reform. The multiple perspectives and work of the other "Fellows" and our on-going conversations over three years influenced my thinking about this project. Thanks to Christelle Estrada, Gloria Ladson-Billings, Diana Lam, Jabari Mahiri, Jessica Gordon Nembhard, Sonia Nieto, and Val Pang. I also want to thank the Annenberg Institute for the fellowship which helped to support my research over three years. The comments of Elaine Simon, Ken Saltman, and Linda McNeil on various pieces of the book helped me sharpen the analysis and clarify my thinking. Thoughtful conversations with my colleagues and friends at De-Paul, particularly Enora Brown, Stephen Haymes, and Ken Saltman have definitely influenced my thinking. I also appreciate the research assistance and substantive contributions of Patricia Hernandez, Lori Huebner, and Julie Warren. DePaul University Research Council also provided two small research grants that helped to make this work possible.

Finally, I owe Michael Apple a debt of gratitude for his intellectual and political support and his confidence in this project. I am honored that the book is part of Michael's series on Critical Social Thought and feel fortunate to have worked with him on this project. Michael championed the book from the very beginning and consistently encouraged me. His sponsorship was invaluable. Moreover, Michael's own theoretical work has helped to shape and clarify my thinking, and his specific suggestions on the manuscript greatly improved its organization and substance. I also want to thank the editors at Routledge. Joe Miranda was enthusiastic about the book and supportive from the outset. Catherine Bernard shepherded the book through the production process, and her editorial suggestions definitely made the manuscript better. There is so much I still don't know or have probably gotten wrong. Obviously, the faults are my responsibility alone.

Last, I need to acknowledge the love, spirit, and unqualified support of my family who are so much a part of anything I accomplish—Sandi, Jesse, Cristina, Rico—thank you.

Pauline Lipman

Earlier drafts of some portions of the book appeared in the following publications:

Lipman, P. (2002). Making the Global City, Making Inequality: The Political Economy and Cultural Politics of Chicago School Policy. *American Educational Research Journal, 39* (2), 379–419.

Lipman, P. (2003). In K. J. Saltman & D. A. Gabbard (Eds), *Education as Enforcement: The militarization and corporatization of schools* (pp. 81–101). New York: Routledge.

Lipman, P. (2003). Chicago School Policy: Regulating Black and Latino Youth in the Global City. *Race, Ethnicity and Education, 6* (4). http://tandf.co.uk/>http://www.tandf.co.uk

I want to thank the publishers for permission to reprint or use this material in revised form.

SERIES EDITOR'S PREFACE

For anyone who has taught or worked in inner city schools, Pauline Lipman's book will be a powerful reminder of the realities that confront educators, students, parents, and activists in these communities every day. For me, it brought back memories that were both compelling and sometimes painful. I began my teaching career in the schools of a decaying urban neighborhood in the largely poor and working-class city in which I had grown up. These were the schools I, too, had attended. For me, reading *High Stakes Education* in many ways was like returning to these schools, reliving the experiences I had as both a student and a teacher there.

In *Educating the "Right" Way* (Apple, 2001), I tell the story of one of these experiences, a story about one of my students, a sensitive but at times troubled boy named Joseph. I want to retell it here since it speaks to what Pauline Lipman has accomplished in this book.

> Joseph sobbed at my desk. He was a tough kid, a hard case, someone who often made life difficult for his teachers. He was all of nine years old and here he was sobbing, holding on to me in public. He had been in my fourth grade class all year, a classroom situated in a decaying building in an east coast city that was among the most impoverished in the nation. There were times when I wondered, seriously, whether I would make it through that year. There were many Josephs in that classroom and I was constantly drained by the demands, the bureaucratic rules, the daily lessons that bounced off of the kids' armor. Yet somehow it was satisfying, compelling, and important, even though the prescribed curriculum and the textbooks that were meant to teach it were often beside the point. They were boring to the kids and boring to me.
>
> I should have realized the first day what it would be like when I opened that city's "Getting Started" suggested lessons for the first few days and it began

with the suggestion that "as a new teacher" I should circle the students' desks and have them introduce each other and tell something about themselves. It's not that I was against this activity; it's just that I didn't have enough unbroken desks (or even chairs) for all of the students. A number of the kids had nowhere to sit. This was my first lesson—but certainly not my last—in understanding that the curriculum and those who planned it lived in an unreal world, a world *fundamentally* disconnected from my life with those children in that inner city classroom.

But here's Joseph. He's still crying. I've worked extremely hard with him all year long. We've eaten lunch together; we've read stories; we've gotten to know each other. There are times when he drives me to despair and other times when I find him to be among the most sensitive children in my class. I just can't give up on this kid. He's just received his report card and it says that he is to repeat fourth grade. The school system has a policy that states that failure in any two subjects (including the "behavior" side of the report card) requires that the student be left back. Joseph was failing "gym" and arithmetic. Even though he had shown improvement, he had trouble keeping awake during arithmetic, had done poorly on the mandatory city-wide tests, and hated gym. One of his parents worked a late shift and Joseph would often stay up, hoping to spend some time with her. And the things that students were asked to do in gym were, to him, "lame."

The thing is, he had made real progress during the year. But I was instructed to keep him back. I knew that things would be worse next year. There would still not be enough desks. The poverty in that community would still be horrible; and health care and sufficient funding for job training and other services would be diminished. I knew that the jobs that were available in this former mill town paid deplorable wages and that even with both of his parents working for pay, Joseph's family income was simply insufficient. I also knew that, given all that I already had to do each day in that classroom and each night at home in preparation for the next day, it would be nearly impossible for me to work any harder than I had already done with Joseph. And there were another 5 children in that class whom I was supposed to leave back.

So Joseph sobbed. Both he and I understood what this meant. There would be no additional help for me—or for children such as Joseph—next year. The promises would remain simply rhetorical. Words would be thrown at the problems. Teachers and parents and children would be blamed. But the school system would look like it believed in and enforced higher standards. The structuring of economic and political power in that community and that state would again go on as "business as usual."

The next year Joseph basically stopped trying. The last time I heard anything about him was that he was in prison.

The personal account I have related here speaks to what might be called a history of the present, a present so well illuminated in *High Stakes Education*. An unyielding demand—perhaps best represented in George W. Bush's policies found in *No Child Left Behind*—for testing, reductive models of accountability, standardization, and strict control over pedagogy and curricula is now the order of the day in schools throughout the country. In urban schools in particular, these policies have been seen as not one alternative, but the *only* option. In many ways, reforms of this type serve as a "political spectacle" rather than as a serious and well thought out set of policy initiatives that deal honestly with the depth of the problems now being faced in schools throughout the nation (Smith, et al., in press). In fact, we are now increasingly aware of a number of the negative and even truly damaging effects of such policies (see, e.g., Apple, 2001; McNeil, 2001; Gillborn & Youdell, 2000). Joseph's story is now being retold in the lives of thousands of children caught in underfunded schools. The global restructuring of markets, of paid and unpaid labor, of housing and health care, of communities large and small and so much more—all of this is having differential effects in terms of race and class and gender. And all of this has had profound effects on the financing and governance of schools, on what is to count as "official knowledge" and "good" teaching, and ultimately on the many Josephs who walk through the halls of the schools of our cities.

This is not only happening in education. In his history of the dismantling of the crucial social and economic programs that enabled many of our fellow citizens to have a chance at a better life, Michael Katz argued that current economic and social policy has "stratified Americans into first- and second-class citizens and has undermined the effective practice of democracy" (Katz, 2001, p. 2).

We cannot understand what has happened unless we connect this to transformations in urban political economies. The social and labor structures of large cities have, in essence, split into "two vastly unequal but intimately linked economies." These economies are intimately linked because jobs that are less well paid, nonunionized, often part time, and with few benefits are required to make urban life attractive to the affluent. This is due not only to an increasingly globalized corporate sector that pits the workers of one nation against those of another and demands ever lower taxes no matter what the social costs to local communities, although such factors are indeed crucial parts of any serious explanation. It is also due to the needs of affluent urban workers "who have created lifestyles that depend on a large pool of low wage workers." In Katz's words again, the result is a new "servant class." "Like corporations, affluent urbanites have outsourced their domestic tasks for much the same reasons of economy and flexibility and with much the same results"—poverty wages and an often heartbreaking exposure to the risks associated with no health care, no insurance, no unions, no child care, and no social benefits (Katz, 2001, p. 37).

Yet, class relations do not totally cover the reasons for this situation. The political economy of race enters in absolutely crucial ways. As Charles

Mills reminds us, underpinning so much of the social structure of American life is an unacknowledged *racial contract* (Mills, 1997). Current neoliberal and neoconservative policies in almost every sphere of society have differential and racializing effects. Although they are often couched in the language of "helping the poor," increasing accountability, giving "choice," and so on, the racial structuring of their outcomes is painful to behold in terms of respectable jobs (or lack of them), in health care, in education, and in so much more. For reasons of economy, health, education, nutrition, and so on, for black children, the American city is often a truly dangerous place not only for their present but for their future as well (Katz, 2001, pp. 43–44). Yet we then ask the school to compensate for all of this.

High Stakes Education provides a detailed examination of what the effects of the dismantling and reconstruction of urban political economies and social networks are on schools in one city, especially on schools that serve poor children of color. Yet, it is much more than a case study, since that city is Chicago. Chicago school reforms have served as a model for the kinds of programs that many cities both inside the United States and beyond its borders are undertaking. Because of this a detailed critical examination of some of the less talked about and hidden effects of widely emulated school reforms is absolutely essential for educators throughout the nation and the industrialized world. Pauline Lipman shows what actually happens to teachers and children when policies involving strict accountability, massive amounts of testing, and similar practices are instituted. The results are striking and should raise serious questions in the mind of all of those who believe that in these sets of policies we have found *the* answers to the problems that beset our schools.

Yet *High Stakes Education* does not end with uncovering the often hidden negative effects of policies that are so reminiscent of *No Child Left Behind*. It also provides hope for a better future by suggesting a more progressive way of envisioning urban schooling. When connected with the rich accounts of successful and socially just school reforms elsewhere (see, e.g., Apple, et al., 2003; Apple & Beane, 1995), this combination—critique and hope—makes this book essential reading for anyone who cares about the future of American education.

Michael W. Apple
John Bascom Professor of
Curriculum and Instruction
   and Educational Policy Studies
University of Wisconsin, Madison

CHAPTER 1

Globalization, Economic Restructuring, and Urban Education

To me it just seems obvious that guiding kids in the process of becoming lifelong critical thinkers, learners, readers, leaders and participants for change is not related and cannot be "measured" on a standardized test bereft of context. My goals (and the goals of my colleagues, too, I think) are so entirely different from the "goals" of the Chicago Board of Education. My instinct is to extrapolate the issues here across the country. These tests are part of a process that produces / cultivates non-thinkers, rote learners, "cogs in wheels." If the ultimate goal of education in the U.S. is to maintain the status quo and create workers to fill needs in our economy then [these policies] are succeeding.
(Teacher testimony, Chicago Teachers for Social Justice,
Policy Forum on High Stakes Testing, November 11, 2000)

African American students and Latino/a students are under-represented in the "college prep track" and over-represented in the "military prep track" and the "prison prep track"
(Generation Y, youth activist organization,
"Tracking in Chicago Public Schools," October 2002)

Where will they go, these poverty-level Chicagoans, mostly black, once invisible in the ghettos, but now inconvenient in the Global City? Probably farther out, into the fringe suburbs, beyond the reach of the global economy.
(Longworth, *Chicago Tribune*, August 25, 2002, p. 8)

These reflections represent the intersection of education policy, the economy, race, globalization, and the city. This book is an effort to examine this intersection. Chicago—the city and its schools, its politics, its economy, its history—is my point of reference. My analysis homes in on this city and its educational policies, but Chicago also epitomizes broad national and international educational trends. In an industrial age it was the city of big shoulders. In the era of big city political machines, the Chicago Democratic machine was canonical. So too are its current school policies. In an era of accountability, high stakes testing, and centralized regulation and militarization of schools, Chicago's school policies are paradigmatic. Through an examination of the political, economic, and cultural dimensions of Chicago school policy, I intend to open a window on the implications of policies that are reshaping education in the United States and in other countries as well.

In 1987, U.S. Secretary of Education, William Bennett visited Chicago and pronounced its schools "the worst in the nation." Bennett chose Chicago public schools to level a charge against urban school districts nationally and to promote his own policy agenda, blaming public schools for the loss of U.S. economic dominance and lobbying for a return to basic skills and "rigor." Just a year later, Chicago again captured national attention with its 1988 School Reform Law, a radical effort to shift some decisions from the school district bureaucracy to local communities and schools. In yet another twist, in 1995 the Illinois State Legislature turned over control of the city's schools to Chicago's mayor, Richard M. Daley. Daley promptly installed a corporatist regime focused on high stakes tests, standards, accountability, and centralized regulation of teachers and schools. These reforms were layered over the "democratic localism" (Bryk, Sebring, Kerbow, Rollow, & Easton, 1998) of the 1988 reform. In an ironic echo of Bennet's earlier pronouncement, in 1998, President Clinton dramatically hailed Chicago's 1995 school reform as "a model for the nation."

Chicago has become a standard bearer for high stakes testing and school accountability, for centralized regulation of teachers and schools, and, less publicly, for increasingly stratified schooling experiences, including the militarization of schooling alongside new, highly selective college preparatory programs (Lipman, 2002). The policies driving the 1995 reform have become the hallmark of big city schools nationally and typify key features of neoliberal education policies in the United Kingdom, Australia, and elsewhere (e.g., Apple, 2001; Ball, 1994; Coffey, 2001; Gillborn & Youdell, 2000; Whitty, Power, & Halpin 1998). Indeed, much of what Chicago's mayor and school district heads have done since 1995 provided a model for George W. Bush's *No Child Left Behind* (2001)—the policy shaping U.S. education at the beginning of the twenty-first century. In short, Chicago has been both a barometer of the state of urban education in the United States and a place to which reformers have turned for lessons on how to change urban schools. For this reason, it has also been a focus of research and changing perspectives on urban education in the United States (e.g.,

Bryk et al., 1998; Hess, 1991; Homel, 1984; Katz, 1992; Katz, Fine, & Simon, 1997; Peterson, 1976; Shipps, 1997; Wrigley, 1982).

Yet, through all the publicity about Chicago's rising test scores and research on outcomes (e.g., Bryk et al., 1998; Roderick, Byrk, Jacob, Easton, & Allensworth, 1999), there is little critical examination of the genesis of these policies; whose interests they serve; their social implications, or their meanings for teachers, communities, and, most of all, the nearly one half million students in Chicago Public Schools, 90 percent of whom are students of color and 84 percent of whom are classified as low income. Front page headlines tell a story about "a vastly improving system," about introduction of order and accountability to chaotic, failing schools. But there has been little attention to what the policies mean for the moral and intellectual life of teachers and students and the social implications of those meanings. There is another story, a story about discouragement and despair, about coercion and disempowerment, about individual blame and disciplined subjectivities, about race and class inequality, and about challenges to these realities. This story is embedded in a larger narrative of globalization and social and economic polarization, of urban displacement and exclusion. This book is an attempt to uncover these converging, and submerged, stories.

Chicago is a concentrated expression of the contradictions of wealth and poverty, centrality and marginality, that typify globalization and its implications in the economy and the cultural politics of race and space in the city. Using Chicago as a case study, in *High Stakes Education* I argue there is a strategic relationship between these economic and social processes and the regime of accountability and educational differentiation governing schools. Contrary to the discourse of equity and the common sense that have been constructed around these policies, I argue that they exacerbate existing educational and social inequalities and contribute to new ones. Drawing on case studies of schools and school district data, I contend that accountability and the centralized regulation of schools and teachers sharpen disparities in curriculum and teaching, widening the gap between schools serving low-income students of color and schools serving mixed- and high-income populations. I also suggest that current policies undermine efforts to help students develop tools of social critique and culturally centered identities that can help them survive and challenge the new inequalities. As students' opportunities to learn and the nature of school knowledge are further differentiated by race, ethnicity, and class, public schooling is contributing to the production of identities closely aligned with the highly stratified workforce of the restructured economy. I also contend that accountability and differentiated schooling concretely and symbolically support the spatial "repolarization" (Smith, 1996) of the

city. This restructuring of urban space is linked to globalization and benefits downtown development and neighborhood gentrification at the expense of working-class communities and communities of color.

I argue that education policies are deeply implicated in a cultural politics
directed to regulating and containing African American and some Latino/a
youth and their communities. They support the policing and exclusion of
youth who have been made superfluous in the new economy and undesir-
able in the public space of the city. Although the policies have led to certain
improvements in some schools and have created additional opportunities
for a small percentage of students, as a whole, they reproduce and intensify
economic and social inequality and racial exclusion and containment.
What is at stake are not only the educational experiences and life chances of
students, but the kind of city and the kind of society we will have.

Chicago school "reform" is a sobering lens through which to view the
implications of Bush's national education agenda of accountability and
high stakes tests and the ground it lays for the privatization of education
when public schools fail. However, I also want to demonstrate through the
Chicago case that any critique of accountability policies must address, in
Gramsci's (1971) terms, the "good sense" in the policies. Support for these
policies needs to be examined, in part, in relation to the organic connections they make with people's daily lives. Understanding this good sense,
and the conditions in which it is rooted, is a crucial aspect of framing alternative educational policy and practice that respond to real problems and
lived experiences. This reinforces the importance of public dialogue that
includes the full participation of those who have been most affected by
urban schools—families, students, and communities of color and committed teachers. Because the hegemony of current policies also represents the
triumph of an agenda that has been constructed as the only alternative to
"the failed policies of the past," creating a viable alternative is all the more
urgent.

In this book, I examine education policy in the context of a constellation of economic, political, and cultural processes linked to globalization
as it unfolds in a major urban context. These include Chicago's restructured, information economy; its drive to become a global city; its urban
development and gentrification; and its new urban geography of centrality
and marginality along lines of race, ethnicity, and social class. I am concerned with systemwide, or macrolevel, dimensions of official policies and
microlevel meanings, how they are experienced by teachers, students, and
principals in schools. Although I focus on the role of capital and the class
interests embedded in Chicago school reforms, I "foreground race as an
explanatory tool for the persistence of inequality" (Ladson-Billings, 1997,
p. 132). I am interested in concrete consequences of policy and in its ideo-

logical force—the ways in which policy discourses shape consciousness about education, specific social groups, and the role of social policy in relation to the common good. In the remaining sections of this chapter, I lay out the political and economic situation underlying the dominant policy agenda, discuss my approach to policy, and briefly describe my research. I conclude with an overview of the book.

Urban Education, Political Economy, and Cultural Politics of Race

The persistent failure of urban schools and repeated efforts to change them have shaped much of the debate about education policy in the United States over the past forty years. The issues have remained stubbornly constant: inadequate funding and resources, unequal educational opportunities, high dropout rates and low academic achievement, student alienation, racial segregation, and race and class inequality within and among urban schools. These failures have, in part, been a product of the evolving crises of cities themselves. Poverty and race have been at the center of these crises, beginning with white, middle-class flight and urban disinvestment in the 1950s. Poverty, urban neglect, and racial isolation were compounded by deindustrialization and further disinvestment in central cities in the 1970s and 1980s and by reduction in federal funding for social programs for the poor beginning in the 1980s (Rury & Mirel, 1997). In the 1990s, the revitalization and gentrification of some urban areas and neglect of others and the highly stratified informational economy widened the gap between rich and poor. This has occurred in ways that are racialized (i.e., white vs. Black and Latino/a), intraracial (i.e., African-American and Latino/a professionals vs. low-income African Americans and Latinos/as) and differentially experienced by various ethnicities and immigrant groups (Bettancur & Gills, 2000). At the same time, intersections of racial oppression and social class and inequities between urban and suburban schools and among city schools have demonstrated the continuing importance of social class in U.S. education. Urban schools remain deeply embedded in these multiple and intersecting inequalities. My analysis of these inequalities begins with the broad social situation—the ensemble of social relations that are shaped by global, national, and local political-economic structures and ideological forces (see Gill, 2003).

Globalization, Global Cities, and Education Policy

> It is impossible to examine education reform in the United States without taking into account continuing forces of globalization and the progressive diversion of capital into financial and speculative channels. (McLaren, 1999, p. 20)

Globalization, a much discussed and contested concept, is at the center of my analysis.[1] My focus is on economic globalization—the global connection of markets, production sites, capital investment, and related processes of labor migration. The world economy over the past thirty years has been defined by mobility of capital nationally and transnationally (Sassen, 1994) and the dramatic contrast between wealth and poverty within nations and on a global scale. "It is this hypermobility of capital that distinguishes the current phase of globalization from that of earlier eras. Against this backdrop, the divide between the global rich and the regional and local poor has never been so great" (Rizvi & Lingard, 2000, p. 420).

At the heart of globalization are the technological capacity to generate knowledge and process information at increasing speeds and efficiencies, a highly integrated and flexible system of production of goods and services built on the global reorganization of the labor process and transnational circuits of labor, and the worldwide primacy of finance and speculative capital (Castells, 1989, 1998; Sassen, 1994). These forces have generated massive transnational movements of money, commodities, and cultures, and a new global division of labor. They are destabilizing populations on a national as well as an international level, setting in motion transnational migrations and circuits of labor, and literally changing the face of national populations. They have also created greater economic integration of national economies and increasing concentrations of power in supranational political bodies such as the World Trade Organization, World Bank, and International Monetary Fund (Burbules & Torres, 2000). Contrary to official applause for the "benefits" of the market and its web of global economic connections, under the global regime of capitalist accumulation, the economic processes and policies associated with globalization are magnifying existing inequalities and creating new ones. They are accelerating the devastation of the environment and the liquidation of languages, cultures, and peoples. The results are a widening global chasm between rich and poor countries, rich and poor regions, and rich and poor people and a steady degradation of life for the vast majority of the world's people (Korten, 1995; Mander & Goldsmith, 1996).

The economic, political, and cultural dimensions of cities are increasingly shaped by these processes. As Feagin (1998) points out, the development of cities is partly shaped by their transnational economic linkages, particularly their connections with the global capitalist economy, dominant transnational companies, and processes of economic restructuring. The new international division of labor, characterized by the shift in the world market for labor and for production sites, is having a profound effect on cities across the globe. The exodus of displaced populations of workers and peasants in some countries is producing increased immigration and cultural diversity in cities like Chicago thousands of miles away. Closing of plants in and around cities in core industrial nations is linked with export of production to Asia, Latin America, and parts of Africa. Disinvestment and unemployment in one urban area are linked with increased investment in another. While some cities or urban sectors have become rusty hulks, reminders of past industrial might, others have emerged as high-tech centers and regions of post-industrial growth. As capitalism is restructured globally, some cities are driven to the margins of the global economy while others fight for position as command centers of that economy (Sassen, 1994). These new inequalities among and within cities, coupled with dramatic demographic changes, have important implications for urban schools and for school policy.

Saskia Sassen (1994) has argued that simultaneous processes of global dispersal of economic activities and global economic integration, under conditions of increasingly concentrated ownership and control, have given cities renewed importance. She argues in this context that "global cities" take on a strategic role as command centers of the global economy (p. 4). Global cities are central marketplaces of global finance, major sites for the production of innovations central to the informational economy, and places where global systems of production are organized and managed. These metropolitan centers require large numbers of highly paid professionals (e.g., corporate lawyers, advertising heads, financial analysts, corporate directors) and concentrations of low-wage workers—immigrants, women, people of color—to service the corporate and financial centers and the leisure and personal needs of highly paid professionals. Paradigmatic global cities include New York, London, Tokyo, São Paulo, Paris, Hong Kong, and Mexico City. In the United States, Los Angeles and Chicago have also been described as global cities (Abu-Lughod, 1999).

Thus, global cities are the strategic terrain on which the contradictions of wealth and poverty, power and marginalization that typify globalization are played out (Sassen, 1998). "We see here an interesting correspondence between great concentrations of corporate power and large concentrations of 'others'" (Sassen, 1994, p. 123). The new immigrants are products of U.S. military interventions as well as global capital's worldwide disruption of local economies and traditional agricultural production. "This global dislocation comes to roost in the 'Third Worlding' of the U.S. city" (Smith, 1996). Terrible economic disparities are paralleled by new forms of social segregation and dislocation and glaring contrasts in the use of, and access to, urban space (Castells, 1989). One striking manifestation is the built environment of global cities which has been, and continues to be, reshaped by massive investment in gentrification and downtown development. These developments both are produced by and contribute to processes of globalization. As global capital floods the real estate market it fuels development. And the influx of high-paid workers at the nerve centers of the global economy creates a massive market for upscale residential and leisure spaces built out of, and over, the homes and factories and neighborhoods of former industrial workforces. The new luxury living and recreation spaces become gated security zones, policed and controlled to ensure the "safety" of their new occupants and global tourists against the presence of menacing "others," particularly disenfranchised youth of color who increasingly have no place in the new economy and refashioned city. "Evicted from the public as well as the private spaces of what is fast becoming a downtown bourgeois playground, minorities, the unemployed and the poorest of the working class are destined for large-scale displacement" (Smith, 1996, p. 28). But new immigrations, coupled with economic and social polarization, also give rise to new contests over culture, language, representation, and place. Sassen (1998) argues that at the same time that immigrants and people of color are politically and economically marginalized, the city becomes a "strategic site for disempowered actors because it enables them to gain presence, emerge as subjects even when they do not attain power" (p. xxi). In Chicago and elsewhere, the drive to become a first-rate global city—with all its contradictions—shapes the social landscape on which the trends and tensions of education policy are played out.

Indeed, education policy has been explicitly tied to global economic competitiveness as the fluidity of investment capital and the global competition for investments and markets have dominated more and more aspects of social life in cities and nations. "Education policy is now often conceptualized as a central plank of national economic planning—the skills of a nation's people being an important factor in attracting peripatetic capital to a specific place" (Rizvi & Lingard, 2000, pp. 423–24). On a world scale, this trend is reflected in the setting of educational standards for developing countries by global capitalist bodies, such as the World Bank, in order to promote an integrated world economy along market lines (Jones, 2000). In the United States, education is being linked directly to the economy through school-to-work programs, the "new" basic skills (working collaboratively, solving problems, improving reading and math skills), and the revitalization of vocational education (Murnane & Levy, 1996; Olson, 1997). Ideologically it is linked through "human capital development" and discourses that define education as workforce preparation (Morrow & Torres, 2000; National Center on Education and the Economy,

1990; Reich, 1991). This "economizing education" (Ozga, 2000) and the emphasis on standards and testing are eroding the concept of education for participation in democracy (McNeil, 2002). Morrow and Torres (2000) summarize this danger: "The overall effect is to shift education toward competence-based skills at the expense of the more fundamental forms of critical competence required for autonomous learning and active citizenship" (p. 47).

Global economic integration and transnational flows of information and culture have also led to more rapid "policy borrowing" (Blackmore, 2000). This is apparent in the convergence of neoliberal[2] policy frameworks in the United Kingdom, Australia, the United States, New Zealand, and elsewhere (see, for example, Burbules & Torres, 2000; Gabbard, 2000; Lingard & Rizvi, 2000; Mickelson, 2000; Stromquist & Monkman, 2000; Taylor & Henry, 2000; Walters, 1997). Chicago's education policies reflect two complementary, though seemingly contradictory, aspects of these frameworks. One is decentralized management (through devolution, school-based management, decentralized governance, Ball, 1994) and opening up of schooling to the market (through school choice, privatization, and direct corporate involvement, Saltman, 2000; Whitty et al., 1998). The other is strong state regulation through centralized regimes of testing, monitoring, and accountability. This trend is reflected in standards, national testing, accountability, and centralized regulation of teachers and curriculum. Framed by the neoliberal discourses of efficiency and quality, these measures are designed to codify, monitor, and rationalize teaching and learning to serve global economic competition (Apple, 2001; Ball, 1994; Gillborn & Youdell, 2000). Since the mid-1980's, nearly every large U.S. school district has adopted some version of accountability and/or market-driven reforms. As in business, the bottom line is a quantitative measure of productivity and success, that is, performance on standardized tests. Bush's *No Child Left Behind* (2001) legislation, Clinton's *Goals 2000*, and Chicago's 1988 and 1995 school reform laws exemplify aspects of these trends.

Economic Restructuring and Education Policy

Global economic expansion and the shift from manufacturing to a service, recreation, and consumption economy in advanced industrial countries have led to a dramatic recomposition of the U.S. labor force. This has had profound implications for economic inequality and, as I shall argue, for education policies. Sanjek (1998) describes the situation succinctly: "The new jobs that appeared during the Reagan years came mainly in two varieties: high-skill, high-pay and low-skill, low-pay. A vast recomposition of the U.S. labor market was under way" (p. 124). The worldwide economic crisis of 1973–74 also precipitated the capitalist drive to undermine the power of labor and achieve greater labor flexibility for a rapidly shifting global market (Castells, 1989). The sweeping effects of these policies are felt in the sustained reversal of real wage gains and health and pension benefits and a dramatic increase in labor subcontracting and part-time and temporary labor. They are also reflected in the rapid growth of the unregulated informal economy (e.g., sweatshops). New labor arrangements pay substandard wages with subminimal health and safety standards. Combined with outright union busting in the 1980s and 1990s, these trends have threatened the wages, benefits, and job security of the salaried and industrial workforce as a whole. As a result, despite increases in earnings at the top of the wages and income scale, the majority of new jobs have lower wages and less social protection than in the recent past (Castells, 1989, 1996; Sanjek, 1998; Sassen, 1994). Salaries of M.B.A.'s have surged, for example, while new jobs have fewer health care and retirement benefits and lower vacation and sick pay benefits. The great majority of the workers in the new low-wage and contingent workforce are immigrants, people of color, and women.

The new labor force is highly segmented and increasingly polarized, a result of the following trends (Castells, 1989, 1996; Sassen, 1994):

a. There is a decrease in basic manufacturing and a shift in its labor structure, with an increase in jobs held by professionals and technicians and a decrease in jobs held by operatives. The downgraded manufacturing sector (e.g., sweatshops, industrial homework, subcontracting) has expanded, and unionized industrial labor with social benefits has declined.

b. There is a massive increase in service jobs that are highly segmented by wages and salaries, education, and benefits with a fast rate of growth in both high-skilled technical, professional, and managerial jobs at the upper end (held primarily by white males) and low-skilled, low-wage jobs at the lower end (held primarily by women and people of color). However, the majority of new jobs are concentrated in low-skilled, low-paid occupations demanding low levels of education (e.g., custodians, clerks, cashiers, waiters).

c. There is a proliferation of contingent labor—part-time and temporary work done mainly by women, people of color, and immigrants working two, three, even four jobs.[3]

d. There is a rapidly growing informal economy employing primarily immigrant and women workers who produce specialized consumer goods and services for the affluent and low-cost goods and services for low-income families.

e. A sector of the potential workforce, mainly African-American and Latino/a youth, can find little work at all in the formal economy.[4]

In short, the result of simultaneous processes of upgrading, downgrading, and exclusion of labor is a workforce that is highly stratified by class, race, national origin, and gender (Castells, 1989).

Although there are variations among firms, regions, and economic sectors, these general trends reinforce race and class polarization and underlie the reality that the traditional working-class road to an improved standard of living—well-paying industrial jobs with benefits and a modicum of security—no longer exists (Newman, 1988). In this context, economic growth is contributing to greater inequality rather than to an increase in the middle class, as in the post–World War II economy (Sassen, 1994; Wolf, 1995).[5] In this new "dual America," the ratio of total chief executive officer (CEO) pay to total worker pay grew from 44.8 times in 1973 to 172.5 times in 1995 while real, average weekly earnings for production and nonsupervisory workers dropped from $479.44 to $395.37 (Castells, 1998, p. 130). There is also increasing polarization of wealth as the richest 1 percent of households increased their marketable wealth by 28.3 percent from 1983 to 1992 while that of the bottom 40 percent declined by 49.7 percent (Wolf, 1996).

In this context, who has access to what knowledge is critical. Although educational stratification is nothing new, tiering of educational experiences and opportunities takes on new meaning in the present context. Knowledge has become far more definitive in shaping one's life chances than in the past, when a high school diploma was sufficient to gain entry to a well-paying, stable job and sense of future.[6] In the informational economy, knowledge is central, and one's education is a key determinant of whether one will be a high-paid knowledge worker or part of the downgraded sector of labor. Flecha (1999) summarizes the implications:

> The prioritizing of intellectual resources in the information society means that cultural factors have great importance. . . . As a consequence of the dual model of society, education . . . is becoming an increasingly important criterion for determining who joins which group. The educational curriculum, therefore, has become a factor in the process of social dualization, the selection of the fittest. (p. 66)

At the same time, privatization and the intrusion of the market are challenging the very viability of public education. The struggle over the direction of education policy is not only a question of who is being prepared for what roles in the economy and society, but of how we define the purpose of education and the kind of society we want to be.

Challenging Discourses of Inevitability

Although globalization and economic restructuring have erected a new set of constraints on education, these constraints are not absolute. "[E]conomic structures set limits on possible forms of politics and ideological structures, and make some of these possible forms more likely than others, but they do not rigidly determine in a mechanistic manner any given form of political and ideological relations" (Wright quoted in Ball, 1990, p. 13). Policy responses are conditioned by the relative strength and mobilization of social forces (e.g., organizations of civil society, working-class organizations, popular social movements) and the political culture of specific contexts. Education policy itself is part of the ideological environment that supports or contests global trends to deepen economic and social polarization and the immiseration of the majority.

This perspective challenges the prevailing "truth" that capitalist globalization and neoliberal social policies are necessary and inevitable. "Everywhere we hear it said, all day long—and this is what gives the dominant discourse its strength—that there is nothing to put forward in opposition to the neoliberal view, that it has succeeded in presenting itself as self-evident" (Bourdieu quoted in Hursh, 2001, p. 3). In fact, globalization and its consequences are deeply contested (Preteceille, 1990). Comparisons of state policies at local and national levels reveal differing responses to global economic pressures and long-term trends in the restructuring of the economy with quite different implications for economic and social polarization in cities (see Logan & Swanstrom, 1990; Ferman, 1996). For example, internationally this is reflected in a comparison of democratic economic and social policies in Brazilian cities under the leadership of the Workers Party (Gandin & Apple, 2003) versus neoliberal policies in Argentina. Education policy is also the product of specific economic and social agendas rather than a necessary outgrowth of an inevitable global economic and social order. Although neoliberal social policy is presented as the inexorable result of the logic of economic imperatives, it is in fact the result of an "ideological convergence—most notable in the English-speaking world—upon neoliberal educational recipes as a specific response to globalization and international competition" (Morrow & Torres, 2000, p. 45). Contention over urban education policy is thus part of the larger struggle over the direction of globalization. Unveiling the global political and economic interests at work in shaping local policies is an important foundation of analysis and critique for the development of alternative educational policies.

Policy and Policy Analysis—Theories and Methods

My analysis borrows from the critical policy scholarship of Grace (1984), Ozga (2000), Ball (1990, 1997b), and others. Grace (1984) defines "critical policy scholarship" as theoretically and socially situated and generative of critical social action (p. 41). This contrasts with the dominant trend in policy analysis, "policy science," which brackets out history and social context and focuses on the "technical and immediately realizable" within-the-system solutions (p. 32). Critical policy scholarship is built on the premise that policy is an expression of values arising out of specific social contexts and relations of power. It "represents a view that a social–historical approach to research can illuminate these cultural and ideological struggles in which schooling is located" (Grace quoted in Ball, 1997b, p. 264). It recognizes the centrality of power in policy and policy making and is grounded in a commitment to transform unjust social relations.

> The personal values and political commitment of the critical policy analyst would be anchored in the vision of a moral order in which justice, equality and individual freedom are uncompromised by the avarice of a few. The critical analyst would endorse political, social and economic arrangements where persons are never treated as means to an end, but treated as ends in their own right. (Prunty quoted in Ball, 1990, p. 2)

Multiple Dimensions of Policy

No decent analysis of urban education can ignore the ways in which urban education systems are shaped by the local and national political economy and the role of the state (Anyon, 1997; Rury & Mirel, 1997). To tackle this question I draw on critical urban sociological perspectives on the role of race and class domination in the development of U.S. cities and urban policy (Feagin, 1998; Feagin & Smith, 1987; Harvey, 1973; Haymes, 1995; Logan & Molotch, 1987; Logan & Swanstrom, 1990). In a world that is being reshaped by globalization, this analysis also needs to take into account the role that global economic and cultural forces play in shaping social policy and cities themselves. Recent theoretical and empirical work focusing on the effects of capitalist restructuring and globalization on cities and the role of cities in the global economy (e.g., Abu-Lughod, 1999; Castells, 1989, 1998; Sassen, 1994, 1998; Smith, 1996) provides a deeper understanding of the economic and cultural processes that are generating new inequalities and new challenges for urban education. This scholarship foregrounds the significance of race, including new forms of racialization, as well as social class in the reshaping of cities. These issues are central to the relationship of education policy and the evolving political economy of cities.

An understanding of how the state works is critical to an analysis of how economic and political power and authority are enacted through education and how social movements around education can challenge arrangements of domination and exploitation. At the core of this understanding is a recognition that the state—governmental bodies, agencies, bureaus, commissions, and organizations at all levels—is neither monolithic nor fixed. As Apple (1996; 2003) has noted (following Gramsci, 1971), the state is "in formation," a site of struggle and shifting compromises among competing interests within the state and between the state and civil society. "State formation typically involves the appearance or the reorganization of monopolies over the means of violence, taxation, administration, and *over symbolic systems* [emphasis original]. In essence, state formation is about the creation, stabilization, and normalization of relations of power and authority" (Apple, 1996, p. 43). This leads us to look at how the alignment and realignment of social forces shape and redefine policy, and how conflicting interests within the state produce differing, even conflicting policies.

In the United States, dominant interests convince the vast majority of people to accept massive social inequality and unequal power relations through processes of cultural hegemony—the construction of "commonsense" understandings, or taken-for-granted assumptions, about social reality that legitimate the social order (Gramsci, 1971; see also Apple, 2003). Hegemony works to impose a particular understanding of social problems and to define the parameters of possible alternatives so as to limit the possibility of thinking otherwise. In this way social inequality and unequal relations of power are legitimated, normalized, and perceived as inevitable. However, because dominant ways of seeing the world conflict with people's real experiences and competing ideologies hegemony is never secure and must be continually reconstructed. The theory of cultural hegemony ties cultural struggles, contests over meaning, conflicting ideologies, political perspectives, and discourses to struggles over social inequality (see Apple, 2003). Conflict over policy is just such a contest about who gets to define social agendas, how they are defined, and what alternatives are presented as viable. In this context, education is an important arena in which dominant interests seek to further their social and political agendas by presenting them as the common interest. This is apparent in the alignment of education systems with the new capitalist economy (a topic I take up again in subsequent chapters) and in the promotion of neoliberal and neoconservative education policies in numerous countries. The theory of cultural hegemony leads us to look closely at how policy discourses are linked to economic, political, and cultural interests and their role in shaping public perspectives on education and wider social agendas. This is not to say that force is *not* used as a form of rule. In periods of social unrest that challenge the existing order or specific ruling class interests the state employs the naked power of the police, military, hired thugs, and prisons. In some communities of color, the repressive force of the state is a daily reality. The legitimation of force can also be an element of policy, as I will suggest.

As Stephen Ball (1994) argues, policy as a power-producing and reproducing social practice operates on multiple levels and dimensions and cannot be limited to the role of the state. Policy is "a set of technologies and practices which are realized and struggled over in local settings. Policy is both text and action, words and deeds, it is what is enacted as well as what is intended" (p.10). In one sense, policies are the official rules or regulations promulgated by various levels of the state to regulate educational practice. Ball conceptualizes policy in this sense as "text" that is "coded" and "decoded" in complex ways. Policy texts are "read" by teachers, principals, and administrators in multiple ways in specific contexts. As people negotiate official policy in these contexts, they "rewrite" it through their own actions. In this sense, policy is "an ongoing process of normative cultural production constituted by diverse actors across diverse social and institutional contexts" (Sutton & Levinson, 2001, p. 1), and local meanings are the result of conflicts and contention in these specific contexts (Grace, 1994). However, the possibility for people at all levels of the school system to reconstruct or redefine policy is not open-ended; it is constrained by circumstances not of their own making.

Policies are also "discourses"—values, practices, ways of talking that shape consciousness and produce social identities (Ball, 1994). In this sense, "policy ensembles, collections of related policies, exercise power through a *production* of 'truth' and 'knowledge'" (p. 21). Following Foucault (1995/1977), policy discourses teach people to become certain kinds of people. "Discourses are 'practices that systematically form the objects of which they speak'" (p. 21). This perspective directs us to analyze how power works through educational practices, social interactions, and the normative language of schooling to construct social identities, social relations, and dominant modes of thought (Gee, Hull, & Lankshear, 1996). As policies work their way through curriculum, instruction, and assessment and through the culture of individual schools, they become a "meaning system" or "operational statements of values" (Ball, 1990). They define who can speak, when, where, and with what authority, elevating some voices (for example, those of state officials and testing experts) while silencing others (for example, those of teachers and students). They influence how people talk and think about schooling; what knowledge, values, and behaviors are considered legitimate; and how educators see their students and their responsibilities to them as well as how students see themselves and their life chances. In this way they work as part of a dominant system of social relations, framing what can be said or thought (Ozga, 2000) and limiting the realm of possibilities for thinking otherwise.

The cultural politics of education policy also plays out through the media and from the podiums of key educational and political leaders. The public rhetoric of policy becomes a political and cultural performance (Smith, Heinecke, & Noble, 2000) that helps shape public consciousness. Through their definition of public problems (Gusfield, 1986) and the solutions they pose, policies organize consciousness around commonsense concepts of education, the work of teachers, the meaning of individual responsibility, and the "place" of various cultures, races, ethnicities, and languages in U.S. society. What is important here is how this common sense connects organically with people's lived experiences and real problems (Gramsci, 1971). Grasping these elements of "good sense" in dominant policies helps clarify why they are supported and how more liberatory policies need to address these issues (Apple, 1996).

Examining policy along these multiple dimensions can begin to account for its complexity and provide a richer, more complicated picture of its social consequences as well as opportunities for agency. Ball suggests that the complexity and scope of policy analysis—from the role of the state and the political economic context, to the cultural politics of policy discourses, to the meaning of policies at the school and classroom level—requires "a toolkit" of theories and methodologies. And Ozga argues that we need to "bring together structural, macro-level analyses of social systems and education policies with micro-level investigation, especially that which takes account of people's perception and experience" (in Ball, 1994, p. 14). Both structural and cultural perspectives are necessary. My intention is to link a political economic and cultural analysis of education policies with ethnographic approaches that examine meanings of official policies in specific local contexts. Through a multilevel analysis, I hope to draw out implications of local meanings in relation to broader contexts and relations of power. My goal is also to explore some of the complexity and cacophony of policy as it is actually interpreted and acted on—or against—in schools.

A Social Justice Framework

My analysis foregrounds the role of education policy in the production of race and class inequality and the reproduction of relations of domination. It is framed by four social justice imperatives: (a) *Equity*—all children should have an intellectually challenging education, including the necessary human and material resources. I claim an expanded definition of equity that emphasizes equality of results and redressing the effects of historical and embedded inequalities and injustice (Tate, 1997). To achieve equity not only must students have equal opportunities and rights, but special efforts must be made to overcome past injustice and historically sedimented inequalities of race, gender, and class. Policies and programs perpetuate social inequality and injustice when they prepare students of specific racial or ethnic, class, or gender groups for different life choices; when they merely extend advantages to a larger percentage of marginalized students; when marginalized students have to compete for scarce advantages (e.g., magnet schools and other highly competitive advanced academic programs); when they expand equality of opportunity or resources without addressing effects of historical inequality; and when they perpetuate knowledge that excludes the perspectives, experiences, and contributions of marginalized groups. (b) *Agency*—education should support students' ability to act on and change personal conditions and social injustice. It should prepare young people to participate actively and critically in public life, support a sense of possibility, and arm young people with tools to survive and thrive in the face of multiple forms of oppression and marginalization (Giroux, 1988). (c) *Cultural relevance*—educators should use students' cultures to support academic success, help students create meaning, develop sociopolitical consciousness, and challenge unjust social conditions (Ladson-Billings, 1994). Cultural relevance operates within a context of critical examination of difference, power, and the multiple histories and experiences of peoples in the United States and globally (Sleeter & McLaren, 1995). (d) *Critical literacy*—students need tools to examine knowledge and their own experience critically and to analyze relationships between ideas and social–historical contexts, or in Freire's words, "read the world" (Freire & Macedo, 1987). This includes grounding curriculum in students' experiences and challenging official knowledge that erases and distorts the histories and interests of subordinated social groups (Macedo, 1994). Obviously, meanings of social justice are multifaceted, evolving, and contextual, hardly reducible to discrete principles. These four imperatives are not inclusive. They simply provide a lens through which to examine implications of education policies.

In foregrounding race, I draw on critical race theory as a lens through which to analyze power relations in the United States. Critical race scholars argue that the normalization of racism as a system of power masks its centrality in all aspects of social life. The power of racism is material (it serves the economic and political interests of capital and white elites and grants privileges to whites in general over people of color) and cultural (it shapes images, perceptions, and discourses about socially constructed "racial" groups so that specific "races" and ethnicities are seen as having distinct and immutable biological, psychological, and moral characteristics). Race, as a form of power, permeates all facets of the political economy and cultural life of the United States, has structured the formation of cities, and continues to be central to the politics of education. Processes of racialization are, however, differential and fluid. Racialized groups are treated differently by the dominant society, and their treatment shifts over time in response to labor market demands and immigration patterns (Keith, 1993), as well as international and national political shifts (e.g., the "war on terrorism"). It is also essential to point out that within processes of differential racialization, African Americans, because of the specific history of enslavement and oppression in the United States, have consistently faced discrimination, racial oppression, and terror at the hands of the state and violent white supremacist groups. Critical race theorists also draw our attention to the epistemic authority of African Americans, Latinos/as, Asians, and Native Americans to speak from lived experience on questions of race. Critical race scholars who share lived experiences of marginalization have a "perspective advantage" from which to critique dominant ways of seeing conditions (Ladson-Billings, 2000). Critical race scholarship exposes the normative whiteness of social institutions and the way color-blind notions of practice and policy operate as a regime of racial power in schools and other institutions. As a white scholar, I take from this work the necessity to make visible taken-for-granted racialized practices and perspectives in schools and to attend to the multiple narratives of people of color as well as to the work of critical race scholars. In particular, I draw on critical race analyses of education (see Ladson-Billings, 1997; Parker, Deyhle, & Villenas, 1999; Tate, 1997 for an overview of critical race theory and education).

The Research

To link structural, macrolevel analyses with microlevel studies of people's perceptions and experiences, I weave together several types and levels of data: policy documents on education, real estate development, and the local economy; descriptive statistics on school and student outcomes and demographics; sociological studies of Chicago's changing economy, workforce trends, racial politics, and neighborhoods[7]; qualitative studies of four Chicago public elementary schools, which I call Grover, Westview, Brewer, and Farley (throughout the book, all proper names are pseudonyms, to protect anonymity).[8] The schools reflect a range of demographic characteristics and levels of academic performance as assessed by the Chicago Public Schools (CPS) accountability system. Despite the temptation to update data constantly, I have had to declare an end point. I use data relevant through the 2000–1 school year (the end of the Paul Vallas era), although I sometimes note important recent developments, and in the epilogue of chapter 3, I assess developments in Chicago school policy after spring 2001. (See the methodological appendix for a fuller description of methods.)

The Plan of the Book

In chapter 2 I establish the political and economic context for Chicago's school "reforms." I begin by describing processes of globalization, economic restructuring, and urban redevelopment in Chicago and the cultural politics of race in the city. I summarize Chicago's 1988 and 1995 school reforms and ways they epitomize major trends in U.S. education policy beginning in the mid-1980s. Chapter 3 presents a district-level picture of accountability, centralized regulation, and the differentiation of schooling. I analyze the implications of these policies in relation to the political economy and cultural politics of the city. This lays the groundwork for the next three chapters, which explore what the policies mean for teachers and students in different elementary schools. These case study chapters circle back to the broader context, examining not only the meanings of the policies in specific contexts but their implications in relation to economic, political, and cultural trends. Chapter 4 is a case study of Grover and Westview Elementary Schools, both of which serve low-income African American students. Although the two schools are very different, I hope to illustrate through them ways accountability and regulatory policies shape teaching and learning and the significance of the policies for the educational trajectories, life chances, social identities, and sense of agency of teachers and students in schools under intense pressures of accountability. I link these implications with the regulation of African American youth and communities and the politics of racial exclusion and regulation. Chapter 5 takes up similar issues at Brewer Elementary School, an immigrant largely Mexican school, but focuses particularly on the material and ideological force of accountability in relation to the politics of language and cultural assimilation. Coauthor, Eric Gutstein, and I attempt to show that these policies are implicated in the production of a stratified and disciplined labor force, processes of development and gentrification, and issues of identity and place in the city. Chapter 6 is a case study of Farley Elementary School, a high-scoring, middle-class-dominated school that illustrates the differential consequences of official policies and ways in which they may actually widen existing disparities in educational experiences. Farley also puts into sharp relief the challenge to develop an agenda that addresses the roots of racial subordination in schools and that prepares all students to think and act critically in a world of deepening inequality and injustice. In the final chapter I recapitulate the main themes of the book and suggest some principles of an alternative education agenda. I describe three quite different educational projects to demonstrate that liberatory education is possible. These examples embody a strategic relationship between education and processes of social transformation. I argue that new activism in education may grow out of emerging social movements. I conclude that the consequences of globalization and the politics of repression in the aftermath of the events of September 11, 2001, make the need for this activist movement all the more urgent.

My Biography and This Project

The theories and epistemological stance I bring to this book are clearly shaped by my own identity (white woman academic and social activist), political commitments, and experiences. I have endeavored to analyze the data systematically and probe rigorously for disconfirming evidence, multiple perspectives, and alternative explanations. Nevertheless, my analysis is shaped by who I am. My inquiry is also not disinterested. I am committed to antiracist, critical, projustice education and to public education as a means of supporting critical democratic participation in society and radical social transformations. I am an education activist as well as an academic. I see education as an arena that has mobilized social movements to challenge existing power arrangements. I am a critic of globalization and economic development that are creating a world of misery for the masses of people alongside untold luxury for a few elites. I am active in a local group of teachers centered on teaching for social justice. I live in Chicago and witness daily how the disparities I write about play out along lines of class, race, ethnicity, and gender. My daughter is a recent graduate of Chicago Public Schools, and my perspective is informed by my experience as a parent, as well. My analysis foregrounds race and ethnicity, yet I recognize the epistemological limitations of my analysis of racism and white supremacy. My perceptions are obviously partial, shaped by my experience as a white educator, parent, and researcher. Yet, it is clear that race must be at the center of the analysis. Race is at the center of Chicago school policies, and the historical legacy and current practice of white supremacy continue to have a powerful impact on educational inequality and public discourse about education and life in the city. This recognition has led me to foreground questions of race, to examine the complexities of race and ethnicity and differential racism, and to draw on the work of critical scholars of color who focus on race and ethnicity. It also has led me to seek out the perspectives of educators of color and to check my perceptions with them.

Throughout five years of working on various aspects of this project, I kept asking myself, "Who am I in relation to these schools, their teachers, students, and communities?" But as I was writing the book I had to look at these issues again. I asked myself whether my predilection for Farley, a mixed-race, mixed-class school (which offered children and adults more independence than the other schools in this study, in my opinion), was the result of my middle-class prejudices. Did the school simply mirror students' privileges and was I blinded to that? And was I failing to identify fully the school's faults in relation to low-income African American students? Was I missing strengths at the more tightly regulated and lower-scoring African American schools in the study? Could I even begin to interpret the complexity of education in a Latino/a immigrant community or in an African American community that was being dismantled? Was my narrative stifling dialogues about race, class, and power (Delpit, 1988)? These questions sent me back to my data, made me suspicious of some of my interpretations, and ultimately restricted what I felt licensed to say. The reader will judge for herself how I take up these issues. As I reviewed my field notes and analytical comments, I recognized that I also had become blind to the blunting of my own critical edge. It was only after I was out of the schools for a while (although I maintain my relationships and contacts with teachers) that I tapped into the lingering questions I had about Farley's goals. What was this school educating students *for*? Because schooling at Farley seemed, in some ways, much "better" than at Grover, and Westview, and to some extent Brewer, it became a point of contrast. Catching myself inside the dominant discourse of individual achievement and acquisition of official knowledge, I was reminded to keep asking, "Literacy for what?" And to return to core issues of social justice to connect the struggle over education to a broader political project.

CHAPTER 2

Chicago School Reform and Its Political, Economic, and Cultural Context

*As the process of uneven development sees both high-growth activities and
downgraded labor concentrated in the largest metropolitan areas, these areas
become the spatial expression of the contrasting social conditions into
which the effects of the restructuring process are ultimately translated.*

(Castells, 1989, p. 203)

Chicago is a "dual city" of increasing inequality and social segregation. In this regard it is like other U.S. cities and U.S. society as a whole. It is my contention that this trend has everything to do with education policies based on accountability, centralized regulation, and differentiated schooling. Chicago's downtown development strategy, its global city agenda, its changing labor force, and the political, economic, and spacial implications of these trends are the context for its 1988 and 1995 school reforms. In this chapter I describe this context and summarize the reforms. I also examine why the policies of the 1995 reform resonate with some teachers, parents, and the broader public.

Chicago, a Dual City

Deindustrialization, white flight, fiscal crises of the state, and racial segregation and abandonment have left inner cities and urban schools underfunded and in decay (see Anyon, 1997; Bettis, 1994; Kozol, 1992; Rury & Mirel, 1997). However, processes of economic restructuring and globalization have also led to *selective* reinvestment and reinvigoration of urban areas. Global cities, in particular, embody the contradictions of disinvestment and reinvestment, poverty and wealth, marginality and centrality, that characterize globalization (Castells, 1989, 1998; Sassen 1994, 1998). They are defined by gentrified neighborhoods and redeveloped downtowns for upscale living, tourism, and leisure alongside deteriorated low-income neighborhoods. These disparities also embody conflicts over representation and the cultural control of urban space. Chicago exemplifies these contradictions and contrasting conditions.

Chicago, a Global City?

In 1989, Mayor Richard M. Daley told *Crain's Chicago Business*: "This city is changing. You're not going to bring factories back. . . . I think you have to look at the financial markets—banking, service industry, the development of O'Hare field, tourism, trade. This is going to be an international city" (Phillips-Fein, 1998, p. 28). In 2002, the Daley administration released its Chicago Central Area Plan for downtown development, announcing, "This plan is driven by a vision of Chicago as a global city" (Central Area Plan, 2002). In fact, Chicago has been on a global city track for the last two decades. By 1983, Chicago's downtown was headquarters to twenty-six Fortune 500 companies. In international banking, Chicago's LaSalle Street was surpassed only by Wall Street, and Chicago's Board of Trade and Mercantile Exchange led the nation in futures and commodities trading (Rast, 1999). Daley has continued to promote the agenda of Chicago's business, financial, and real estate interests. However, in order to legitimize his administration,[1] the mayor has had to widen his circle of allies and political functionaries and has had to make some concessions to African Americans and Latinos/as and to neighborhood development. I will argue that, to some extent, the tension between these dual functions, capital accumulation and legitimation, is also manifested in education policy.

Despite some concessions to neighborhood development, Chicago fits many of the criteria of a global city, that is, concentration of sophisticated producer services, international markets, and corporate headquarters (Abu-Lughod, 1999). Perhaps it is best characterized as second-tier behind paradigmatic global cities such as New York, London, and Tokyo. Since the 1990s, Chicago has become a financial center and home to producer services and eighteen headquarters of top 500 transnational companies (Betancur & Gills, 2000a). In 2002 it was second to New York in headquarters of companies with more than 2500 employers (Metropolis Index, 2002). Its fastest growing job sectors are business services, software, and tourism (Regional Realities, 2001, p. 17). The city has seven of the top fifty U.S. exporters, and Chicago firms are among the top ten in the world in pharmaceuticals, oil, electronics, telecommunications, leisure services, and food processing (Moberg, 1997). Chicago has been called a "first order international financial center" (Reed in Betancur & Gills, 2000a, p. 27), with the value of the financial transactions of the Chicago Mercantile Exchange far out-weighing those of any other world city, including New York (Abu-Lughod, 1999). Chicago also dominates the global market in futures and options trading (Sassen, 1994). By 1999, the city had also become the nation's fourth largest high-tech center. Specialized services required by global financial centers (e.g., legal, technological, and consulting services) are expanding. Meanwhile, the Daley administration's development policies have fed a boom in upscale housing, restaurants, and other "lifestyle" amenities designed to attract the highly paid technical, professional, and managerial workers essential to a global city economy (Betancur & Gills, 2000a; Longworth & Burns, 1999). Whether Chicago qualifies as a global city or not, financial elites and city political leaders are clearly promoting the global city agenda to justify corporate and real estate development policy (Sanjek, 1998).[2]

The dominant narrative about global cities highlights high-income knowledge workers, luxury living, downtown skyscrapers, tourism, and corporate culture. This narrative writes out the legions of low-paid workers, the working-class neighborhoods where they live, and the cultural diversity they bring to the city (Sassen, 1994). Because global cities are command centers for global networks of production and capital mobility, they concentrate high-paid professionals, such as informational technology specialists, lawyers, advertising professionals, and stock analysts, who are primarily white and male. However, the high volume of this work also requires thousands of low-paid workers to enter data, clean corporate offices, staff messenger services, and perform other essential but low-paid work. These workers are primarily immigrants, women, and people of color. Although the high-income knowledge workers and professionals are not a ruling class, they are a culturally hegemonic class that "shapes civil society" by appropriating urban space through real estate acquisition and a culture of consumption (Castells, 1989). This stratum crystallizes in a lifestyle that is markedly distinct from that of low-paid workers but is made possible through their low-paid personal services as dog walkers, nannies, gardeners, house cleaners, personal shoppers, preparers of gourmet take-out foods, and customized clothing makers. They are also the low-paid employees who work in leisure and retail outlets as restaurant workers, sales clerks, and cashiers. Many of these service jobs demand certain dispositions and perceived characteristics (compliance and a "pleasant manner") that are part of the cultural process of racial differentiation—the inclusion of some immigrant groups and the exclusion of African Americans and some Latinos/as. As Abu-Lughod (1999) points out, becoming a global city has only widened the gap between the haves and have-nots in

Chicago and increased economic disparities between whites, on the one hand, and African Americans and Latinos/as on the other, as demonstrated by the 2000 census.[3] These disparities are also linked to the restructuring of Chicago's labor force.

Economic Restructuring, the New Labor Force, and Inequality

Feagin and Smith (1987) note, "The unfolding of capital restructuring creates profoundly destabilizing conditions of everyday life in the cities most immediately affected" (p. 24). This observation aptly describes Chicago. The city exemplifies the deepening inequalities and social disruption precipitated by the restructuring of the economy from manufacturing to information and service work. From 1967 to 1990, Chicago manufacturing jobs shrank from 546,500 (nearly 41 percent of all local jobs) to 216,190 (18 percent of total jobs) while nonmanufacturing jobs went from 797,867 (59 percent) in 1967 to 983,580 (82 percent) in 1990 (Betancur & Gills 2000a, p. 27). From 1970 to 1992 the larger Chicago metropolitan region lost almost a half-million manufacturing jobs primarily as a result of competition and relocation for cheaper labor. For dislocated manufacturing workers, primarily African Americans and Latinos/as, the alternative is often a low-wage service job, if they can find work at all.

According to Illinois Employment Security Agency data for 1998, 76 percent of the jobs with the most growth in Illinois paid less than a livable wage, calculated at $33,739 a year for a family of four, and 51 percent of these jobs paid below half a livable wage (National Priorities Project, 1998). When we compare average weekly wages for all workers and exclude "supervisory workers," manufacturing workers earn $562 compared with $400 for service and $248 for retail workers (Phillips-Fein, 1998, p. 30). According to the Midwest Center for Labor Research, in 1999, Chicago manufacturing jobs paying an average of $37,000 a year had been replaced with service jobs paying $26,000 (Longworth & Burns, 1999). Since unionized workers are more likely to have health insurance and pension plans, the shift to primarily non-union service work has compounded wage losses with fewer benefits and less security. Moreover, manufacturers that have stayed in the Chicago area have tended to automate their plants and restructure for just-in-time production with greatly reduced workforces that often require more sophisticated skills but at stagnant or reduced wages (Moberg, 1997). While some workers are recycled through the new labor positions, others even less fortunate, are forced into the informal economy or the ranks of the unemployed. The results of simultaneous upgrading, downgrading, and exclusion of labor (Castells, 1989) are a highly segmented workforce[4] and a social structure polarized on the basis of class, race, national origin, and gender.

Economic restructuring intersects with racism to produce increasing racial inequality, especially for African Americans.[5] The Chicago metro area now outstrips all others in economic disparities between whites and African Americans, who have the lowest incomes and occupational levels in the city (Abu-Lughod, 1999). Average wages for African Americans for all occupations dropped from 66 percent of wages of whites in 1970 to 56 percent in 1990. Latinos/as, on average, earned 64 percent of whites' wages in 1970 and 60 percent in 1990 (Betancur & Gills, 2000a, p. 28). Moreover, manufacturing jobs declined most for African Americans and Latinos/as, who, if able to find work at all, are pushed from manufacturing to the bottom of the service economy, where wages are lowest, benefits often nonexistent, and work temporary and part-time. Importantly, this downward spiral is linked to globalization and export of manufacturing. Ranny (cited in Betancur & Gills, 2000, p. 29) estimates that 62 percent of job loss in large manufacturing plants in the Chicago area between 1979 and 1989 was due to moving operations to other countries.

Downtown Development and Gentrification—a Geography of Inequality

In Chicago, economic restructuring and the drive to become a global city are linked to a corporate-center development strategy nearly fifty years old. This strategy had its roots in the administration of Mayor Richard J. Daley (1955–76) and his alliance with real estate, banking, and corporate interests (Rast, 1999). Within the framework of capitalism, a small group of powerful actors (real estate developers, banks and other financial institutions, corporate heads, speculators) working with key elements of the state (mayors, development commissions) shape real estate markets and development and land use policies (Feagin, 1998). The strategy of this powerful coalition of interlocking business associations and government units, or "growth machine" (Logan & Molotch, 1987), is to develop central business districts and their surrounding areas, displacing local manufacturing and working-class housing. Logan and Molotch (1987) provide evidence that wherever this strategy prevails, it intensifies economic disparities and supplants alternative visions of the role of city government and the meaning of community. Between 1955 and 1983, Chicago's growth machine squeezed out small and medium manufacturers and low- to medium-income residential areas and replaced them with corporate headquarters, business services, and expensive residential developments.[6] Richard J. Daley's Democratic Party machine eliminated potential opposition and funneled city resources to corporate center development through zoning ordinances, tax policies, publicly financed infrastructure improvements, federal Urban Development Action Grants, and financial incentives (Rast, 1999).

These policies facilitated massive public subsidies to corporate, banking, and real estate interests. Rast (1999) presents compelling evidence to support the claim that this was not simply a response to structural changes in the economy, but a conscious political decision. According to Rast, these policies were responsible for the loss of thousands of working-class jobs and disinvestment in low-income and working-class neighborhoods (see also Squires et al., 1987). In 1973, the Commercial Club of Chicago (CCC)—an activist association of the city's top business, financial, philanthropic, and civic leaders—published the *Chicago 21 Plan*, with an introduction by Daley. The plan called for a sweeping redevelopment of the center city and its environs as a nucleus of corporate headquarters, upscale living, recreation, and tourism, including upgrading the lakefront and development of Navy Pier as an amusement and tourist center. To facilitate this transformation, the *21 Plan* called for the demolition of African American neighborhoods south of the downtown (or "Loop") and working-class areas to the west, which were to be replaced by a campus of the University of Illinois and middle-class residences.

More than thirty years later, much of the *21 Plan* has become reality, largely through the leadership of two Mayor Daleys in alliance with downtown business, financial, and real estate interests (see also Joseph, 1990). Despite grassroots opposition, since the early 1970s, the face of today's downtown Chicago and the ring around it is marked by high-end lofts and shops carved out of converted manufacturing space, new condo developments, and a central core corporate and convention center with expensive retail outlets, cultural venues, and parks. The not-so-public face is a city of deindustrialization, displacement of settled working-class and low-income neighborhoods, and socially isolated, deeply impoverished communities (Betancur & Gills, 2000a).[7] As are other major international cities, Chicago is a dual city spatially as well as socially and economically.

The driving force remains a powerful coalition that includes the current Daley administration, corporate and banking leaders, legal and architectural firms, and real estate developers that control development in the city (Betancur & Gills, 2000a; Ferman, 1996; Logan & Molotch, 1987; Squires et al., 1987). The strategy is to continue to build Chicago's Loop as a tourist and convention center[8] and to continue to gentrify its outer ring and working-class neighborhoods spreading north, west, and south of the central city along the lake and key public transportation routes. In the Loop and its fringes, luxury loft conversions and new town-home and condo sales in projects of ten units or more increased from 1,006 in 1995 to 2,577 through just the first three quarters of 1998 (Allen & Richards, 1999). The Brookings Institute projects a 32 percent increase in residential use of the downtown from 2000 to 2010 (Katz & Nguyen,

1998). In July 2002, the mayor's office released a plan to expand downtown development dramatically, increasing downtown workers from 650,000 to 900,000 by 2020 and downtown residents from 83,000 to 150,000, building new parks, riverfront walks, lakeshore recreation, and rapid transit in the Loop. Transit alone is expected to cost billions of dollars (Washburn, 2002).

The explosion of gentrification in Chicago is integrally linked with globalization. Globalization has given real estate development increased importance as a source of profit and a means of dominating the city culturally. This is a result of the flood of transnational investment capital into real estate in key cities, the need for upscale housing and recreation for the new high-paid professionals, and the role of gentrification in recolonizing the city as a space of white affluence and corporate culture. Neal Smith (1996) argues that the relationship of gentrification to economic and cultural processes of globalization has made it a central force redefining the city:

> Systematic gentrification since the 1960s and 1970s is simultaneously a response and contributor to a series of wider global transformations: global economic expansion in the 1980s; the restructuring of national and urban economies in advanced capitalist countries toward services, recreation, and consumption; and the emergence of a global hierarchy of world, national, and regional cities. These shifts have propelled gentrification from a comparatively marginal preoccupation in a certain niche of the real estate industry to the cutting edge of urban change. (pp. 6, 8)

Under Richard M. Daley, Tax Increment Financing zones, or TIFs are a key tool of city government to seize land and facilitate development. An area is declared by the city to be "blighted," a TIF is created, and taxes are diverted from schools, libraries, and other publicly funded services to subsidize developers and the infrastructure that facilitates development. For example, the North Loop TIF district is expected to produce $33 million annually for individual development projects and infrastructure to support development (Podmolik, 1998). The TIFs represent a massive transfer of public funds to banks, realtors, and major contractors and create the conditions for multimillion-dollar profits in real estate sales and speculation. Once an area is declared a TIF zone, the city can also force owners to sell homes and businesses under the right of eminent domain, clearing the way for development. The mayor's capital budget has also heavily favored downtown development. During the 1990s, downtown wards were slated to receive an annual average of $19.4 million in economic development infrastructure funds compared with just $1.5 million or less in capital development funds for forty-two of the city's other forty-nine wards (Rast, 1999, p. 151).

Gentrifying areas are booming at the expense of working-class residents priced out, through increases in property taxes and rents, of the neighborhoods where they have raised families, shopped, and established relationships. In "hot" neighborhoods, housing prices shot up 25 to 40 percent from 1993 to 1995 (Schmid, 1998). In 1997, 93 percent of the city's new houses were built in just seven of the city's community areas (Phillips-Fein, 1998). A typical case is the Near South Side, just south of the Loop, where half the African American households earned less than $14,173 in 1999 while the upper-middle-class residents (mainly white) who have moved into the newly gentrifying area averaged $88,489 (Skertic, Guerrero, & Herguth, 2002). Whole neighborhoods, including small businesses, are being supplanted by new brick condos, rehabs, and upscale corporate chains such as Starbucks coffee stores, which have proliferated across the city. While Chicago is diverting taxes from schools, libraries, and other public services to infrastructure for development in select areas, low-income neighborhoods and housing have been allowed to deteriorate (Podmolik, 1998). The boom in condos has exacerbated the crisis in affordable rental housing. According to a report produced by the Catholic Archdiocese of Chicago, in the Chicago area, 245,000 low-income renters compete for 115,000 units of affordable housing; meanwhile, there are more than eight thousand abandoned buildings in Chicago that could be rehabbed for low-income housing (Catholic Charities, 1999). In particular, African Americans and Latinos/as are being forced out of rapidly gentrifying areas and segregated in parts of the city and suburbs with the most depressed economic conditions, little public transportation, and inadequate social services (Betancur & Gills, 2000a). Between 1980 and 1999, the share of people living in concentrated low-income areas of the city decreased from 8 percent to about 5.6 percent while the number of concentrated high-income census tracts more than quintupled (Regional Realities, 2001, p.8).

Chicago public housing is a prime example. Left by the city to decay for decades,[9] public housing is characterized by deplorable conditions that have become the justification for tearing them down and displacing thousands of residents to substandard rent-subsidized apartments or out of the city altogether. The vacated land then becomes prime property for real estate developers. One example of many is the Cabrini Green public housing complex, adjacent to the upper-class lakefront Gold Coast, which is now the site of new luxury townhouses. Second grade African American children who attend an elementary school in the Cabrini Green area look out their classroom windows at new $1.3 million townhouses.

Race and Development
Race was, and is, central to downtown development strategy, to the global city agenda, and to the educational policies that are implicated in these

goals. In the late 1960s, business leaders allied with Richard J. Daley planned the removal of the African American population adjacent to downtown to create a "buffer zone" between the Loop and large African American communities to the west and south of downtown. This design was laid out bluntly by a prominent real estate developer at the time: "I'll tell you what's wrong with the Loop. It's people's conception of it. And the conception they have about it is one word: Black. B-L-A-C-K. Black" (quoted in Rast, 1999, p. 31). It is symbolic that Mayor Richard M. Daley now lives in Dearborn Park, the "buffer zone" of upscale housing south of the Loop planned by his late father and the city's business elite.

As the preceding plan illustrates, although capital accumulation is a driving force in these urban development programs (Harvey, 1973), culture is also central in the production of the built environment of cities (Haymes, 1997). Urban space is both a place and a cultural context of human actions. Spatial forms are imbued with meaning. Stephen Haymes (1995) has powerfully argued that specific urban places gain significance as people assign meaning to them in relation to the construction of cultural identities, survival strategies, and social struggles that grow out of their daily experiences. Thus, Haymes argues, in the context of white racial domination, cities have been an important site for Black identity construction, place making, and resistance. Black public spaces in cities are "crucial to blacks creating a culture and politics of resistance" (p. 71). Following this line of argument, in Chicago and other urban centers, massive redevelopment of the city center and surrounding areas and the resulting displacement of African American communities are propelled by financial speculation and real estate profits *and* fueled by the cultural politics of white supremacy. Black urban places are defined in the white imagination as pathological (perverse, irrational, dangerous, beyond repair), thus justifying "taking them back" as spaces of middle-class stability, whiteness, and rationality. Employing the vocabulary of the "urban frontier," new "urban pioneers," real estate speculators, and city officials rationalize gentrification and displacement of communities of color as the "taming" of urban neighborhoods (Smith, 1996). I will argue that the cultural politics of race is pivotal in the relationship of education policies and the politics of development in the city.

Against the Discourse of Inevitability

Counter to discourses of economic determinism and inevitability that dominate discussions about globalization and economic restructuring, the downtown development strategy and global city policies that began to unfold more than fifty years ago were not simply an inevitable result of macroeconomic processes and international economic trends. They were, and are, policy choices by political actors representing specific race and class interests and ideologies. Chicago today is the culmination of actions by a post–World War II racist progrowth alliance of downtown business interests and the state that preceded the perceivable economic shift from manufacturing to service. As Feagin (1998, p. 7) notes: "Economic systems and governments do not develop out of an inevitable structural necessity but rather in a contingent manner. They result from conscious actions taken by individual decision makers in certain class and racial groups acting in particular historical circumstances."

Even within the framework of capitalism, there are alternatives to the corporate center development strategy. This was exemplified by the proposals of grassroots coalitions that challenged the *Chicago 21 Plan* in the 1970s. Their plan focused on job creation and preservation of neighborhood housing and manufacturing, rather than real estate development. Rast (1999) argues that by the time of Chicago's 1983 mayoral election, the growing strength, sophistication, and political mobilization of multiracial neighborhood development coalitions posed a genuine challenge to the political power of the progrowth alliance and its ability to define economic development. These coalitions crystallized in the election of Harold Washington, the city's first African American mayor, in 1983. Washington's administration supported more balanced, redistributive economic development policies; neighborhood-based job growth; measures to stop plant closings; and balanced growth of the downtown and neighborhoods (see Betancur & Gills, 2000b; Clavel & Kleniewski, 1990; Ferman, 1996; Giloth & Meir, 1989; Rast, 1999; Squires et al., 1987). In a break with the back room deals of the Democratic Party machine, Washington opened up economic development policy to public debate and supported neighborhood-initiated economic development plans (Rast, 1999). After his sudden death in 1987, this emergent agenda was derailed along with the collapse of his nascent political coalition of African Americans, Latinos/as, and progressive whites (see Rivlin, 1992).

Though limited and short-lived, the Washington years signaled that corporate development strategy is subject to contention by grassroots social movements. Although his coalition broke up, in neighborhoods and communities, working-class people, people of color, and immigrants continue to struggle to make the city their own—to contest gentrification and displacement and to redefine the city on their own terms.

Chicago's School Reforms

In the 1960s through the 1980s, African Americans and Latinos/as organized mass protests against racial segregation, school overcrowding, inequitable resources, school violence, and high dropout rates. They demanded better college preparation, more African American and Latino/a principals, bilingual education, and African American, Chicano/a, and Puerto Rican history and representation in the curriculum. A full account of this history is beyond the scope of what I can accomplish here, but the flavor of these struggles is crucial to understanding the 1988 and 1995 Chicago school reforms. In the present, when the status quo has become a new regime of truth, the history of these social movements for school reform provides an important counterdiscourse about schooling and social justice and about democratic participation and activism in redefining social policy. Although only partly successful in achieving their goals, these movements linked education reform to wider social change.

African American and Latino/a Social Movements
In the 1960s, influenced by the Civil Rights and Black Power movements, African American parents, students, and communities built a mass social movement to force change in Chicago schools (Danns, 2002). According to Danns, in 1957 the National Association for the Advancement of Colored People (NAACP) reported that more than 90 percent of Chicago's students attended segregated schools. Many of these schools on the South and West Sides were overcrowded, run-down, and deprived of the resources available to many white schools. By the early 1960s, Black parents had reached the boiling point over these conditions. In 1963 and 1964, the Coordinating Council of Community Organizations, an umbrella organization of Chicago's Civil Rights movement, organized massive school boycotts against overcrowding, segregation, and the administration of Superintendent of Schools, Benjamin Willis. In October 1963, 225,000 African American students boycotted their schools and twenty thousand parents and students surrounded city hall demanding Willis's resignation. In particular, they were protesting portable trailers, dubbed "Willis Wagons," that the Willis administration erected to deal with overcrowding in African American schools while schools in white neighborhoods were half-empty (see also Rivlin, 1992). By the late 1960s, as the Black Power movement took hold, parents, teachers, and students organized conferences, boycotts, and student walkouts and sit-ins to protest overcrowding, racist curricula, racist teachers, unresponsive principals, and poorly prepared graduates. They demanded community control of schools, teaching of African American history, hiring of more Black teachers and administrators, and the general academic improvement of their schools, including the elimination of tracking, increased school funding, reenrollment of dropouts, language labs, more rigorous classes, and more homework. The political tenor of this movement was reflected in the theme of a 1968 conference, "Judgement Day for Racism in West Side Schools," organized by Black parents on the West Side of Chicago. To enforce their demands, on October 14, 1968, between 27,000 and 35,000 Black high school students boycotted their

schools while others went to the central office and demanded to speak to the superintendent. This action was followed by more boycotts, walkouts, and an attempted sit-in. Although concrete gains were limited—African American and Latino/a principals were hired and the board established African American history courses in high schools—the more substantive though less visible gain was the development of political consciousness and solidarity.

The African American movement was followed by mobilizations of Latinos/as in the next decades. In the late 1970s and early 1980s, several studies began revealing the Chicago Public Schools' (CPS's) high dropout rates, especially among Latinos/as. In 1984, Latino/a parents marched on Clemente High School in the largely Puerto Rican Humboldt Park community demanding action on the Latino/a dropout problem and on gang violence in schools. This was followed in 1985 by public hearings on Latino/a dropout rates held by the Hispanic Drop-out Task Force. There were also four teachers' strikes between 1980 and 1987, largely because state and local governments refused to fund decent salary increases and needed school improvements. During the 1987 strike, the longest in Chicago history, parents' long-standing frustrations coalesced in major demonstrations. The People's Coalition for Educational Reform, a coalition of African American and Latino/a parents, set up freedom schools and demanded the mayor resolve the strike. Another community group, Parents United for Responsible Education (PURE), circled city hall in protest against the mayor's failure to act. Shortly after the strike, the People's Coalition formed a human chain across the Loop calling for thoroughgoing school reform (Kyle & Kantowicz, 1992).

Despite some gains as a result of these movements, on balance CPS has persistently failed to provide an equitable, meaningful, safe, and relevant education for the vast majority of its system's students, most of whom are African American and Latino/a. In 1990, Gary Orfield, a political scientist at the University of Chicago, whose research has followed Chicago school policy, declared, "The great majority of Black and Hispanic youths in metropolitan Chicago today attend schools that prepare them for neither college nor a decent job" (p. 131). During the 1970s and 1980s, CPS also went through major financial crises. In 1979 CPS declared bankruptcy. The superintendent resigned; the governor arranged a bailout, and the state legislature established the Chicago School Finance Authority (SFA), chaired by a major business leader, to oversee CPS finances. Programs and staff were cut to pay off bondholders, and teachers had the first payless payday since the Great Depression. As of 1990, some programs and curricula had not yet been restored (Orfield, 1990). At the same time, business groups complained that the schools were not preparing students with workforce skills for the new economy. The convergence of all these factors catalyzed the 1988 Chicago school reform.

The 1988 and 1995 Reforms

After a period of intense negotiations with a coalition of Chicago school reformers, business interests, organized parents, and community activists, the Illinois State Legislature passed the 1988 Chicago School Reform Act (see Hess, 1991; Kyle & Kantowicz, 1992). The law established unprecedented democratic participation in school governance through elected local school councils (LSCs) with a majority parents and community residents. LSCs were given the power to hire and fire principals, approve annual school improvement plans, and allocate the school's discretionary budget (Federal Title 1 and State Chapter 1 funds). The law also awarded the mayor authority to appoint an Interim School Board (Daley chose seven business and civic leaders). The School Finance Authority won expanded oversight of central office and the Board.

The bill itself was spearheaded by Chicagoans United to Reform Education (CURE), a racially mixed group of community activists and educators, in alliance with professional school reform organizations.[10] From their standpoint, decentralization and grassroots participation would stimulate innovation and school improvement (Bryk et al., 1998; Katz, 1992). Parent and community groups,[11] with support from Mayor Washington, were a key force behind the 1988 reform (Kyle & Kantowicz, 1992); the law was also spurred by corruption scandals at the central office, the 1987 teachers' strike, and support from a segment of business interests and downstate Republicans. One explanation for business support is that after years of instability and failure, they were looking for a dramatic solution to turn around a school system that deterred investment and failed to provide the skills needed in the new economy. Mirel (1993) suggests that the CURE plan also fit corporate decentralization strategies fashionable at the time. Although known as a decentralization reform, the 1988 Reform actually gave business more central office oversight through the mayor and the School Finance Authority (Shipps, Kahne, & Smylie, 1999).[12]

As LSCs were voted in, went through "training," and began to carry out their responsibilities, there was substantial variability in their effectiveness, their level of participation, and the degree to which they sparked change (Bryk, et al., 1998; Shipps, 1997). This may be partly explained by the fact that although LSCs were all "empowered," no additional resources were provided, despite differential existing resources within school communities, including ability to obtain grants, expertise in managing budgets, and levels of community organization. Nonetheless, at least in its first few years, the 1988 reform energized broad grassroots participation in school reform (Katz et al., 1997; Catalyst, 1990, 1991).

However, in 1995, the Illinois State Legislature passed a second Chicago school reform law recentralizing control of the Chicago Public Schools in the mayor's office. The mayor was given the power to appoint a five-person Board of Trustees and a chief executive officer (CEO) to run the schools. The new administration had broad powers to hold local schools accountable for performance, including the authority to decide which schools required central intervention and the power to fire or reassign school personnel, dissolve Local School Councils when deemed necessary, and cancel union contracts and outsource and privatize work done by unionized school district employees. This gave the mayor control over millions of dollars in CPS contracts. The law also redirected all increases in state Chapter 1 funds to the district, freezing funds to LSCs at 1994 levels. Teacher strikes were prohibited for eighteen months, and a number of educational and quality of work issues (e.g., class size) were eliminated as union bargaining issues. In short, the 1995 law consolidated power, authority, and money in Daley's office and in the offices of his appointed managers.

Mayor Daley appointed his chief of staff, Gery Chico, to head the CPS Board of Trustees and his budget director, Paul Vallas, as CEO. (When test scores leveled off in spring 2001, Vallas and Chico resigned and Daley appointed Michael Scott, a vice president at AT&T, Board president and Arne Duncan, Vallas's deputy chief of staff, CEO.) The Vallas/Chico administration installed a corporate, regulatory regime centered on high stakes tests, standards, and remediation. Schools that failed to perform at minimal levels on the Iowa Test of Basic Skills (ITBS) in the elementary grades and Test of Academic Proficiency (TAP) in high school were put on a warning list, on probation, or their leadership and staff were reconstituted by the central office. Low test scores also carried severe consequences for students, including retention at benchmark grades three, six, and eight and mandatory summer school. Eighth graders, fifteen years or older, who failed the ITBS in summer school were assigned to remedial high schools initially called Transition Schools and later renamed Academic Preparation Centers. Bilingual education was effectively limited to three years, after which students were to be tested in English with the same consequences as monolingual English students. Accountability measures were backed up by new after-school and summer remedial programs. The Board also created new academically differentiated schools and programs. In 1997, it established academic standards and curriculum frameworks to standardize the knowledge and skills to be taught in each grade.

Under the current system, teachers' work is increasingly governed by the technical rationality of teaching specific skills, employing centrally mandated curricula, and, in some low-scoring schools, using scripted direct instruction. Beginning in fall 1999, the board issued a semiscripted standard curriculum for grades kindergarten to twelve based on its mandated summer school curriculum. Although it was optional, Vallas predicted that in five years 80 percent of teachers would be using it. In addition, a new high school test for core academic subjects, the Chicago Academic Standards Exam, was phased in as 25 percent of students' final grade, thereby dictating a significant portion of what was to be taught in high school core subjects.

Shifting Alliances, Changing Political Context

If we think of education policy as originating in three sectors—the economy, the state apparatus, and the institutions of civil society—then specific policies can be understood by looking at the alignment of these sectors and their responses to global and national political, economic, and ideological forces (Ozga, 2000). From this perspective, the 1988 reform reflected the relative strength of organized groups in civil society and their proactive response to the long-standing failure of the state to deal effectively with educational crises in Chicago. This development coalesced with the actions of the local state, under Washington, who was more supportive of social movements and community based empowerment than any mayor in recent memory. Washington's administration encouraged the coalition of school reformers, community based organizations, and local political organizations. Business interests, concerned about Chicago's competitiveness in a globalized economy, formed a tactical alliance with these forces to support the 1988 reform. Business support was grounded in the idea that improving Chicago Public Schools would strengthen economic competitiveness and that decentralization would spur innovation. The 1988 reform also fit the national business-supported trend of school restructuring and site-based management, although it was arguably more far-reaching. But the coalition of community and school reform groups was developing its own, more democratic version of school-based management. It believed that change should be locally directed because each school needed to develop an agenda that was responsive to its own context, constituency, and issues (Hess, 1991).

Race was also a central issue in the alignment of social forces in support of the 1988 reform. The Washington elections demonstrated the strength of African Americans and Latinos/as a social force in the city, as did previous mass movements for education reform. They were the backbone of community organizations and parent groups who led the reform and saw it as a vehicle to strengthen community organizing. On the other hand, Lewis and Nakagawa (1995) argue that by targeting bureaucracy as the problem, the 1988 reform diverted attention from the state's failure to address racial inequality in schools. By denying necessary additional funding for local school councils in the most impoverished areas, the reform created organizational empowerment without providing the actual resources to improve schools in African American communities. It devolved responsibility without additional resources. It also decentralized the voice of communities, arguably diminishing their political power vis-a-vis the central administration (Shipps, 1997). The bill was also supported by key Democratic leaders in the state legislature, perhaps as a way to legitimate this branch of state government after years of failing to address problems in the Chicago Public School system while shifting responsibility to local schools (Lewis & Nakagawa, 1995).

But by 1995, the insurgent grassroots movement that put Washington in the mayor's office was divided and weakened. Mayor Daley and business leaders were impatient with the pace of school reform, CPS's fiscal instability, lack of school accountability, and ongoing contention with the unions (Ships, 1997). This time they took charge. The national policy discourse had also shifted to accountability and privatization, and Daley had locked in political control of the City Council and domination of the city's economic agenda in close alliance with major business, financial, and real estate interests. Chicago's global city agenda was full blown, and its economy had fully rounded the corner from large-scale industry to service, finance, tourism, business services, and technology-driven companies. Seizing control of the schools provided the mayor with a huge source of funds with which to allocate contracts (CPS has the largest budget and number of employees of any public agency in the state) and gain leverage over labor. But most important, the schools were an arena to institute policies supportive of his larger economic and urban development agenda. The 1995 reform was a means to undercut the power of LSCs that can be a vehicle for local communities to gain a share of city resources and potentially to organize politically around other issues, including in opposition to Daley's downtown development, global city agenda. The 1995 reform also coincided with the desire of the new Republican majority in the state legislature to weaken the Chicago Teachers Union. They collaborated to centralize the system's management under the mayor.[13] These changing conditions, shifting relations of power, and differing responses of the local state help explain the shift from local democratic reform of schools to corporatist centralization of CPS.

The "democratic localism" of the 1988 reform (Bryk et al., 1998) continues in tandem with centralization, albeit in an increasingly weakened form.[14] The relationship of democratic local control and centralized accountability is varied and complex. The pages of *Catalyst,* a monthly magazine that has chronicled Chicago school reform since 1990, record wide variation in the vitality of LSCs since 1995. The influence of centralized policies on schools also varies. The variation in LSCs is a barometer of the strength of communities and the relative influence of the centralized policies on local schools. I take up this issue in subsequent chapters. However, reports in the *Catalyst* and my own data indicate that, in general, grassroots participation and local power (embodied in LSCs) have been substantially compromised by the overriding impact of recentralization and accountability. LSCs have lost power in principal selection, budgeting, and opportunities for training (Lewis, 1997; Williams, 2000). In fact, some school reform activists argue that the agenda of the mayor, CPS leaders, and business is to get rid of LSCs altogether.[15]

The "Good Sense" in CPS Policies

It is important to consider not only what is wrong with Chicago's accountability and centralized regulation but also what is right with it, in Gramsci's (1971) terms, the "good sense" in the policies. What organic connections do they make with people's real problems and lived experience? In part, the policies make sense because finally school leaders are taking decisive action against a status quo that has failed to educate the majority of students. When Vallas and Chico took power, they immediately signaled a new take-charge attitude. They uncovered gross mismanagement in the central office (hundreds of new computers were found stored in a warehouse) and announced that the city's predominantly African American and Latino/a student population would no longer be allowed simply to pass from grade to grade without making academic progress. Chicago Public Schools would teach all children, and students, teachers, and administrators alike would be held to the same high standards of performance. Failing schools were put on probation with external oversight, ineffectual principals were replaced, schools were reconstituted, thousands of students were sent to summer school, and many were retained because of low test scores in reading and math. Schools were finally being held accountable for doing more than holding students in school buildings six hours a day. As a result, there is a new sense of urgency and a press to focus on instruction, planning, and curriculum coherence. As one veteran African American educator put it: "For decades Chicago Public Schools haven't even tried to educate Black kids. This is the first time, under Paul Vallas, they are doing something about it. That's why I support him." To appreciate the import of this comment, it is important to note that the same issues parents and students organized around over the past thirty years still plague Chicago schools today.

But CPS leaders have succeeded in framing their agenda as the only choice against "the failed policies of the past." There has been no public discussion of the social, economic, political, and educational roots of the failure to educate so many of Chicago's children. Through the first six years of accountability policies, there was little public discussion of any viable alternative to accountability. The Vallas administration denounced any critique as support for the failed status quo. Recently, alternative proposals of school reform organizations and parent, student, and teacher organizations have begun to filter into media accounts.[16] Yet, resonant with dominant neoliberal policy discourses, CPS policies have powerfully reframed the meaning of educational equity and justice as standards and accountability. The system is equitable because all students are evaluated by "the same test" and "held to the same standards," and the retention of thousands of students is described as "ending the injustice of social promotion" (Vallas, 2000, p. 5). Powerfully disseminated through the media (including the mayor's TV station and CPS's mass-circulation newsletter), the policies impose a narrow instrumental definition of the purpose of education, the nature of curriculum and assessment, and processes of human and institutional change. In this way, policy discourse becomes a "discourse policy"

> turned through the media, toward society as a whole, whether at the national or local level, as part of the work of hegemony. . . . Politicians and state institutions, central and local, state their capacity to recognize social problems, impose their legitimate definition and solutions, which will in turn contribute to structuring the way people, as well as other economic and political actors, think of those problems and define their actions. (Preteceille, 1990, p. 45).

Moreover, the discourse is convincing because there have been concrete results. In the first six years of the policies, there were gains in test scores, although they flattened out in 2001. Some teachers and administrators who have held very low academic expectations for students and/or exerted little effort or accepted little responsibility for their learning have been forced to teach or have been removed. The district's semiscripted curriculum does provide a guide for ineffectual or inexperienced teachers, and my own data provide evidence that classroom instruction has become more systematic in some schools as a result of standards and centralized oversight. As one veteran teacher said, "At least now they're teaching *something.*"

Yet, there is a more complicated story about the meaning of the policies for teaching and learning, for the intellectual and social experiences of students, for the agency of adults and children, and for equity and social justice. In the following chapters, I explore that story through an overview of district policies and a close look at what has happened in four schools. However, we also need to pay attention to the ways in which accountability policies resonate with anger and frustration at decades of CPS failure to educate all students. Change is long overdue. The good sense in the policies points to the urgency to resolve in a substantive and liberatory way the issues the current policy agenda purports to address.

CHAPTER **3**

Accountability, Social Differentiation, and Racialized Social Control

The NRC Committee [National Research Council, Committee on Appropriate Testing] concluded that Chicago's regular year and summer school curricula were so closely geared to the ITBS [Iowa Test of Basic Skills] that it was impossible to distinguish real subject mastery from mastery of skills and knowledge useful for passing this particular test.
(Hauser, 1999, p. 1)

"If you weren't in IB [International Baccalaureate], Honors, or had a certain GPA [grade point average], the school either didn't care about helping you go to college or they tried to get you to join the military."
(Araceli Huerta, graduate of Kelly High School, *Higher Learning*, 2002).

Introduction

These comments capture some of the central issues of Chicago's accountability system and its differentiated educational "opportunities." This chapter examines Chicago's education policies across the school system and the relationship of these policies to the city's political economy and cultural politics of race. I begin by discussing systemwide implications of accountability, standards, and remediation for teaching and for students' educational experiences. I also discuss the ideological force of these policies as a regime of surveillance and self-blame. The policies are coupled with a newly differentiated system of educational experiences or "choices" that constitute new forms of internalized tracking within an already highly stratified system. These new forms of educational differentiation increase educational inequality and exclusion, and they are tied to development strategies in the city. A specific case—military high schools—are part of an ensemble of policies that produce new forms of punishment, criminalization, and regulation of African American and some Latino/a youth. Again, I relate these policies to the larger political economic and cultural context, examining their consequences for the place of African Americans and Latinos/as in the city. In the same fashion, I argue that accountability and stratified schooling are linked with the skills and dispositions required for a stratified labor force. Further, I suggest that these education policies and the cultural politics of race in which they are complicit serve global city development. I conclude with an epilogue on CPS policy after 2001, the end of the Vallas administration.

Accountability, Remediation, and Standards

Underneath claims of a vastly improving school system in Chicago (*Trending Up*, n.d.), there is evidence of a far less rosy picture than the one painted by the mayor and CPS leaders. This is the case even according to CPS's own criteria. Over seven years of accountability, the gap remains between a relatively few elite, selective, high-scoring schools and the widespread failure of the majority. Results for 2001–2 showed that in 67 percent of elementary schools and 85 percent of high schools fewer than half the students met national norms in reading (based on the city's high stakes tests) (Olszewski & Little, 2002) while selective academic schools scored above 90 percent. But the larger story is what is happening to raise test scores and the implications for teaching and learning and equity.

Accountability and Test Prep

The press for academic achievement is driven by penalties for low test scores and is linked to the Iowa Test of Basic Skills (ITBS) in elementary schools and the Test of Academic Proficiency (TAP) in high schools. The principal consequence of the extraordinary emphasis on accountability has been to steer teaching toward test preparation, especially in low-scoring schools. (This is exemplified by Grover and Westview, in chapter 4.) Across the city, teachers teach to the test, focusing on specific skills, concepts, and items that students have failed in the past. Much time is also spent practicing test-taking techniques—timed practice tests and bubbling in answer sheets with a number two pencil. As reflected in the opening quotation from the National Research Council (NRC), improved scores may have more relation to test preparation than to learning. Even more troubling is the widespread knowledge that the obsession with test scores has encouraged a form of educational triage. Teachers and administrators report that central office administrators have advised them to focus instruction on the students who are near to passing the standardized tests, paying less attention to those well above the 50th percentile (the national norm CPS is trying to reach) and those with no hope of reaching it. This is a tactic to raise a school's overall scores. At one school, in the weeks before the test, the desks of "bubble kids" (those near to passing) line the halls as the children are pulled out of their classes to spend extra time working with tutors on test preparation. Educational triage, in force across the city, runs directly counter to claims that current policies promote equity. (See Gillborn & Youdell, 2000, for similar practices in the United Kingdom.)

Teaching and learning and daily life in school are most dominated by test preparation in the lowest-scoring schools. This is an inevitable result of the district's policy. These are the schools that hold Iowa Test pep rallies in the spring, that focus professional development on passing "the Iowa" and Illinois State Achievement Test (ISAT), that substitute test prep books for the regular curriculum, that decorate hallways with posters and banners urging students to "Zap the Iowa." To the extent the new policies prompt schools to overemphasize standardized tests and basic skills (as opposed to an intensive effort to develop more thoughtful, intellectually challenging pedagogies), they widen educational inequalities by institutionalizing a narrowed curriculum and less intellectually challenging work. Not surprisingly, Newmann, Bryk, and Nagaoka (2001) concluded that CPS students in classrooms that organized instruction around "authentic intellectual work"[1] versus basic skills produced more intellectually complex work. Smith, Lee, and Newmann (2001) also found that "didactic instruction," in which "student's time is typically spent: (1) listening to the teacher, (2) reciting answers to questions, or (3) practicing skills and information retrieval by completing worksheets or exercises," was more common in classrooms with low achievement, in "problem classrooms" (read: discipline issues), in classrooms with irregular attendance, in schools with more low-income students, and in schools with low achievement levels. (See McNeil, 2000, for similar findings in Texas.)

Concretely, these are schools serving primarily low-income African Americans and Latinos/as. This is reflected in demographics of probation schools, scripted direct instruction schools, transition high schools (now called Academic Preparatory Centers [APCs]), and remedial programs. Probation schools are overwhelmingly, and disproportionately, African American; a few are Latino/a or mixed African American and Latino/a, and very few white students are in schools on probation.[2] In 2002 only two schools on probation had 1 percent or more white students—one had 9.2 percent white students, the other, 7 percent white students (CPS Office of Accountability, 2002). When CPS placed 109 schools on probation in 1996, the average poverty level of the seventy-one elementary probation schools was about 94 percent (PURE, 1999). The fifty-nine schools employing scripted direct instruction (Personal communication, CPS Office of Accountability staff November, 2001) follow the same demographic pattern as probation schools. The program is described by its staff as following a special education model. According to the information CPS provides to scripted direct instruction teachers, the goal is to improve the "basic education of children from economically disadvantaged backgrounds" (Becker, 1977/2001).[3] Students in the seven APCs are disproportionately African American, Latino/a, and low-income.[4] Clearly, a basic education for students who have historically been denied an enriched and intellectually rigorous education is hardly a solution to entrenched inequities.

As schooling is reduced to test preparation, the policies have also spawned intense regulation and deskilling of teachers with devastating consequences for their morale, confidence, and commitment. The emphasis on accountability and standardized tests and the pressure to act against their own best judgment has undermined and demoralized committed teachers across the system, and especially in low-scoring schools. It is not an exaggeration to say many Chicago teachers face an existential crisis as they question their own competence and find that their own actions in the classroom are in conflict with the very reasons they became teachers. There are no official channels to voice this crisis. Written testimony at a Chicago Teachers for Social Justice forum on high stakes testing in spring of 2000[5] reflected the discouragement, anger, and cynicism that the current policies have generated. A high school teacher in a school that was "reengineered" (directly supervised by external administrators) wrote:

> Each year as accountability increases, the pressure to teach to the test is increased. This year as our school is getting re-engineered, we have been told that we must put test preparation on the top of our priority list. Discussion of testing monopolizes faculty meetings, department meetings, and all forms of staff development. I think one of the biggest effects is on school morale. Teachers, administrators, and students alike see the absurdity and quickly become cynical. The tests distract attention from all the ways in which our school is truly failing to prepare our students for the world. By the time they reach high school most of our students have been beaten down by the tests.

Another teacher wrote:

> My concerns, and why I am here today, are not only with high stakes testing in CPS but with the entire top-down management system. . . . I am especially concerned with the loss of control (but as a new teacher, maybe "loss" is wrong) that teachers are experiencing. There are mandates, and policies, and tons of procedures that I am given with no discussion at all. I, too, see the fantastically damaging effect of fear that teachers are experiencing.

The pressure on everyone to raise test scores was illustrated in fall 2002 when teachers at seven schools were accused of helping students cheat on the ITBS. The new CPS CEO, Arne Duncan, announced that if the charges were proved, the teachers would be fired, but the president of the teachers' union, while unequivocally condemning cheating, questioned why teachers were being scapegoated and called on CPS to join the union in a task force to study the overreliance on standardized tests (President Lynch, 2002). While some of the weakest teachers have been pushed to focus more on instruction (sometimes by following the district scripted curriculum), paradoxically, these pressures are also driving out some of the most respected and committed teachers. This is very serious because strong teachers are a potential nucleus of substantive improvement in teaching and school change. This issue reverberates in the next chapters.

Consequences for students can also be devastating. Among assessment experts there is a consensus that using standardized tests to make high stakes decisions about individual students is inappropriate and inequitable, particularly since all students do not have an equal opportunity to learn (Heubert & Hauser, 1999). Yet, based on their scores on a single test, tens of thousands of Chicago students have been sent to summer school, retained in grade for as long as three years, precluded from eighth grade graduation, and assigned to remedial transition high schools. These consequences have fallen heavily on African American and Latino/a students. For example, in 1997, 4 percent of whites, 18 percent of African Americans, and 11 percent of Latinos/as were retained (Designs for Change, 1999). In 2000, Parents United for Responsible Education (PURE) won a civil rights complaint against CPS for adverse discriminatory impact of the retention policy on African Americans and Latinos/as. In 1998, the district ratio of African Americans to whites was 5:1, and the ratio of Latinos/as to whites was 3:1. However, in transition high schools for over-age eighth graders who failed the ITBS, the ratio of African Americans to whites was 27:1, and the ratio of Latinos/as to whites was 10:1 (PURE, 1999). Moreover, while citywide, test scores have increased for nonretained students, retained students' scores have not improved. Roderick and colleagues concluded in 1999: "The goal of CPS efforts during the retained year is to address poor performance among students who do not meet the minimum test cutoff. This goal is clearly not being met" (p. 39). Those retained in 1997 were doing no better than previously "socially promoted" students, in many cases they were doing worse, and nearly one third of retained eighth graders in 1997 dropped out by fall 1999 (Roderick, Nagaoka, Bacon, & Easton, 2000). Looking at long term effects of similar policies in Texas, Haney (2000) found that accountability and high stakes tests correlated with increased dropout rates, especially among African Americans and Latinos/as.[6]

Ideological Force of Accountability

Ideologically, accountability reframes education as performance on achievement tests, undermining broader and more liberatory purposes.

Practice for multiple choice, one-right-answer, and timed tests undermines a classroom culture that encourages students to question their texts,
the teacher, and the authority of official knowledge. Accountability policies also devalue whatever is not tested, including curricula and pedagogies rooted in the language, culture, lived experiences, and identities of
students. For example, the three-year-and-out bilingual education policy
both concretely and symbolically privileges English language acquisition
over bilingualism and biculturalism and devalues students' first language.
(I explore this further in chapter 5.)

Accountability policies constitute an insidious mode of social discipline
merging Foucault's (1995/1977) notion of discipline as "spectacle" (social
control through the observation of the few by the many) and discipline as
"surveillance" (social control through the observation of the many by the
few) (Vinson & Ross, 2001). Probation, retention, publication of schools'
test scores, and constant media monitoring of test results have become a
public spectacle of failure. Students who fail are marked by assignment to
remedial programs and grade retention. Teachers and administrators, as
well as students and their communities, are publicly chastised by being
placed under the authority of central administrators and outside agents
contracted by the board to supervise and "help" them. At the same time,
the policies promote a panoptic order of intense monitoring and surveillance. Central office administrators monitor principals, principals monitor teachers, teachers and staff monitor students and parents. It is
important to be clear that this is not a policy that promotes engaged public
attention to inequity in the system; nor is it a policy that encourages collective examination of the problems in schools. Accountability has been instituted without public discussion and without the participation of teachers,
local administrators, students, and parents working together to improve
children's education. Rather, this is a process of powerful city and school
officials holding up certain schools (and by extension, their communities),
teachers, and students as public exemplars of failure and monitoring them.
Despite the appearance of uniform treatment, concretely, the schools
under close scrutiny are in low-income communities of color. This is social
discipline primarily directed at African American and Latino/a students,
schools, and communities and their teachers.

Top-down accountability also shifts responsibility for the failure of
public education from the state to individuals (cf. Katz, 2001). In Chicago,
the high stakes nature of accountability and sanctions against individuals
and schools feeds a pervasive culture of individual blame. When students
fail, they blame themselves and/or complain about their teachers; teachers
denounce students and parents; central administrators accuse school administrators, teachers, students, and parents. This mentality is instantiated

in the CPS parent report card, initiated in fall 2000, on which primary teachers were to grade parents' support for their children's education. While the ideology of individual responsibility absolves the state of responsibility, accountability policies have given the state a new tool to sort students for selective academic programs and regulate them for the labor market—all in the guise of equity.

Remediation

CPS leaders contend that the harshness of accountability is offset by new remedial "supports" (CPS Promotes Retained Students, 1999), including after-school remedial classes, mandatory summer "Bridge" classes for failing students, and transition high schools. However, these remedial programs are explicitly aimed at the ITBS. The after-school programs use a board curriculum that "focuses on boosting standardized test scores for 3rd, 6th, and 8th graders not meeting promotion standards" (Public Schools Receive $2.25 Million, 1998). The ITBS is the capstone for summer Bridge and APC high schools. And counter to the Board's claim of "state of the art" curricula, a review of the semiscripted 1999 summer Bridge curriculum for eighth grade math revealed a series of rather disconnected lessons generally aligned with the ITBS. The teachers' manual for eighth grade math had approximately one error per lesson (Gutstein, 1999). This is particularly troubling because many summer school teachers are not experts in the content area they are assigned to teach. In fact, some are learning along with the students. Moreover, students who fail the ITBS in one subject, reading or math, are required (supposedly for administrative reasons) to attend summer school in both subjects, so many students are sitting through instruction to prepare them for a test they have already passed.

The pared-down course of study at transition high schools consists of math, English, and world studies and revolves around intensive ITBS preparation (see Duffrin, 1999a, b). Former Brewer students reported that their transition center English class had no discussion of literature but a steady diet of worksheets primarily geared to the ITBS. The "library" had no books, and gym classes were held in an empty room with no equipment (Gutstein, 2001). A teacher at another transition center said, "We try to boil the concepts down to the point where if they just pay attention, they will succeed" (Duffrin, 1999a, p.6). The impoverishment and redundancy of this basic skills education for students the school district has defined as "behind" can hardly be construed as an antidote for the inequities of the system, particularly as African Americans and Latinos/as are disproportionately assigned to this type of schooling.[7] Mandating a rudimentary curriculum that few middle-class parents would choose for their own children publicly signals that low-income children and children of color are deficient.

Standards

The Chicago Academic Standards (CAS) and Curriculum Frameworks Statements (CFS) putatively ensure that all students are taught the same challenging academic content (Board of Education, 1997). However, whereas most teachers I interviewed supported the concept of a common curriculum framework for each grade, the standards were imposed with little discussion or professional development and with little attention to the complexity and judgment intrinsic in teaching (see Sheldon & Riddle, 1998). Unlike content and pedagogical frameworks developed by national professional organizations, such as the National Council of Teachers of Mathematics, the CAS and CFS are *performance standards,* essentially lists of what is to be learned at each grade level in each subject area.[8] The point is that education cannot be left to teachers, and the overall effect is to reduce teaching to the model of the industrial workplace (Morrow & Torres, 2000). The technical rationality undergirding the establishment of these standards encourages teachers to focus on specific skills and information rather than rich content. This is evident in the common practice of teachers simply checking off the required skills in their lesson plans. Furthermore, skills mandated by the frameworks are not necessarily tested by the ITBS, nor the ISAT (the state mandated test), so teachers have to focus on three sets of sometimes unrelated skills and concepts.

Most important, setting standards does not address how they are to be met in the context of Chicago's entrenched inequalities in resources, opportunities to learn, and teachers' knowledge. Without addressing these inequalities, standards may intensify inequality (Apple, 1996). Without support for students and teachers and without reconceptualizing curriculum, pedagogy, and assessment, failure to meet the standards can deepen school failure and students' sense of inadequacy and justify remedial experiences such as summer school and transition high schools. In fact, the emphasis on standards as a path to equity is part of a shift away from the responsibility of the state to provide additional resources to make up for past discrimination (Tate, 1997). As others have argued (e.g., Apple, 1988; 1996; Bohn & Sleeter, 2000), standards also elevate the knowledge and cultural capital of privileged groups and devalue the cultural capital of low-income students, particularly students of color. As do high stakes tests, the standards help legitimate a system that, as a whole, continues to produce inequality, and they may actually exacerbate inequality.

Differentiated Schooling

Since 1995, CPS has initiated a variety of differentiated programs, schools, and instructional approaches with significant implications in Chicago's current economic context. For purposes of analysis, I have divided programs and schools into "plus" and "minus." My analysis is primarily based on data from the 1999–2000 school year. Although some percentages have shifted, for example, some college prep magnets have reached full enrollment, the pattern remains the same. In the plus category I include programs and schools that purport to offer a college preparatory course of study and intellectually challenging curricula.

- Plus programs that predate the 1995 reforms are elementary magnet schools, regional gifted centers, and classical schools; grade seven to twelve Academic Centers for "academically advanced students"; and traditional magnet high schools.
- New (post-1995) plus programs/schools are expanded International Baccalaureate (IB) programs, College Prep Regional Magnet High Schools, and Math, Science, Technology Academies (MSTAs). (The latter began to be phased out in 2002.)

In the minus category I include programs/schools that focus on vocational education, restricted (basic skills) curricula, and intensified regimentation of instruction and/or control of students.

- Pre-1995 minus schools are vocational high schools and elementary schools using scripted direct instruction (DI).[9] Not to be confused with direct teaching of specific skills and concepts, DI employs teacher-read scripts and mastery of a fixed sequence of skills. Its philosophical underpinnings are behaviorism and a deficit model of "economically disadvantaged" students (Becker, 1977).
- Post-1995 minus programs/schools include expansion of DI schools and Education-to-Career Academies (ETCs). The ETCs are examples of the "new vocationalism" that closely links applied vocationalism and academics (Carlson, 1997). I also include military high schools because they are highly regimented although CPS labels them college prep.

I have not categorized some programs because, in my observations, they vary widely and may exist in name only (e.g., a "Science Academy" with no special science program) and some, such as magnet clusters, were designated with little or no knowledge of principals and no programmatic development.[10] A few schools have plus and minus programs.[11]

The school district is divided as a layer cake is, from north to south, into six administrative regions (see maps 1 and 2). (I discuss the 2002 subdivision of regions in the epilogue to this chapter.) The area along Lake Michigan, from the middle of region 1 to the northern border of region 5, is a band of high-income and/or increasingly gentrified neighborhoods. These upper-middle-class and upper-class areas along the lake are spreading west into working-class neighborhoods and abandoned industrial corridors.[12] Region 1 has the largest concentration of middle- to upper-income families,[13] and gentrification is progressing through the region's mix of immigrant, working-class, and low-income neighborhoods. Region 2 includes the elite Gold Coast along the lakeshore and expanding middle- and upper-income areas to the west. Regions 3 to 6 include the largest concentrations of very-low-income African Americans and Latinos/as in the city. However, the fringes of the center city (the Loop) along the lake in Region 3 are exploding with upper-income residential developments, and there is gentrification and an upper-middle class community along the lake in Region 4. In addition to large concentrations of very-low-income Latinos/as, African Americans, and whites in Region 6, this region also has middle-income areas. In sum, wealthy and gentrified/gentrifying areas are primarily along the lake in Regions 1 to 4 and are expanding westward. Low-income areas are concentrated in large West and South Side tracts of the city, primarily in Regions 3 to 6.

Map 1 shows that pre-1995 plus and minus programs/schools were distributed across the city and within each region. The wide distribution of plus programs primarily reflects magnet elementary schools and gifted centers, many of which originated in the board's early 1980s desegregation plan. Map 1 also shows several patterns: (a) a concentration of plus programs and schools in a relatively small upper-income white area along the north lake shore in Regions 1 and 2; (b) a cluster of minus programs/schools in very-low to low-income African American and Latino/a areas of Regions 2, 3, and 4; (c) no plus programs/schools in the large tracts of low-to very-low-income African Americans in Region 5. (Region 5 has no Regional Gifted Center, Academic Center, or Classical School.)

When we look at the geographic distribution of *new* plus and minus programs created under the 1995 reforms (map 2) and examine which were operational and involved all the students in the school and which were not operational or involved only a small percentage of the students in the school in 2000, the data reveal an interesting pattern. First, the only new plus whole schools are Regional College Prep Magnet High Schools. Four (Regions 1, 2, 3, 4) are located in, or draw from, upper-income and/or gentrifying neighborhoods, and three are in prime lakeshore areas. The Region 6 magnet is in a middle- to low-income African American community. The Region 5 magnet, in the heart of a very low- to low-income African American community, is the only one of the six schools that is not in a new or rehabbed building. There is no regional magnet college prep high school in the extensive low-income African American and Latino/a

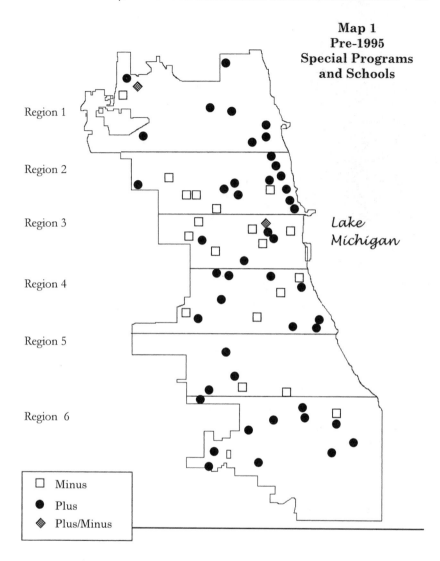

Map 1
Pre-1995
Special Programs
and Schools

Region 1

Region 2

Region 3

Region 4

Region 5

Region 6

Lake
Michigan

☐ Minus

● Plus

◈ Plus/Minus

West Side. It is notable that two of the new schools, Northside Prep (Region 1) and Payton (Region 2), are in lavish new buildings. Northside cost $47 million and Payton $33 million (Martinez, 1999). Both are in neighborhoods with median home prices eight to ten times those in the neighborhoods of Region 5 and 6 magnets (Williams, 2000). In fall 2002, Jones (Region 3) completed an extensive $50 million renovation. In addition to unequal facilities, principals reported dramatic north–south disparities in resources and time to design curriculum and recruit teachers (see *Catalyst,*

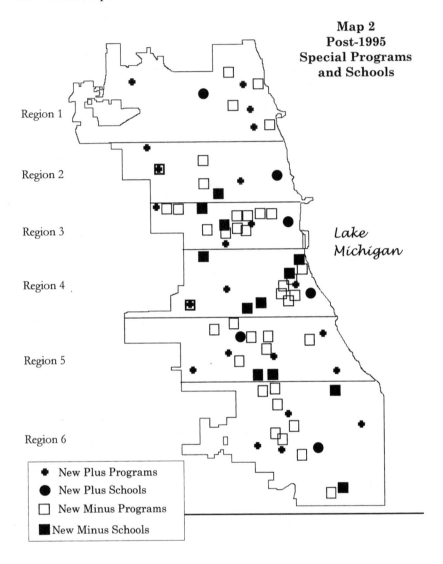

Map 2
Post-1995
Special Programs
and Schools

Region 1

Region 2

Region 3

Region 4

Region 5

Region 6

Lake
Michigan

✚ New Plus Programs
● New Plus Schools
☐ New Minus Programs
■ New Minus Schools

2000). Pressure from South Side African American leaders reportedly pushed the board to increase the Region 6 magnet's original renovation budget from $1.5 million to $33 million (Williams, 2000). However, as of February 2003, the renovation had not been done and there were reports the funding was no longer available.

Second, new selective academic programs/schools expand very little the small percentage of students enrolled in selective academic programs. I calculated that in the 1999–2000 academic year, only 8.31 percent of all 95,235 enrolled high school students were in special college prep high school programs—including magnet high schools (5.86 percent), high school IB programs (1.89 percent), and MSTAs (0.56 percent) (CPS website; Allensworth & Rosenkranz, 2000). This included three college prep magnet high schools and one IB program that existed before 1995. Students in all *new* high school college prep programs combined in 1999–2000 (regional magnets, IBs, MSTAs) totaled only 4,541, or less than 5 percent of all high school students. By fall 2002, students in the *new* programs/schools increased to 6.24 percent of all high school students.[14] IB programs, although distributed equitably, two per region, were funded for just thirty students at each high school grade. By fall 2002, when the new IBs were mostly operational in fourteen high schools, they involved a little more than 1 percent of all high school students. A total of only 11.5 percent of all high school students were in selective college prep programs/schools in fall 2002—this included the magnets and IBs existing before 1995. Beyond this, there are special college prep programs in other high schools, small high schools and charter schools, and advanced academic courses available in high schools across the city, but in most neighborhood high schools these offerings are quite limited. Access to these programs is skewed in favor of white students. The youth organization Generation Y reported that in 2002, African Americans made up 51 percent of CPS high school students but only 42 percent of students in advanced college prep classes[15]; Latinos/as were about 33 percent of students but less than 27 percent of those in college prep classes. White students, however, were 11 percent of high school students but 20 percent of students in college prep track classes (2002).

Historically, magnet schools have increased class differences in urban education systems, including Chicago (Kantor & Brenzel, 1993). The new Regional College Prep Magnet High Schools are no exception. They provide little additional access to challenging academic courses of study for the majority of students. The new high schools are so exclusive that, according to news reports, only 3 to 5 percent of students who applied and tested for admission were admitted to the three North Side regional magnets in 2001 (Rossi, 2001). The schools are allowed to bypass desegregation goals and enroll more than 35 percent white students in a district that is 11 percent white. For example, in 2002, Northside Prep was nearly 50 percent white and only 21 percent low-income in a district less than 10 percent white and more than 85 percent low-income (Illinois State School Report Cards, 2002). Moreover, since the development of the regional magnets, the rate at which high-achieving students have been leaving CPS has declined. If at least part of the enrollment in the new high schools comprises students who would otherwise have left CPS (see Allensworth & Rosen-kranz, 2000), then these schools represent even less expansion of opportunity for students who do not have the option to leave the CPS system.

Third, there is a proliferation of minus programs and schools in Regions 3, 4, 5, and 6 in low- and very-low-income African American and Latino/a areas. These mainly reflect ETCs and expansion of DI schools from seven before 1995 to forty-five in 2001 (Personal communication, CPS Office of Accountability, October 2001). Many of the new minus programs/schools are operational and involve all students in the school (all ETCs, military high schools, and some DI schools).[16] (On Map 2, I mark DI schools as programs because schoolwide implementation varies.) Both Chicago Military Academy and Carver Military High School are in the heart of the largely low-income, African American South Side. The MSTA college-prep math/science program seemed to run counter to the dominant pattern of race and class distribution of new programs. Seven of the eight MSTAs were in high schools on probation and served primarily low-income African Americans and Latinos/as, and each MSTA was planned to enroll four hundred students eventually. However, there was inadequate staff development and preparation in middle schools, and in 2002 CPS began phasing out MSTAs.[17] At the same time there has been an expansion of minus programs, particularly Direct Instruction. This program is tightly linked to improving test scores, as revealed by its location in the CPS Office of Accountability—not Curriculum.

"Good" Schools, Gentrification, and Legitimation

"Good" schools are real estate anchors in gentrifying neighborhoods. The intersection of CPS policies and the interests of developers and real estate companies is apparent in the geographical location of four of the new college-prep magnet high schools. The future of the Region 3 Jones College Prep magnet, which opened in fall 1998, is with the massive new upscale South Loop development where it is located. This was clear to the Jones parents, students, and local school council, who protested its conversion from a business high school widely supported by working-class families destined to be largely excluded from the new school. "It's real obvious that it's tied to the gentrification of the neighborhood," one teacher said. "They want a school that they can point to and say, 'Here's a school for your kids'" (Phuong Le & Malone, 1998, p. 2). The displacement of the previous students was itself a process of gentrification, removing the working-class high school students who fought to keep it open much as working-class families have battled developers in the neighborhood. Although the school was a vocational high school, it was one of few options for working class students to gain access to more skilled jobs in downtown corporations that sometimes provided college tuition as a job benefit (Personal communication, Jones teacher, April 2003).

Another case is the Region 1 magnet Northside College Prep (opened fall 1999), which draws from six of the fifteen "hottest" neighborhoods (those with the greatest increases in real estate values) (Pitt, 1998) and three more areas that realtors predicted would be "future hot spots" in the next ten years (Pitt, Sept.1, 1998). Payton, the Region 2 magnet, is in the upper-income Gold Coast area, with median house prices at $271,000 in 2000 (Williams, 2000), just north of the gentrifying North Loop and east of the redeveloped Cabrini Green public housing project, now the site of $1.3 million townhouses. It also draws from upper-income Lincoln Park as well as newly gentrifying near northwest side neighborhoods. King, the Region 4 magnet, is in the Kenwood neighborhood, where "distinguished new residences" are advertised just blocks from boarded-up housing projects. King is also near Hyde Park, home of the University of Chicago. From 1995 to 1998, median prices for detached single-family houses went up 50 percent in Kenwood and 67 percent in Hyde Park (Pitt, 1998, p. 9). Only Region 5 and Region 6 magnets are in nongentrifying areas, and Lindbolm (Region 5) has received little support and resources (*Catalyst,* 2000). As a whole, the regional magnet high schools reflect dual functions of the state. They support capital accumulation through their strategic location in key gentrifying and upper-income neighborhoods while legitimating city government and CPS administration by being "fairly" allocated to all region of the school district.

In short, when we examine the distribution of new programs against CPS's claim to expand educational opportunity, we find that although high-profile, allegedly academically challenging programs and schools are scattered throughout the city, almost all whole-school college-prep programs initiated since 1995 are clustered in middle-class, white, or gentrifying areas. This has been a huge investment by the city. According to the *Catalyst* (Schaeffer, 2000, p. 13), the new regional magnets got almost half of CPS construction and renovation money between 1996 and 1999. Meanwhile, most academically challenging programs in low-income communities involve only a portion of the students, and vocational, military, and DI schools—most involving all students in the school—are clustered in low-income African American and Latino/a areas. Thus, programs created and expanded under the 1995 policy agenda have reinforced the inequitable distribution of challenging academic programs, and they support gentrification, displacement, and spatial dualization.

Educational Exclusion and the Illusion of Choice

From the standpoint of equity, within existing school systems the issue is not whether some students and parents may want vocational or military schools and some teachers champion DI, or whether these programs are an improvement over existing schools and programs. The issue is whether *all* children, and especially those historically excluded, have access to important knowledge; are prepared for and encouraged to pursue an academically challenging, thoughtful, college-bound program; *and* have the support of the school system to succeed in that program. To achieve this goal requires special efforts and additional resources to overcome past inequities that have caused working-class students and children of color to be assigned to low-level vocational programs, basic tracks, and academically and materially inferior schools. When low-income children and children of color continue to be the target of vocational and military programs, and when these students have few alternatives, the programs clearly perpetuate, if not exacerbate, inequality. Moreover, these inequalities take on new dimensions in the context of the informational economy.

New academically challenging programs serve a dual purpose. First, they are an incentive for professional and middle-class families to live in the city, especially in areas of budding gentrification, where they provide access to a *separate* high-status-knowledge program. As one CPS official said, the IBs are intended to "attract more [middle-class] students to CPS. There aren't enough academic offerings for parents—they're all going to private schools. That's why this [IBs] went out" (Personal communication, February 16, 2000). Yet, politically, big city mayors, such as the Daley administration, cannot ignore economically and racially marginalized populations. Hence a second purpose—small, highly publicized college-prep programs and magnet high schools paint a veneer of equity and opportunity on a vastly unequal system.

I am not imputing to all those involved an intention to develop programs that serve real estate development and legitimate inequality, nor do all programs do this. Policy is contested at all levels of the system. For example, MSTAs may have reflected the desire of some CPS staff to extend challenging academic programs to historically disenfranchised students. Moreover, the city's demographics compel the mayor and CPS leaders to make concessions to African American and Latino/a communities. A case in point is the board's capitulation to community pressure to fund modernization of Gwendolyn Brooks, the Region 6 Magnet High School. However, this gain was taken back when, three years later, improvements had not yet been made and a local legislator reported that money allocated by the board for Brooks was spent elsewhere. Despite some concessions, in the context of a vastly unequal school system and Chicago's global city agenda, the aggregate effect of new programs and schools is to exacerbate educational inequality and heightened economic and social dualities. This is legitimated by the discourse of choice. Presenting a plethora of "options" masks the selectivity of a few elite programs, "constructing selectivity within a framework that claims inclusivity" (Ozga, 2000, p. 204). As Wells, Slayton, and Scott (2002) note, neoliberalism defines democracy as the freedom to consume within a capitalist economy. Chicago's differentiated schools are "equitable" because everyone has a choice of "options."

Even more to the point, plus programs/schools, and even ETCs and military academies, are the *upper tiers* of public schooling in Chicago. They are layered over a bottom tier that is actually the majority of neighborhood elementary and general high schools with very limited advanced course offerings. The new academic programs and schools represent a new form of tracking. The academic track is more differentiated from the other tracks and more spatially separate than in the old comprehensive high school, stripping academic track students from the general high school (Carlson, 1997). One of the major complaints of teachers in regular high schools is that the magnets and specialty programs have drawn away most of the high-achieving students, leaving everyone demoralized as neighborhood high schools are perceived to be "for losers" (as one teacher put it). Carlson (1997) notes that because of the importance of knowledge production in the informational economy, there is more interest in constructivist curricula in upper-tier schools. For example, all Northside Prep math classes use the *Integrated Mathematics Program*, a conceptual, constructivist curriculum. As the general elementary and high schools become more oriented to basic skills, the gulf between them and the new academic programs grows. In short, schooling in Chicago is arranged in a pyramid of opportunities with a few selective programs at the peak, college prep programs and vocational education in the next tiers, and the majority spread out along the wide base of rudimentary schooling.

Finally, a large percentage of students do not make it through the system at all. The Consortium on Chicago School Research calculated that the cohort dropout rate (following students from age thirteen to nineteen) was 41.8 percent in 2000, down only slightly from 44.3 percent in 1997 (Allensworth & Easton, 2001). As an example, at Juarez, a general high school in a Mexican neighborhood, enrollment of the class of 2002 at the end of the first semester of ninth grade was 547. The graduating class was 260, a completion rate of 48 percent (Personal communication, Eric Gutstein, August 15, 2002). Other students never made it beyond eighth grade to enroll at Juarez or entered an APC only to drop out. Including students who have dropped out citywide is central to grasping the magnitude of inequality in Chicago Public Schools.

"Military Prep" and "Prison Prep": Regulating and Controlling Youth of Color

Military schools are one element in an ensemble of policies that, as a whole, regulate and sort youth of color, criminalizing some while selecting others as exemplars of the positive effects of discipline. Other elements of this ensemble include CPS's Zero Tolerance discipline policy, which mandates automatic suspension and expulsion for specific offenses; Safe Schools, which segregate youth who have been involved in the criminal justice system; and Chicago's antigang loitering ordinance, which authorizes police to disperse groups of three or more in public places if the police believe they are gang affiliated.

In 1999, Vallas called school military programs "the wave of the future" (Quintanilla, 1999). In addition to two public military high schools, CPS has instituted a military middle school and expanded Junior Reserve Officer Training Programs in neighborhood high schools. Both military high schools, Chicago Military Academy and Carver Military High School, are in African American communities, and their enrollments are more than 80 percent African American, with the remainder mainly Latino/a. (Less than 1 percent of Carver and less than 5 percent of Chicago Military is white, Asian, or Native American.) The schools are a partnership between CPS and the United States Army, which has high visibility in the schools. The Chicago Military Academy is led by military officers; teachers wear military uniforms and are referred to as "Captain." Military recruiters meet with all juniors and offer them the army admission test, which is administered in the school, and some students join the army and go through basic training before graduating high school. In fact, the military high school admission process is a first screening to identify youth who will conform to military discipline. Parents and students must sign a contract agreeing to obey the military discipline code with its own set of punishments for failure to follow directions or complete homework, for example, doing ush-ups, running laps, scrubbing school walls. Administrators say the instructional program is modeled on basic training. As the CPS Board of Trustees head, Gery Chico said when Chicago Military Academy opened: "It's a school based on rules and conduct. This is a very good thing" (Quintanilla, 1999, p. 16).

The schools emphasize unquestioning obedience to hierarchical authority and undermine solidarity. This emphasis is embodied in the cadet system, which promotes those who exhibit the strongest military values and behaviors and show the greatest enthusiasm for military activities. Youth who advance to "colonel" have considerable responsibility and authority over their fellow students. A Carver administrator described a system that requires youth to refuse to compromise military discipline for solidarity with their friends: "You have to be kind of conceited, show off your skills. . . . There is no time for friends because if you have too many friends you can't lead. You can have friends but you have to do your job. . . . If you are too close to people then you can't go against them if you have to as a commander" (Personal communication). The schools speak to young people's desires to win respect, take on responsibility, and develop leadership—experiences so lacking in most public schools—but construct them as the exercise of authority over others. There is no place here for learning self-determination, collectivity, critical analysis of the world and one's place in it, or self-control for ethical ends. Rooted in the ideology of competitive individualism, the schools "help the kids who help themselves" (School administrator, August 2001).

While these youth are drilled in rules and authority, thousands of others like them are pushed out of school through Zero Tolerance discipline policies. Data collected by the Chicago youth activist organization Generation Y demonstrate that under Zero Tolerance students are being suspended primarily for minor, nonviolent infractions and attendance-related issues. Targeting and criminalizing students of color, especially African Americans, has intensified under Zero Tolerance. CPS data, obtained by Generation Y (2001), show that in 1994, the year before Zero Tolerance began, African American students made up 55 percent of CPS enrollment but had 66 percent of suspensions and expulsions. In 2001, African Americans were less than 52 percent of all CPS students, but they received more than 73 percent of all suspensions and expulsions. Although enrollment in CPS increased by only 665 students between 1999 and 2000, suspensions increased from 21,000 to nearly 37,000. "The biggest increases were among students of color, especially African-American students—where the suspension rate increased from less than 7% up to 12%" (Generation Y, 2001). In 2000–1 suspensions reached a nine-year high of 52,684 with 94 percent to students of color (Generation Y, 2002). Expulsions have also surged. Again, African Americans have been the main target. According to the *Chicago Reporter* magazine, between 1995 and 1999, African American students represented 73 percent of expulsions though they were 53 percent of CPS enrollment (Rogal, 2001). This pattern of racial exclusion is reflected in the quarantining of youth involved in the criminal justice system in "Safe Schools" isolated from the general school population. School discipline policies parallel the containment and policing of African American and Latino/a youth in their neighborhoods through Chicago's anti-gang loitering ordinance.[18] The law, championed by Mayor Daley, supports legalized harassment and street sweeps of youth and is a powerful signifier that youth of color are dangerous and justifiably contained. Between 1993 and 1995, the police arrested 43,000 people under the ordinance (High Court Is the Final Chapter, 1998).

Military schools single out some youth for their successful accommodation to a system of race and class discipline and set them apart from others criminalized by Zero Tolerance, Safe Schools, and the antigang law. Those newly disciplined by the army are explicitly defined by their difference from others like them who are, by implication, out of control and menacing. As a military officer at one of the academies put it, "*Our* gang colors are green, *our* gang is the army [emphases original]." The fact that military programs can turn these youth into models signifies that it is the youth (and their families and communities), not racism, not economic policies of disinvestment, not real estate developers, not demonization in the media, that are responsible for their lack of a productive future. Molding of these youth into obedient citizens supports the demonization of others. The binary opposition of positive versus negative images of African American youth is a form of collaboration with white supremacy, in which achievement and hard work are associated with whiteness (Haymes, 1995). "[T]he partial nature of the process of racialization as criminalization may simultaneously allow the evolution of a symbolically more successful racialized fraction which serves publicly to rebuke the immiserated majority and divest white society of any responsibility for such immiseration" (Keith, 1993, p. 207). Of course, this distinction may be largely symbolic because African American and Latino/a youth in military schools (and, in fact, in magnet schools) are also potential victims of police gang sweeps and zero-tolerance policies.

Economic restructuring and neoliberal social policies have made sectors of African American and some Latino/a communities "surplus populations." They are part of a new globalization-induced "Fourth World . . . made up of multiple black holes of social exclusion throughout the planet" (Castells, 1998, p. 164) that must be controlled directly. Christian Parenti (1999) argues that there is an intensification of the spectacle of naked state power and police terror aimed at African American and some Latino/a communities. "A growing stratum of 'surplus people' is not being efficiently used by the economy. So instead they must be controlled and contained and, in a very limited way, rendered economically useful as raw material for a growing corrections complex" (Parenti, 1999, p. 137). Thus there is a direct link between zero tolerance and antigang policies and the thriving prison industrial complex. Military schools and criminalization are part of a process of racialized social control that involves simultaneous inclusion and exclusion, self-regulation and direct force. Capital needs both "disciplined communities and flexible workplaces. The racism expressed in the imagery of a criminalized underclass coexists alongside a form of racism, different in form if not in kind, which constructs racial divisions of labor" (Keith, 1993, p. 207). These policies also help secure the new urban professionals' claims on urban space much as spear-tipped iron fences and electronic security systems fortify upscale residences. School policy is part of the regulation, containment, and eviction of marginalized "others" from the city.

CPS Policies and the New Urban Workforce

Education reform has been a consistent priority for Chicago's corporate and financial elite. This is clear from a brief overview of the Commercial Club of Chicago's (CCC) economic development proposals since the mid 1980's. The CCC is an extraordinarily active organization of the city's business and financial elite whose influence extends to direct involvement in Chicago-area policy, including education. In its 1984 long-term strategic plan, *Make No Little Plans: Jobs for Metropolitan Chicago*, the CCC called for making Chicago a leading financial services center, noting that although Chicago would have an abundance of workers, these workers needed constant upgrading of skills.[19] In a 1990 update (*Jobs for Metropolitan Chicago*), the CCC asserted, "The failures of Chicago's public schools in previous years have left us with hundreds of thousands of people untrained and ill equipped to fill the jobs of the new economy" (p. 4). The report went on to say that although good progress had been made since the 1988 school reform, education should be at the top of the city's agenda. Again in *Chicago Metropolis 2020*, published in 1998, the CCC identified lack of education and skills training as the first of three key impediments to the Chicago area's becoming a "global metropolis."

Stratified Schooling for Stratified Jobs

What kind of training is the CCC talking about? Although there is a perception that the new economy demands significantly upgraded skills for everyone (Murnane & Levy, 1996; National Center on Education & the Economy, 1990) in fact, many of the new low-wage service jobs require basic literacies, the ability to follow directions, and accommodating disposition toward work (Castells, 1996). Although a majority of rapid-growth occupations are projected to require education or training beyond high school, there is expected to be only a modest change in educational levels for all new jobs created in 1992–2005 (Castells, 1996). This is confirmed by a Bureau of Labor Statistics' prediction that between 1992 and 2005 there would be overall 6.2 million new professional workers and 6.5 million new low-wage service workers (Castells, 1996, p. 225; also Apple, 1996). In Chicago, a CCC report defined the need for "ever-more-skilled employees" required by the new economy as people "who can, at the minimum, read instruction manuals, do basic math and communicate well" (Johnson, 1998, p. 6). The report also noted that "minorities" in low-performing schools will become a greater part of the workforce and will need these new basic competencies. These competencies are corroborated by Rosenbaum and Binder's (1997) interviews with fifty-one urban and suburban Chicago employers, the majority of whom said they needed employees with "eighth grade math skills and better than eighth grade reading and writing skills."

Carlson (1996) summarizes this trend: "The 'basic skills' restructuring of urban schools around standardized testing and a skill-based curriculum has been a response to the changing character of work in post-industrial America, and it has participated in the construction of a new postindustrial working class . . . of clerical, data processing, janitorial, and service industry jobs" (pp. 282–83). Further, in the era of Fordist assembly line production, manufacturing workers needed very specific skills (e.g., welding), but through rapid technological advances, specific tasks are increasingly accomplished by computers and robotics, and these jobs are constantly being redefined. The new low-wage service and post-Fordist manufacturing jobs, as well as the large number of jobs filled by part-time and temporary labor, require the flexibility to adapt to changing job requirements. Basic reading and math literacy is essential to this learning. The overwhelming majority of Chicago high school students, largely students of color, are enrolled in neighborhood high schools organized around these competencies.

Another tier of high schools, ETCs, are linked to skill-specific manufacturing and service work, for example, automotive technology, hospitality management, mechanical design, cosmetology, and secretarial science. The ETCs are coordinated with local businesses and vocational programs at community colleges. Some ETC programs prepare students for entry-level jobs, and others, such as some health services, require further training or education. The goal of ETCs is to prepare students with "a solid background of vocational training in their field" (Personal communication, CPS official, April 12, 2000) or to prepare them to attend a postsecondary vocational program. But in an economy of simultaneously higher-skilled and downgraded labor, many of the jobs ETCs target may not include the benefits or security of unionized industrial jobs of the past. For example, whereas clerical work today demands new skills, it is often part-time and temporary. Other ETC courses, such as hospitality management, have a nonacademic curriculum core, and entry-level jobs are likely to be low-wage. At the same time, college prep magnets and IBs prepare the top tier of students for four-year colleges and universities and orient them toward technical and professional knowledge work. (The goal is not to prepare these students specifically for Chicago jobs, but to keep their middle-class parents in the city.) At the opposite end, the more than 40 percent of students who do not graduate may have little opportunity at all in the formal economy.

Tracking, differentiated curricula, and magnet schools are not new (Oakes, 1985). However, differentiated schooling has new significance in an economy in which knowledge is far more decisive than in the past. In the informational economy, one's education is a key determinant of whether one will be a high-paid knowledge worker or part of the downgraded sector of labor. The differentiation of schools and academic programs results in differential access to specific courses of study with significant implications for students' preparation for college, such as the rigor and level of high school math and science classes taken by students at the college prep magnets versus general high schools. Because of the dualization of the economy, education is becoming an increasingly important determinant of which stratum of the labor force one will enter. Ozga (2000) argues that the closer linkage of education and the economy "has produced the attempted redesign of education systems along less inclusive, more selective lines, with the purpose of reproducing and mirroring the differentiated flexible workforces of the future" (p. 24). Although I am not suggesting a simple correspondence between schooling and the workforce, there is a striking relationship between evolving educational differentiation in CPS and the stratification of labor.

Producing Differentiated Identities

Equally important, the discourses of different schools and programs apprentice students to particular ways of being, behaving, and thinking. In this sense, a *discourse* "is composed of talking, listening, reading, writing, interacting, believing, valuing . . . so as to display or to recognize a particular social identity" Gee et al., 1996, p. 10):

> Immersion inside the practices—learning *inside* the procedures, rather than overtly *about* [emphases original] them—ensures that a learner takes on the perspectives, adopts a world view, accepts a set of core values, and masters an identity without a great deal of critical and reflective awareness about these matters, or indeed about the Discourse itself. (p. 13)

Students construct identities from many social–cultural resources, but disparate school experiences provide them with disparate resources on which to draw.

Scripted direct instruction programs, IBs, ETCs, military academies, college prep magnet high schools, and so on, constitute social practices that "teach" students particular identities. In the "new capitalism [which] requires a core of relatively well paid knowledge leaders and workers supplemented by a bevy of people 'servicing' them for the least possible price" (Gee et al., 1996, p. 47), this has profound implications. The open and relaxed environment of Northside Prep, where students lounge in spacious hallways and participate in Wednesday afternoon colloquia, teaches students social roles and expectations quite different from those the military discipline at Chicago Military Academy teaches, I want to emphasize that this is not necessarily purposeful; nor is it determined. Teachers and administrators I have talked with who champion DI, military schools, and ETCs are generally dedicated to improving the academic performance and future of their students, but they see few alternatives. It is the ideological effect of differentiated learning that is the point here.

Differentiated programs, curricula, and pedagogies also have a symbolic function. The prestigious IB program with its stringent admission requirements and diploma "recognized worldwide" has a cachet quite different from that of the Military Academy's enforced subordination to authority. The ideological force of racially coded "basic skills," scripted instruction, probation, and military schools is publicly to define African American and Latino/a youth as requiring special forms of discipline and regimentation. Despite Daley's claim that military schools simply offer students "another option," the schools were established with much public fanfare in low-income African American communities—not white or middle-class communities. The media coverage of the schools' boot camp discipline commends them for putting under control "dangerous" and "unruly" youth (Johnson, 2002) and turning around "at-risk" students by exposing them to "order and discipline" (Quintanilla, 2001). Media accounts are filled with stories of failing and undisciplined youth who do not speak "proper English" and are members of "dysfunctional" homes who have been transformed through the military academies into young men and women who work hard in school, help out at home, respect adults, and even learn to speak "correctly." The schools are exemplars of a new "truth"—if schooling is going to work for many urban youth of color, it will need to be highly regimented and be separate, and distinct from college prep schools like Northside.

CPS policies also frame schooling in a language business understands—regulation, accountability, and quality assurance (see Mickelson, Ray, & Smith, 1994). The steps for education reform outlined by a consortium of top business organizations in 1996 (*Common Agenda for Improving American Education*) read as a blueprint for Chicago: "First, helping educators and policy makers set tough academic standards . . . ; second, assessing student and school-system performance against those standards; and third, using that information to improve schools and create accountability, including rewards for success and consequences for failure" (quoted in Sheldon & Riddle, 1998, p. 164). High stakes tests define education as a commodity that can be quantified, regulated, and designed much as any other commodity. Symbolically, as well as practically, a tough retention policy, standardized tests, and discipline and control of both students and schools certify for Chicago business that CPS graduates will have the specific literacies and dispositions it demands. The retention policy, for example, stamps a seal of approval on students who pass to the next grade, confirming that they meet "industry" standards.

This symbolism is highly racialized. In addition to basic mathematical and print literacy, employers are particularly concerned with future workers' attitudes and "work ethic" (Ray & Mickelson, 1993), their reliability, trustworthiness, ability to take directions, and, in the case of in-person service workers, pleasant manner (Gee et al., 1996). Eighty percent of the business leaders sampled by the Commission on the Skills of the American Workforce said they were seeking a stronger work ethic, appropriate social behavior, and a good attitude in their new workers (Ray & Mickelson, 1993). Moberg (1997) argues that Chicago is at a disadvantage in attracting new firms because there is a widespread perception that Chicago's workforce is "ill-educated, untrained, and difficult to manage," and that this perception "especially affects the hiring of black men" (p. 79). Interestingly, the description of ETCs, including "job-readiness" and "employability skills," addresses this "problem," as does CPS's overall focus on discipline and individual responsibility.

Public perception and the actual production of a disciplined workforce are constructed through a set of policies and a rhetoric that emphasize hard work and personal responsibility, individual achievement, regulation, and control. This is the pedagogy of scripted instruction, basic skills, test preparation, and discipline through which students are trained to follow directions and learn according to a strict protocol. Programs and policies that discipline, regulate, and control also teach students their "place" in a race and class hierarchy (cf. Bartlett & Lutz, 1998). They are a powerful selection mechanism, bringing in line those who comply and pushing those who do not outside the bounds of formal work and legitimated social intercourse. But parental support for military academies, ETCs, and emphasis on test scores is also rooted in a realistic assessment of the limited opportunities available to low-income students of color. In the absence of good high schools, resources to attend college, or prospects for a good job, as well as the threat of gangs in high schools, military academies (like military service itself) and ETCs are viable choices in a world of limited options. And parents are well aware that test scores are a potent selection mechanism, particularly for students who do not possess the social networks and dominant cultural capital that are the hidden advantages of middle-class white students. This good sense speaks to the urgency to create equitable alternatives to restrictive and militarized "choices."

School Policy, Global City Development, and the Cultural Politics of Race

School improvement is also central to Chicago's image as a global city. In its 1998 report, the Commercial Club praised the mayor's school reforms and identified education as one of three top priorities to realize its vision of a multicentered region of "knowledge, expertise, and economic opportunity" (Johnson, 1998, p. 3). State of the art schools are key to attracting high-paid, high-skilled workers. New York City, for example, has an established upper tier of elite public as well as private schools. A series of articles in the *Chicago Tribune* on Chicago's bid to become a global city noted that key business spokespeople consistently identify the need to "fix" the schools, "both to provide a pool of good workers and to persuade middle-class and upper-class families to settle in the city" (Longworth, & Burns, 1999, p. A14). CPS leaders have been quite explicit about this. Gery Chico, head of the CPS Board of Trustees, said in a CPS press release announcing three new magnet high schools, "Students who are ready for a challenging academic program will be able to find it at a school in their area" (Three More Schools, 1999). And a 1998 *Chicago Tribune* article on the "hottest" real estate markets in the city noted that "Chicago's improving public school system is making young families less leery of rearing their children in the city" (Pitt, 1998). CPS's open appeal to middle-class families is seen as legitimate, in part because it is taken for granted that middle-class children are essential to a good school system. As in the argument for mixed-income housing, the assumption is that there cannot be good working-class schools (or good working-class neighborhoods).

Epilogue: CPS Policy after Vallas

When test scores flattened out in spring 2001, Vallas and Chico resigned and Daley appointed Michael Scott (vice president at AT&T) as board president, Arne Duncan (Vallas's deputy chief of staff) as CEO, and Barbara Eason-Watkins (a well-known elementary school principal) as chief education officer. The new leadership has taken a more open approach when compared with Vallas's authoritarian and blatantly corporate leadership style. There is a general sense among education advocates and principals I talked with that the new administration is interested in teaching and learning. In spring 2002, central administrators held a series of focus group discussions that included some education reformers excluded by the Vallas administration. Duncan also extended the district's reading initiative by assigning reading specialists to the lowest-scoring schools, and in fall 2002 the board decentralized the regions to twenty-four new Instructional Areas. To emphasize the new focus on instruction, "highly successful" principals were appointed Area Instructional Officers (AIOs) to head the areas and work directly with principals.

However, fundamentally, the core policies and their consequences remain unchanged. The district has maintained the trend of differentiated education. CPS is dropping MSTAs, the single high school initiative under

Vallas that offered the potential for a challenging academic education for at least a quarter of the students in a few neighborhood high schools. At the same time, a budget crunch and the enormous spending on the regional magnets raise the specter that CPS may not have the funds to build long-promised neighborhood schools in low-income areas where students attend dramatically overcrowded schools. For example, parents in Little Village, a Mexican immigrant community where mothers conducted a hunger strike for a new high school, are very pessimistic. Promised extensive renovation of the far South Side college prep magnet high school, Gwendolyn Brooks, has been put on hold, maybe indefinitely, according to a state legislator who broke the news to parents and students in a January 2003 meeting. This was to have been a concession wrung from the Daley administration by African American elected officials.

Post-2001 policies have continued to further gentrification and displacement, appealing to, and advantaging, the middle class at the expense of low-income families. In April 2002, without warning, Duncan closed three "low-performing" schools (Dodge, Terrell, and Williams) on the African American West and South Sides over furious protests by families and teachers. CPS announced the schools will be reopened as "Renaissance Schools" after a thorough academic transformation (Chicago Public Schools Announce, 2002). Interestingly, Duncan had visited Dodge just a month earlier to praise its academic improvement. In November 2001 he told Williams teachers their school could be a "model school," and in March 2002 Daley and Duncan praised the school (Personal communication, Williams teacher, April 2003). In April, Duncan announced he was closing it. The grassroots analysis of community residents and teachers is that Dodge and Williams were closed to force out African American families in order to pave the way for gentrification. Williams served the Dearborn Homes housing project in an area swamped by gentrification, Terrell served a housing project under demolition, and Dodge is in a near West Side neighborhood ripe for gentrification. A community organizer commented to the *Catalyst*: "You close the schools that serve those communities, you can be sure [residents] are not going to stick around. . . . Get rid of the kids and you get rid of the families" (Weissmann, 2002, p. 17). Despite promises of significant community input in the schools' redesign, reports are that parents and long-time community members have been closed out of the process (Weissmann, 2002). These events suggest CPS's continued complicity with developers and the strategy to remove low-income African Americans from prime real estate areas.

Accountability and surveillance have also intensified, in part to satisfy *No Child Left Behind* legislation mandating high stakes standardized tests at every grade level. A close analysis of CPS's *Every Child, Every School* (2002), CPS's new education plan under Duncan and Scott, suggests that the aim is to improve teaching toward the Illinois State Achievement Test (ISAT). Independent school reform advocates have been predicting for several years that CPS would replace the ITBS with the ISAT as its high stakes test. This would put Chicago fully in line with the state's use of the ISAT for accountability under Bush's national policy. Although the goal of *Every Child* is to build "strong instructional programs and supportive school environments," the plan's core elements—"building instructional capacity, high quality teaching and leadership, engaged learning, and challenging assignments"—are geared to improvement on the ISAT, despite that there are undoubtedly CPS administrators who embrace these goals and see an opportunity to further them. The ISAT has a few more open-ended questions than the ITBS, hence concern in *Every Child* that children engage in "interpretation and analysis." Decentralizing the regions facilitates the plan's implementation, particularly its focus on professional development toward the ISAT goals.

On one hand, potentially, the new education plan sets better conditions for educators to pose alternatives to the status quo and to contest narrow educational goals and pedagogies. One Area Instructional Officer told me it represented a "window of opportunity." But in the context of ongoing coercion of accountability and a climate of hierarchical inspection and control, some teachers report that, so far, the decentralization has only intensified surveillance at their schools. With more superintendents (AIOs) going out to schools, teachers report that their principals are initiating frantic preparations to get grade books in a specific format, objectives on the board, and student work posted in prescribed fashion ahead of an AIO visit. In a further institutionalization of incentives and punishments, *Every Child* also refined and expanded accountability by instituting rewards as well as punishments. In 2002, CPS leaders gave sixty schools $10,000 each for demonstrating the greatest improvement on standardized tests, developing accountability benchmarks, and realigning local school improvement plans with CPS goals. (The latter policy directly undermines the power of parents, communities, and teachers to set school goals.) Meanwhile, in 2001–2, the highest percentage of third, sixth, and eighth graders was retained since the policy began—nearly 41 percent—almost double the percentage retained at the inception of the retention policy in 1997 (Gewertz 2002, October 9). In short, the evidence suggests that the current leadership is continuing in the policy direction set by Vallas—accountability, sorting, and control—despite more discussion of teaching and learning.

Conclusion

As a whole, the CPS policy agenda and the discourses that surround it are part of a politics of race and class that serves global city development and economic restructuring and has a life of its own rooted in Chicago's racialized history. Magnet high schools, IB programs, and publicity about rising test scores are complemented by policies that emphasize regulation and centralized control, primarily of students of color. School policies that discipline African American and Latino/a youth not only certify the production of a disciplined workforce, they signify that city leaders are "taking back" the city as a space of middle-class rationality and whiteness from African Americans and Latinos/as whose neighborhoods, "place-making practices" (Haymes, 1995), and identities are a threat to "stability." The white supremacist myth of African Americans as dangerous in the city is realized in the imagery of education policies and programs that discipline and regulate these youth. As does the vocabulary of the "urban frontier" that rationalizes gentrification and displacement as the taming of urban neighborhoods (Smith, 1996), racially coded "basic skills," scripted instruction, probation and reconstitution of schools, and military high schools legitimate the segregation and/or dispersal of low-income communities of color. These policies (the "flip side" of elite high schools) instill order and help make the city "safe" for new upscale enclaves, much as "the new urban pioneers seek to scrub the city clean of its working-class geography and history . . . its class and race contours rubbed smooth" (Smith, pp. 26–27). The discourse of control and authority may also be a preemptive response to an urban context simmering with potentially explosive contradictions of wealth and poverty, development and abandonment, and blatant economic and social power alongside disempowerment.

CHAPTER **4**

"Like a Hammer
Just Knocking Them Down"

Regulating African American Schools

The children are being knocked down to a test score and the teachers, with their variety of skills and talents, are just being wasted because they are just so zoned into this test.

(Grover teacher, April 1999)

Introduction

Despite their apparently universal application, Chicago's 1995 school reform policies—accountability, centralized regulation, standards, educational "choices"—are deployed selectively as a racialized, class-specific ensemble of messages and social practices. In this and the next two chapters, I examine what these policies mean in four different local school contexts. This chapter explores these messages and social practices at Grover and Westview, two low-income African American elementary schools serving public housing projects. I argue that the thrust of centralized control and accountability in these schools is to regulate students and teachers and to redefine education around the skills, information, procedures, and results of standardized tests. This kind of schooling prepares people for low-skilled jobs. But it is also a racialized discourse that disciplines African American students and their teachers and constructs African Americans in general as people in need of social control. I will argue that these policies contribute to the formation of white supremacist culture and consciousness and the construction of an urban mythology of middle-class normalcy and whiteness that justifies the removal of African American urban communities no longer needed as a source of industrial labor. Yet, schools are "paradoxical institutions" (Ball, 1997a), and despite the hegemony of accountability discourses, no unitary story can be told about Westview and Grover. There is resistance, and dominant discourses are complicated by alternative ideologies and mediated by specific contexts. Yet, despite these contradictions, in the end, I have to conclude that educational disparities are hardened, and in the most beleaguered and regulated context, we see demoralization and flight. The starting point of my discussion is the schools and their communities.

Grover and Westview: The Schools and Their Communities

More than 95 percent of Grover and Westview students are classified as low-income; 100 percent are African American. During my research, most of the children lived in public housing complexes in areas with high rates of unemployment and poverty and few to no commercial or public resources such as parks and recreational facilities, banks, grocery stores, and other businesses. Families who live in these housing projects epitomize the city's "expendable" population. These are communities that have been on a steep economic decline over the past twenty-five years and were untouched by the "boom" of the 1990s. Welfare "reform" and the demolition of public housing have compounded this crisis and put extraordinary pressures on families. Grasping these conditions and the persistent educational inequalities facing African Americans is essential to an understanding of implications of education policies for Grover and Westview.

Demolition of Public Housing—"The Land Is Valuable and the Present Tenants Are Not"[1]

During the 1980s, both communities were hit hard by the massive deindustrialization and disinvestment that changed the face of Chicago and other cities across the United States. As a result, average annual income in both areas today is around seven thousand dollars, unemployment is around 98 percent, and poverty, lack of community resources, and expressways have essentially isolated residents from the rest of the city. Chicago's crumbling public housing is iconic for the disinvestment, lack of maintenance, and corrupt management of public housing in the United States. Once-stable, working-class public housing projects, with high levels of employment, became warehouses for some of the most economically impoverished people in the United States. The Chicago Housing Authority (CHA) let the buildings decay to the point of being uninhabitable— sewage backed up in kitchens, no heat in the dead of winter, and nonoperational showers, toilets, and elevators are facts of life. Having systematically neglected the buildings and the people living in them, the federal and local state created the logic for their demolition.[2] With economic and material decline, the projects became sites of violence and permanent police occupation and terror. They also became ideological sites for the demonization of African Americans. Dehumanizing conditions created by the state were ascribed to the people living there, who were defined in the media as "criminal" and "savage." Having established the logic for the dispersal of residents, the city and federal authorities who demolish the buildings are now construed as humanitarian.

However, less benevolent motives are more plausible explanations for the decline and razing of public housing in the city. The proximity of both housing projects to gentrifying areas and expressways and the nearness of one to a university have made the building sites prime real estate. Articles in the real estate section of the *Chicago Tribune* note that the areas "have potential."[3] A spokesman for Chicago's Department of Planning and Development said of one of the communities, "There's a lot of companies in the city looking for space, and if CHA made that land available, being right on the expressway, it would be very attractive for an industrial park." Demolition is creating the conditions to move the residents out of the city altogether. Affordable housing advocates contend there is not enough replacement housing available for residents and the demolition of CHA buildings is increasing homelessness. Although the city promised to find or build replacement housing for displaced residents, 7,327 units were demolished between 2000 and 2001, but only fifty-six new units were actually constructed (Community Renewal Society, 2002). A 2002 study by the Lawyers Committee for Better Housing found that landlords denied housing to tenants with Housing and Urban Development (HUD) vouchers[4] in up to 70 percent of cases (Community Renewal Society). This is compounded by Chicago's extreme crisis in affordable housing (Catholic Charities, 1999). Most former recipients of public assistance cannot find jobs above a minimum wage, and "it takes 76% of a minimum wage earner's monthly paycheck to cover the cost of a two-bedroom apartment at fair market rent" in the Chicago area (Catholic Charities, 1999). Data published by the *Chicago Tribune* indicate that most displaced residents move to other high-poverty areas or out of the city to impoverished ring suburbs with dilapidated housing and little or no public transportation. A member of the Coalition to Save Public Housing put it succinctly, "Now there is no use for us either as labor or votes, we are being moved out to the suburbs" (Haney & Shiller, 1997).

As the buildings go down one by one, children do not know when they will be moved out, where they will be living, or even with whom, as some families are forced to parcel out their children to relatives because it is so difficult to find adequate housing using the HUD subsidized rent vouchers that residents are left with. The sense of abandonment is so total that one parent told a teacher she believed soon the city would not even provide education for her community. Contrary to the imagery of the "urban jungle" in which families at Westview and Grover are depicted in the white supremacist imagination, veteran teachers say the projects used to be like small towns. Everyone knew almost everyone else in "the buildings," and teachers taught siblings and knew parents and grandparents. Now as families are "deported" (as one tenant leader put it), these bonds are further shattered. Teachers say that over the past four years they have seen a marked increase in the stress on children and families. In 1997, both schools enrolled about eight hundred students. By fall 2000, although Westview's enrollment remained stable, Grover's had been cut in half as a result of families' being moved out of the school's attendance area.

Grover Elementary School

Grover is a pre-kindergarten through eighth grade neighborhood school located in one of the most impoverished census tracts in the United States. The school provides three hot meals a day, and, as the principal said, the fact there is no food left over "tells you a lot." Grover sits right across the street from the high-rise housing project where almost all the students live. The school is in a squat rectangular building with no architectural features to distinguish it from other brick and concrete schools built in the city in the early 1960s. Inside it feels mostly drab and institutional with cement block walls and hallways with little decoration other than classroom bulletin boards. Grover is orderly, although discipline is a constant topic of discussion among teachers and administrators. The school has a strict discipline regimen, and a few moms and grandmothers are hired to keep order in the cafeteria and hallways and to monitor anyone who walks through the front door. There are no spaces for children or teachers to congregate and relax, and there is zero tolerance for noise or spontaneity in hallways. The teachers' lunch room is a cramped, cheerless room filled with lunch tables and lined on one wall with shelves of handouts from the school's probation partner (external agency contracted by CPS to oversee the school) and a few random textbooks.

Grover was in the first wave of schools to be put on probation by the Vallas administration in 1996. In 1998, the board removed Grover's veteran Polish American principal, Ms. Lipinski, and replaced her with Dr. Thomas, an African American staff development person in the central office. Although Grover was one of the lowest-scoring schools in the district (less than 20 percent of students were reading at or above national norms, as measured by the ITBS), in a 1997 interview, Lipinski said that if the school provided a safe haven for the children, she felt it was doing a good job. Until 2000 the school had no playground, almost no working computers, few classroom libraries, and no full-day kindergarten; the library was closed, its books moldering and absurdly out-of-date. There were more than thirty students per class. In 2001 there was still no gym or art class and a talented veteran music teacher left and could not be replaced, eliminating music. Only about 25 percent of students scored at or above national norms on the ITBS. Despite the obvious need, teachers and administrators saw Reading Recovery or some other early intervention reading program and reduced class size as pipe dreams because they would "cost too much." Repeatedly, teachers talked about the need for a full-time social worker and other social support programs in the school. According to the principal, much needed resources, "enrichment classes," and instructional materials must be financed by the school's existing funds. By fall 2000, Dr. Thomas had juggled the budget to buy calculators, math manipulatives, a new primary reading series, and new blackboards and to reopen and revitalize the library. He also pressured the board to build a long-promised playground. The school's external probation partner was a university-sponsored organization called Better City Schools (BCS) that had a multimillion-dollar contract with CPS to oversee school improvement for a number of schools on probation. BCS received more than $1 million for its oversight of Grover. BCS's program focused on structured scope and sequence of instruction, grade level curriculum coordination, and weekly and monthly lesson plans and assessments tied to CPS Standards and standardized tests. Teachers were required to use BCS instructional schema, charts, designated topics, and mottos. BCS monitored teachers, led professional development sessions, and had the power to approve the School Improvement Plan, discretionary budget, and administrative decisions. Grover had an extraordinarily high teacher turnover rate, as much as one third of the staff in 1999. Each year the principal scrambled to find last-minute replacements, and the LSC did not have enough parents and community members for a quorum.

Westview Elementary School

Westview is also a pre-kindergarten to grade eight neighborhood school located beside a CHA high-rise. In 1997 the school had more than eight hundred students; about 94 percent were classified as low-income. Enrollment remained fairly constant through 2001. Westview is an airy glass and steel structure. Its entranceway and halls are alive with student artwork (much of it produced under a previous principal), African cultural artifacts, colorful posters and banners, and bulletin boards displaying student work. The teachers' lounge and lunchroom is an open, roomy space with a couch, lunch tables, and a few lounge chairs. By 8:00 A.M., the aroma of frying bacon, eggs, and pancakes wafts through the first floor, signaling the daily breakfast, where many teachers meet to finish last-minute work, plan activities, and connect before the start of the schoolday. Despite its pleasant ambiance, Westview had no art or music, no reading specialist, and a computer room that is a hodgepodge of outdated, mismatched computers.

Westview is known as one of the strongest elementary schools in the community. I heard many explanations: the leadership of a legendary former principal, a relatively stable student population, outside funding and community partnerships, a dedicated, well-educated corps of teachers. However, in 1997, Westview's test scores dropped, and a second drop would have put it on probation. In the following years the scores improved by almost 25 percent, and by 2000 almost 50 percent of students were scoring at or above national norms in reading and math. (The story of this test-score recovery is part of my discussion in this chapter.) The school's principal, Ms. Grimes, is an African American woman with a long history in the school. Westview is in many ways "her" school, the teachers are "her" staff, the parents "her" parents, and the students hers, as well. In my observations, she seemed to know the name of every student she reprimanded, cajoled, or praised in the hallways or school office. On the face of it, her leadership seemed disorganized (she invariably forgot appointments and made last-minute schedule changes) but was actually grounded in her relationship with a core of veteran, mostly African American teachers who could be counted on to head up committees, anchor grade-level teams, and fill in to handle daily emergencies. The school also had a number of energetic, capable young teachers. There was very little teacher turnover. Generally, teachers described Westview as a good place to teach. Unlike at Grover, the principal's support for professional development had been strong. When I began my research, seven teachers had just completed a graduate program in reading and others were beginning. The LSC president reported there was an active core of about a dozen parents, whom Ms. Grimes described as "involved" and "supportive."

Education as Test Scores

The discourse of high stakes tests and accountability dominated both Grover and Westview in ways both similar and different. There were also counterdiscourses and resistance. Standardized tests governed daily life at both schools. Although Grover administrators believed accountability was necessary to prod negligent teachers, people at both schools linked the importance of the tests not to improved learning, but to their punitive consequences. When Westview's scores went down, the whole school was consumed by the ITBS. After the school raised its scores, the goal became raising them further. For Grover, "getting off probation" was the mantra throughout. The culture of both schools, although complex and contradictory, was increasingly saturated with practices, language, and values shaped by increasing performance on standardized tests. This discourse became normalized and shaped the way people defined education.

"We're Test Driven"—Remaking Educational Practice

> Oh boy, if these scores go down this year, I tell you Miss [Grimes] will have a fit. She's really on the teachers this year. And that's why she's really focusing on the [teams]. She'll really be working and be on for how the children are learning, what they're learning, what they're doing. ;. . . If these kids go down this year, whew. Be very critical. (Westview teacher, March 2000)

When we asked teachers and administrators at both schools, over four years, what their school's main goals were, they consistently answered "improving test scores," and when we asked them what internal and external factors were the main influences on their school, they consistently identified "standardized tests." Talk about standardized tests peppered my interviews:

> Grover teacher: "Fifty percent of my day is spent teaching either out of an IGAP [ISAT][5] math book or language arts book." (February 1998)
> Grover teacher: "I've been at this school for five years, and the emphasis on standardized tests weighs more heavily than it ever has in my career." (December 1998)
> Grover teacher: "Half the day is spent practicing for the test, but learning things too, but it's really geared to the test, the test, the test." (December 1998)
> Grover teacher talking about teachers of benchmark grades (third, sixth, eighth): "I think that they spend the majority of their time doing Iowa [ITBS] practice things." (May 2000)
> Grover administrator: "the scores on the test drive a lot of what we're doing." (November 2000)
> Westview teacher: "We are test driven . . . everything is test driven." (March 2000)
> Westview teacher: "Testing, yeah, because you know that's the basic focus." (February 2000)

Grover went all out to make sure students attended during the week of the tests:

> They were actually sending people over to their houses to make sure that they came to school, sending security guards out to go and get kids. Which just tells you if they had this effort and energy throughout the whole year when kids are truant over 20 days, the kids would get to school and they would learn. But it's all about the test. (Teacher, May 1999)

One obvious manifestation was that teachers taught to specific parts of the test that students did poorly on the previous year. At both schools, the faculty reviewed a detailed item analysis of the ITBS and ISAT. Each teacher received a printout of her students' scores for each item and was expected to gear instruction to rectifying weaknesses. For example, at both schools, the test item analysis pointed to problems making inferences from reading passages, so staff development and classroom exercises often focused on "inferencing." "Inference was our big thing this year. I think all the teachers focused on inference" (Ms. Barnes, Westview teacher, May 1998).

Although CPS cites rising test scores as evidence that "reform is working," and, by implication, students are learning more, in fact, improved scores may have more relation to drilling for the tests than to learning (Hauser, 1999). From my observations, Westview's extraordinary concentration on test preparation is a plausible explanation for its big increase in scores between 1997 and 1998. Teachers said the test pressure was so intense that they did breathing exercises and meditation with students to relieve anxiety. A consultant working at Westview commented: "There's more emphasis in that school on test scores certainly than at [Grover], certainly more than any school I've ever been in, to the point where the week following the Iowa tests the kids were saying, 'That's it. School's out.'... The teachers kind of had that attitude too" (Interview, June 1998). A seventh grade teacher said, "It's been drilled into us that this is the most important thing for this year." An eighth grade teacher said, "with all the teaching strategies that have been going on—teaching them how to take the tests. I have tested them to death to tell you the truth about it." Although the big push occurred after the winter holidays (testing is in late winter and spring), test prep was year-round. "[T]hat's what our principal is really on, standardized tests. And even though we test frequently, we do test-taking [practice], well I do, at least once a week" (Ms. Waller, Westview teacher, March 2000).

One implication is that this emphasis undermines more potentially rich educational experiences. In some classrooms *Test Best* and *Test Ready* books *were* the curriculum, day in and day out, for weeks. In others, teachers used them once a week throughout the year or for a few weeks before the test. In a few cases, in kindergarten through second grade, they were not used. But at the key benchmark grades, the Westview principal required teachers to substitute test preparation materials for the standard curriculum for twelve to fifteen weeks. For example, Ms. Washington's third graders worked cooperatively in groups, developed projects, and used a literature-based reading text, but she spent about a third of the year mostly on test preparation. During that time, the students put away their novels, basal readers, and math manipulatives, and she rearranged clusters of desks into rows and forbade students to work together because that would be cheating on the ITBS and ISAT. She used the test preparation books exclusively for reading and math during this time. "The principal's like, I don't want to see that basal [reading textbook] out. I want you to really focus on using test practice materials to get these kids where they need to be" (March 2000). Test prep also involved practice in taking tests. Most teachers reported they used timed tests regularly. Three Westview teachers attended a meeting at the board's Office of Accountability in November 1999 and were advised to stress "test taking tips daily." They were told that third graders should practice using two sheets of paper (one with test questions, one an answer sheet) all year. In fact, students spent hours taking mock tests, practicing filling in bubbles in scantron sheets, developing familiarity with the layout of the tests and the kinds of questions that are asked, and learning "tricks" for eliminating incorrect answers (e.g., "Three *b*'s in a row, no, no, no").

Redefining Education

Over the period of my research, preparing for standardized tests dominated talk about schooling. Classroom talk was shaped by test preparation, and phrases like "That's the kind of question you will have on the test [ITBS]" or "You will need to know this for the test [ITBS]" ran through teachers' commentary with their students. As one Grover administrator summed up: "We are looking at how to teach reading to get off probation in place of how to teach reading for lifelong learners" (December 1998). Despite her broader educational goals and multifaceted approach to literacy, Ms. Washington, at Westview, began to see the test prep books as valuable because they reinforced the "knowledge" tested on the ITBS: "[*Test Best*] has given me a chance to use small passages and shorter stories to focus on how to find answers and how to understand the story with my students" (February 2000). A writing lab teacher at Westview said she used to let fifth grade students experiment with a variety of genres, but because the ISAT required a five-paragraph persuasive essay, all her writing labs focused on that. This was apparent on the second floor bulletin board, where all thirty fifth grade essays on display had exactly five paragraphs and followed the same formulaic structure. The teacher introduced other genres of writing, such as narratives and poetry, only after the tests were finished in the spring. Squeezing open-ended and creative assignments or longer or more engaging texts into the beginning and end of the school year was a recurring theme in my data. The emphasis on testing reading and math also pushed out arts and other subjects, except in the specific grades when they were tested on the ISAT. "After Christmas, unless your grade level is being tested in social studies, they stop teaching it and concentrate on reading and math to push the scores. . . . They don't see or hear about any social studies from January through May, and nothing after that" (Grover teacher, December 2000). When Westview's scores dropped, teachers voted to use money allocated for incorporating arts in the curriculum to purchase test-prep books.

The emphasis on analyzing and preparing for standardized tests; the intense pressure on administrators, teachers, and students to raise scores; the substitution of test-preparation materials for the existing curriculum; practice in test-taking skills as a legitimate classroom activity—these constitute a meaning system that reinforces the definition of education as the production of "objective," measurable, and discrete outcomes. This culture is ritualized in the weeks immediately preceding the ITBS, when schools across the city cover bulletin boards with messages like "Zap the Iowa," students make posters and write essays about how they will pass the test, and whole schools are assembled for Iowa test pep rallies. A teacher described test-prep fever at Grover:

> As the test came closer and closer, as the weeks before the test came around, over the intercom [they were] saying, "You know that we are on probation at the school, we all need to try our best to pass this test, and we are on probation, and so you don't have to stay in your same grade." And then the Friday before the test started, they had a big ITBS pep rally and had the kids in the gym chanting about how they were going to do so great on the ITBS and had the cheerleaders doing cheers about the Iowa test. (April 2000)

As accountability measures exert real authority over students, teachers, and school administrators and permeate instruction, "words and concepts change their meaning and their effects" as they are deployed within the discourse of accountability and standardized testing (Ball, 1990, p. 18). A staff development session on "critical thinking skills" at Westview was about teaching children how to think about test questions. A Grover probation partner's example of making students "part of the educational process" was students' making up their own multiple-choice test questions like those on the ISAT and ITBS. A Grover administrator gave this example of a critical approach to knowledge: "[BCS, the external probation partner] encourages students to be critical insofar as they make up their own—now I'm talking about in terms of their reading material. They're supposed to read the material and things like this and they make up their own tests, multiple-choice tests and things like this" (Interview, March 2000). Some Grover teachers said the arts program was not "relevant"—equating "relevance" with preparation for the ITBS. BCS even led an in-service on writing poetry that circled back to the ITBS: "This is what you have the kids do, you have them write poetry and then you have them make up Iowa test questions about their poetry" (Teacher interview, April 2000). Westview's principal defined *educational success* as "when our children are able to read, write, do math, and also able to do critical thinking. And [when] all of this is done at the 50th percentile, I think our children are successful" (Interview, December 1998). Achieving high test scores was equated with good teaching. The Grover teacher with the highest scores received an award in a public ceremony whereas a teacher who had won a prestigious state teaching award received no public recognition.

After sitting through weeks of test preparation, Iowa test pep rallies, and daily talk about gearing up for the tests, students also learn inside these procedures that education is about discrete skills, measurable results, externally validated right answers, and test scores. Ms. Kopke, who was critical of the process, said:

> Suddenly the classroom is a place where you get better test scores, you learn to get better test scores instead of learning. I have seen children who used to just love learning, love reading, love dance, love science and math run up to me now and they are in 5th and 6th grade and say "I got better test scores." And that is the first thing out of their mouth and I will say, "Are you feeling smarter these days? Have you read any good books lately? What have you done in your community to improve things? Do you have any new goals in your life?" They sort of look at me, "Wow nobody has asked me that in a long time or nobody has talked about that or focused on that in a long time." (Grover teacher, May 2000).

Not all schools are immersed in this discourse. Neoliberal restructuring of education has given new authority to standardization and quantification of learning, but this discourse has differential consequences based on race, ethnicity, and social class. The importance of standardized tests is greatest in schools like Grover and Westview that are under the greatest pressure to raise their scores. Concretely, these schools serve low-income African American and Latino/a students. Seemingly objective and color-blind policies have racialized consequences (Gillborn & Youdell, 2000). To quote a principal of a relatively high-scoring school, "They [central office] mostly leave us alone. They're too busy with the low-scoring schools." If the new policies reinforce a narrow curriculum and promote education as test preparation, then students historically denied an equal opportunity to learn, who are the supposed beneficiaries of the new policies, continue to be denied access to an intellectually powerful education. Moreover, they are immersed in a discourse that is contrary to critical social thought, complex analysis, and preparation for intellectual leadership while those who are more privileged are relatively more immune to this discourse, as I argue in chapter 6. Ideologically, students who are subjected to the intensified boredom and regimentation associated with weeks of test preparation and an additional two hours a day after school have the daily experience of powerlessness, teaching them their "place" within a race and class hierarchy (Carlson, 1996; Haymes, 1996).

Educational Triage

The accountability regime also encouraged the educational triage that I described in chapter 3. At Grover, administrators distributed a form for teachers to identify students who were at stanine 4 or 5 (students near to or just above the 50th percentile on the ITBS who could potentially raise the number of students in the school scoring above the 50th percentile). These students were to be singled out for extra attention. A central office supervisor advised the teachers to focus on these students:

> They tell us, at least in 1st and 2nd grade, to pick 5 kids from your room to go to summer school. "We don't want high kids and we don't want the lowest kids, we want the kids that are just about to pass the IOWA test." So here you have a third or a fourth of your classroom really needs help to be ready for that next grade level and they don't get to go. We had [name] the head of our district, our region, come and tell us, "when you are walking around your classroom and the kids are working, the kids whose shoulders you need to lean over and give a little extra help are the kids who have stanine 4 and 5." (Grover teacher, May 2000)

At a Westview faculty meeting in 1997–98, one teacher suggested they identify the "kids who score high and carry the school" and make sure those students are "being serviced" (provided with counseling so they would not transfer to another school). The assistant principal also reported that the principal would identify all students close to passing so they could be pulled out of the classroom for extra work (Field notes, January 1998).

In practice, many teachers refused to sort their students as if they were the wounded on a battlefield. Outside the walls of their schools or behind closed doors, they were quietly outraged. But teachers were also caught in the intense pressure to raise scores. Jobs, careers, reputations were on the line, but, more important, educators wanted to escape the intense scrutiny and oversight that mark probation and low-scoring schools. Teachers talked about triage as a short-term strategy, yet they were implicated in processes of "rationing education" (Gillbourn & Youdell, 2000) contrary to basic principles of fairness and the very mission of teaching. In a cynical twist, a system of high stakes accountability, supposedly imposed to ensure that "no child will be left behind," has become a means and rationale for slighting those students who need the most help.

What About "Bad" Teachers?

An important argument for accountability and standards is that there are too many teachers who simply are not teaching, cannot teach, or are willing to pass students just to be done with them. For these teachers accountability is meant to be a potent motivator to change or get out of the system, and for principals, an impetus to supervise teachers more closely and ensure that they have necessary pedagogical and content knowledge. For weak or uncommitted teachers, critiques of accountability's constraints on curriculum and pedagogy are beside the point. They need mandates, benchmarks, and sanctions. In schools where there is a substantial portion of very ineffective or uncommitted teachers, these urgent measures are necessary to ensure improvement, and these schools are the primary target of the policies. This is the argument.

To some extent, this argument was supported by my data from Grover and Westview. Probation provided the rationale for the board to replace Ms. Lipinski, an apparently well-meaning but status quo principal, with Dr. Thomas, an authoritarian figure who certainly had the force of the central office and the probation partner at his back, compelling him to act. One result was that, between 1998 and 2000, Dr. Thomas removed at least four veteran teachers who had little control of their classrooms and/or very weak content and pedagogical knowledge. He also did not rehire at least five interns who, he judged, were not competent. The BCS program and district semiscripted curriculum also provided a scaffolding and techniques for teachers who were having trouble. For example, Ms. Brown, an intermediate grades teacher, liked the BCS graphic organizers: "They emphasize a lot of webs, and, you know, like, charts. Then we have [pause] they have the comparison and contrast. We have the Ven Diagram" (May 1998). She went on to say:

> I'm happy for this, you know, because I've been teaching a long time. And I know that, you know, the student—without reading, without, if you can't read, you're just, you're really messed up, you know, in life. And you need to read, so I welcome any kind of help. . . . I don't have a problem with that. . . . I'm glad for somebody to come and help me.

But my observations indicated that this kind of technical and prescriptive help did not take teachers far. From a summary of field notes, the following describes Ms. Brown's intermediate grade class in November 2000:

> This was a reading lesson. There were two foci: (1) listening to a story on tape and completing a story map worksheet [BCS activity], (2) reading a selection from the text on Benjamin Banneker and completing a time line worksheet [BCS activity]. Students focused on finding right answers from tape or story. Mostly Ms. Brown sat at her desk. Sometimes she walked around and repeated a question on the worksheet. Once a student got the "right" answer, she said, "OK, write that down." Two boys read the whole story (5 pages) others read only 2–3 pages in 26 minutes. Ones who didn't finish, Ms. Brown directed to look ahead and find answers, "like on the Iowa." To one boy she said, "Alan, you're working too slow." There was no discussion or activities directed to comprehending the story as a whole, no introduction or context set although Banneker was a famous African American mathematician.

This pattern was representative of many classes we observed at Grover. Although teachers were using more explicit and varied strategies, a good deal of the instruction we observed continued to be at a slow pace and involved what we judged to be superficial coverage of content. (This is reflected in the later discussion of BCS professional development.) Almost half the lessons emphasized basic skills and transfer of basic information, and this proportion remained consistent over the four years of observations across grade levels. In short, there was little evidence that accountability and centralized regulation supported substantive teacher development at Grover. It was a very simplistic response to a complex set of problems that included the need for stronger pedagogical and content knowledge, the failure to root curriculum and pedagogy in students' social–cultural contexts, deficit notions about students and families, a culture of blame, and lack of necessary resources and material and intellectual conditions.

The Political Economy and Racial Politics of Education as Test Preparation

Among some teachers, educational triage provoked cynicism and provided evidence for the political insight that, as a Grover teacher put it, "Everything in CPS is for show. It's all PR for political goals." Development, investment, and global city dreams are linked to certifying that Chicago schools are producing a literate workforce. Rising test scores, coupled with highly publicized selective schools and programs, are the leading edge of Daley's claim that Chicago schools are improving. These scores are being raised at the expense of African American students and other students of color in lieu of transformative changes that are urgently needed in all Chicago schools and especially in schools like Grover and Westview. There is a hidden chain connecting city hall and real estate, business, and financial interests with what is happening at Grover and Westview and other schools serving African Americans and other low-income students of color.

As I have argued, differential access to the knowledge and dispositions that prepare one to create knowledge and process information has significant consequences for social inequality in an information-based economy. The focus on test preparation runs counter to the problem-solving and open-ended thinking required for upper-tier professional, managerial, and technical jobs (National Center, 1990). Rather than promoting greater equality, the dispositions and skills fostered by education as test preparation are more likely to prepare Grover and Westview students for the abundance of low-level, low-skill, low-paid jobs in Chicago's growing service economy. As probation schools and low-scoring schools serving low-income students of color are defined by test preparation, accountability policies widen the existing gap between them and schools serving middle-class and white student populations. Although test scores may go up in some schools, as they did at Westview, the policies further consolidate a two-tier school system differentiated by race, ethnicity, and social class. Further, a triage system that sorts out children deemed beyond resuscitation is likely to lead to their exodus from school. The tedium of test preparation and the assault on students' self-respect by a system of individual blame and punishment can only further alienate youth who already find school largely irrelevant to their interests, lived experiences, and future. These are also youth most likely to be "superfluous" in the formal economy, channeled into military and prison tracks.

The narrowly instrumental pedagogy, curriculum, and assessment that I observed at Westview and Grover would never be tolerated at selective private or public schools. They are, however, deemed appropriate for "inner city schools," which are coded Black. Defining the problems of the schools as the problem of race justifies their regulation (Haymes, 1995). Racially coded test-prep education is part of a cultural politics of race that designates routinized, skill-driven schooling for African American and some Latino/a students and in turn defines them by this kind of schooling. It is no accident that youth at Grover and Westview are consistently subjected to police terror and police occupation of their communities. These schools illustrate how public schooling contributes to racialized social control through dual processes of coercion and ideological regulation.

Standards and Standardization

The Chicago Academic Standards (CAS) and Curriculum Frameworks Statements (CFS) are supposed to ensure that all students are taught the same academic content (Board of Education, 1997). On the face of it, this is a step toward equity in a system with wide disparities in the opportunity to learn challenging curriculum. Ms. Williams, a Grover teacher, summarized this logic: "[They] provide a vehicle for teachers that they have to teach these certain skills so the children will have the same success or the same knowledge as other students all over the school system" (Interview, March 2000). There seemed to be general agreement among teachers that consistency across the school district is important. Ms. Kopke said: "I think that we need something going on in the city that sort of keeps us abreast of what happens in grade levels. If I teach 2nd grade I want the 1st graders to be able to do certain things and it's good for me to be able to look back and see what they should do" (May 2000).

However, I found little evidence that the Standards (I use this term generically to refer to CAS and CFS) had much real impact on teaching at

Grover and Westview. At Westview, neither teachers nor the principal talked much about them because there was little monitoring. At Grover, where BCS's strategy was to align curriculum with the Standards and high stakes tests, teachers were required to indicate in each lesson plan and on the chalkboard each day which CAS and CFS they were covering. They became part of a system of surveillance—rather than use them to guide curriculum planning, teachers plugged them in mechanically *after* they wrote their lesson plans. This is illustrated by my notes from a grade-level weekly planning meeting of four teachers at Grover in 2000. The teachers began by discussing which story to read in the basal reader, moved on to talk about individual students, discussed activities that had "worked" the previous week, and wrote a lesson plan for the next week following the BCS protocol. In the remaining few minutes one teacher said, "Okay, we've got to have the standards in there." They quickly went through and inserted standards that seemed to fit what had already been decided. "Okay, we can put number A1 in here. C1 might fit story mapping" (Field notes, February 2000). Ms. Kopke's critique corresponds to my observations:

> I think they get used more so like a checklist like well we did that, check, instead of having the learning constantly folding back and spiraling and scaffolding so that what we learned this last week but now I am going to take it to another level. . . . I have actually seen physical check marks in people's books saying "check we did that," and unfortunately I have actually seen people who have said "I've taught everything in there and we are kind of done, we are just going to do this or that for the rest of the school year." (May 2000)

At Grover, for inexperienced teachers or those without a clear instructional plan, the Standards seemed to provide a welcome list of skills and concepts. However, in neither school was there evidence that the Standards provoked thinking or discussion about selection of knowledge or pedagogical decisions. Ms. Kopke:

> I think that the other reason why they are not used productively is because they are so simplistic and so people can feel like they can just check it off. If they were more complex and if they required the children to think more deeply and to synthesize, people couldn't check, you would have to spend a whole year teaching children to evaluate a situation and to make past judgments or what have you. If it was written for each grade level in a spiral then you couldn't check and at the end of the year you couldn't check it, you could just say we have worked on this, we've done this and you create examples of how your students have worked on that through literature, experiments, situations and community work, what have you. (May 2000)

I observed only a few teachers who used the standards critically. Ms. Kopke was one of the few:

I don't pull mine [CAS] out on a daily basis or anything like that, but I do browse over them and sort of see where I have holes. . . . They are really written in the most skeletal form possible, which for me, I actually appreciate that because it allows me a lot of space to plug in the kinds of things that I really want my students to be doing, that I think are valuable and that come from the kids themselves. (May 2000)

Evidence from these schools puts in question the claim that the CAS and CFS actually promote more rigorous content across the district. In fact, the mandated formal equality of standards masks sedimented educational inequalities and deficit ideologies that have contributed to the long term failure to ensure that all children engage rigorous intellectual content. Some teachers argued that the Standards were harmful because they provided no curricular scaffolding or intensive support for students who lacked necessary prior knowledge and skills. Teachers said they were forced to move on to the next standard even when students lacked background knowledge, leaving them even further behind. What the Standards have done is shift the terrain of discussion about race and equity to standards-based outcomes (Tate, 1997). As in high stakes testing, the symbolic equality of standards helps legitimate a school system that, as a whole, continues to produce inequality.

Moreover, the Standards further eroded teachers' control of classroom knowledge (to the extent they ever had any) and foreclosed debate about the curriculum. They were imposed without discussion and with little attention to the complexity of teaching or the diversity of students' cultures, languages, and experiences. This system not only deprofessionalizes teaching, it obscures the political nature of school knowledge. The Standards were presented as a conclusive compendium of what children should know, masking the politics of the selection of what counts as knowledge (see Apple, 1996). In fact, the Standards opposed some teachers' conception of an excellent education for African American children. Several Grover teachers believed it was important that the curriculum examine the history and cultural production of African Americans and their relationship to other social groups in the United States. To some extent, these teachers were silenced by the prevailing discourse of test scores, standards, and technical procedures. "Discourses are, therefore, about what can be said, and thought, but also about who can speak, when, where and with what authority" (Ball, 1990, p. 17). This silencing was an important contributor to teachers' demoralization at Grover. Ms. Jones describes this experience:

This year has been the worst year since I have been teaching, period. It is because a lot of people are afraid to do things if they're not a certain way. . . . If it doesn't fit into the framework, if it doesn't fit into the Standards, if it doesn't fit into this, if someone from the state comes past, if you're not doing what they feel is teaching. . . . I feel under pressure because this is the first time in a long, long time since I was a child that I really feel I'm compromising my beliefs. (Feburary 1998)

Contradictions, Competing Discourses, and Resistance

The meaning of CPS policies is constructed in the intersection of dominant forms of curriculum, instruction, and assessment, on the one hand, and the culture of individual schools and teachers' ideologies, on the other. Within the dominant policy framework, the day to day reality at both schools was complex and contradictory as dominant policies were assimilated, redefined, and resisted. In this section, I describe some of this complexity and how the school contexts and teachers' ideologies shaped teachers' responses to the dominant agenda.

At Grover there was a small subset of teachers who maintained their own agenda in the face of accountability. At Westview, residual ideologies and practices reasserted themselves to some extent after the big push to raise test scores in 1997–98. Although improving test scores continued to be the goal, it operated alongside broader goals (caring for the whole child, using African American–centered texts, and choosing topics related to students' experiences). Contradictory tendencies within the CPS administration and the state Department of Education played out in the schools as well. In part, these contradictions reflected the infiltration of strategies directed to different (but complementary) workforce trends: collaboration, open-ended problem solving, and continuous learning for the new post-Fordist workforce and routinized learning and basic skills for low-skilled jobs. Ball (1994) argues that these apparent contradictions reflect the state's dual role of supporting capital accumulation (e.g., training students for flexible work) and exerting social regulation (e.g., through routinized education and state regulation). Although the targets of these opposing strategies may be different social class and racial and ethnic groups, their deployment is actually more diffused, and it is this diffusion that creates contradictions. These strategies are picked up in diverse contexts, sometimes simultaneously. How, and whether, they are taken up depend on particularities of these contexts. This process is illustrated by the unfolding of professional development at Grover and Westview.

Overlapping Discourses: The Example of Professional Development

In general, lack of ongoing substantive professional education and failure to recruit and retain the most competent teachers are among the reasons that schools like Grover and Westview are shortchanged. However, Westview had a strong tradition of support for teacher development and teacher collaboration. In my first interview with the principal, Ms. Grimes, she said the school's greatest strengths were the knowledge and commitment of the teachers. (I did not find this claim to apply to all teachers.) Teachers taking advanced courses periodically led teacher workshops, and there seemed to be an informal practice of teachers' exchanging expertise and ideas. On the other hand, at Grover, Dr. Thomas quickly identified professional development as a critical weakness: "The teachers are only addressing basic skills in math. . . . There are teachers who have been teaching 20 years with a B.A. They don't have the knowledge. They are afraid of math" (Interview, October 1998). In his first year (1997), he reallocated funds to send teachers to professional conferences and encouraged them to enroll in graduate programs.

The content of professional development at both schools reflected contradictory, but overlapping, paradigms—prescriptive instruction and test-prep alongside constructivist and conceptually grounded pedagogies. These contradictory trends played out differently in each school, and these differences reflect the role of local context in the implementation of dominant agendas. At Westview, in 1997, some teachers were attending workshops on portfolio assessments at the central office at the very time *Test Best* books were consuming the curriculum. Seven teachers had just completed a graduate program in reading instruction, and others were enrolled. The program preceded the era of high stakes testing. It favored rich literacies and multiple approaches to reading instruction. Several teachers were enrolled in conceptually based mathematics education programs. Meanwhile, teacher in-services focused on using *Test Best* books and test-prep drills.

At Grover, a handful of teachers had been working with two university-based professional development projects—an arts program (ARTS) and a conceptually based mathematics curriculum (Math Works). Both projects engaged teachers in regular dialogue about curriculum and instruction and children's thinking. They modeled practices, co-taught lessons, and helped teachers reflect on their teaching. One involved teacher research. Both expected teachers and students to think in complex, open-ended ways and to engage in sustained inquiry. Although project staff worked with only a few interested teachers, the projects held the potential to change the way teachers thought about pedagogy. These professional development activities, supported by a few people in the central office, nibbled at the edges of the dominant CPS agenda. At the same time, BCS's regular teacher workshops focused on prescriptions for teaching embodied in charts, formulaic lesson plans, graphic organizers, routines, and curriculum alignment—all keyed to CPS Standards and standardized tests. Field notes from a BCS workshop in February 2000 illustrate the BCS "process":

> Dr. Odett of BCS begins by handing out a pink sheet, going over the agenda: "Number one, tool kits. Teachers need tools. Number two, teachers make

things work. . . . Number three [one thing you need is] a tool kit on asking questions. Number four, graphic organizers are a way for students to think about the kind of question. . . . [Grover] should be a dynamic museum filled with graphic organizers of knowledge. . . . We've been getting ready for the tests since August. [Standardized tests are given in the spring; teachers start the school year at the end of August.] We've been on a journey all along. Now what you have to do is make connections." She outlines some connections. "Continuity in the curriculum. What are the tests about and are you teaching it?" Thinking strategically when taking tests is another topic. "Focus, ask, report. They should be doing it all the time so they're prepared for the tests." She goes on to discuss different types of questions asked on the ITBS, how students can identify them, and urges teachers to practice these using classroom texts. [She spends about 30 minutes on this topic.]. . . . Discussion of timed tests. "Kids aren't pacing themselves. They need test-taking skills." The principal volunteers that they will "run off reams of multiple choice answer sheets" so kids can practice filling them out. . . . Odett lectures on test-taking tips [15 minutes].

Although some teachers I interviewed liked BCS's system, most said it was condescending and repetitive. Ms. Bouvet, a kindergarten teacher: "The ones [workshops] that were conducted by [BCS], if you ask any teacher in this school they will tell you that they are ready to walk out. . . . Each time she has shown the same table of Bloom's taxonomy and it's insulting" (February 1998).

Mr. Collins, a fourth grade teacher, described the BCS program: "The strategies are to get charts up on the wall to organize our students' learning. Those are the strategies in addition to Iowa and IGAP [ISAT] test taking techniques. Fifty percent of my day is spent teaching either out of an IGAP math or language arts book" (February 1998). BCS required teachers to follow a weekly schedule of teach, review, test, and retest. In my observations, the suggested instructional approaches were so formulaic that they resulted in mechanical, slow-paced lessons, regardless of students' actual understanding. BCS emphasized that teachers needed to follow each instructional step, like a map. An example was a third grade math lesson. The topic was "adding groups." First, the teacher had students go to the front of the room to model grouping in twos; then she asked them to list things that occur in groups of two, share their lists with each other, and read their lists; next they did a math array with groups of two; then they made up their own word problem involving multiplying groups of two. After the first four minutes several students said, "Miss [name], can we do things that come in threes?" She said, "Not yet." Despite the class's obvious grasp of the concept, the exercises continued for seventy-eight minutes. Students became more fidgety and bored as the lesson proceeded and asked several times whether they could move on. Afterward, the teacher told me she was following a lesson modeled by BCS (Field notes, November 2000).

Despite Dr. Thomas's interest in high-quality professional development, "problem solving," and "critical thinking," between 1997 and 2001, ARTS and Math Works were increasingly forced to work in the margins of the probation partner's agenda. BCS simply overrode the other projects. Trying to hold onto a space at Grover, the ARTS director located his project within the dominant paradigm by defining ARTS' goal as increasing the number of students at or above grade level on the ITBS and ISAT by 5 percent annually (Interview, June 1998). Even this instrumental strategy did not work for some teachers, who dropped out because they did not see an immediate payoff in test scores. In 2000 Grover did not renew the grant with Math Works. The director described the contradiction between his project's constructivism and BCS's focus on accountability:

> Their program does not work well with ours, and so we've had huge problems at the schools that use [BCS]. . . . Their big thing is getting those ISAT and ITBS, so you see this is what the teachers are given and every single thing is on testing. . . . We are not philosophically aligned in any way. (Interview, March 2000).

Although the education rhetoric of problem solving and continuous learning (linked to flexible work) (Gee et al., 1996; National Center on Education and the Economy, 1990) was deployed broadly through Math Works and ARTS and the principal's own rhetoric, in practice it was subordinated to the goals of regulating and certifying basic literacies. For a few teachers ARTS and Math Works were "what keep me going." But for most they were largely irrelevant to the central task, raising test scores. Some, including Ms. Bouvet and several other capable young teachers, left Grover because they said they were fed up with BCS. Although teachers and administrators cited ARTS as evidence Grover was committed to "problem solving" and "multiple intelligences," it was actually marginalized yet gave legitimacy to the larger basic skills agenda. The school's weak history of support for professional development was not conducive to more thoughtful approaches to teaching, and probation was such a powerful force it exacerbated this tendency, contributing to teacher demoralization. Thus, probation worked together with a weak culture of professional development to undermine more potentially enriching professional education.

Westview's stronger history of support for professional development and collaboration and its fewer constraints were the basis for a more schizophrenic response. In 2000, Westview joined a national school reform project that emphasized inquiry-based instruction. Still, the principal maintained that her most important goal was that all students score above the 50th percentile on the ITBS and ISAT. In 2001, a Westview teacher doing graduate work in mathematics education recommended the school purchase a conceptually rich mathematics textbook series, even though the text did not focus on the computation and procedural knowledge emphasized by the ITBS. After the big test-prep push in 1997–98, Westview was a walking contradiction—weeks of test preparation but also a stress on what the principal called "critical thinking." She continued to support substantive professional development and purchased the math texts but also required teachers to use *Test Best*. Despite its contradictions, this dual focus created the space for a subset of teachers to use approaches grounded in substantive pedagogical knowledge. Because Westview was not under the constant surveillance Grover teachers faced, as long as test scores continued to rise, the administration was relatively more free to support a richer professional culture. Thus, probation actually reinforced the disparity in the professional development cultures of the two schools.

Conditions for Teacher Resistance

Teachers at both schools had conflicting responses to the dominant CPS agenda. Some complied. Others tried to negotiate test-prep activities alongside the "real" curriculum—McNeil (2000) describes this as "double entry teaching." Some claimed allegiance to contradictory goals, the hegemonic discourse overlapping a broader educational mission. For example, a Westview administrator repeatedly said her goals were for "teachers to ask thought-provoking questions," to have students involved in "engaged learning," and "to have 50% of students at or above grade level on the ITBS. Anytime you are below 50%, that's your main goal." Ms. Washington's goal was "teaching them to be independent readers and writers," but she also said she liked the *Test Best* books with their short reading passages and multiple choice questions. Some teachers felt compelled to focus on high stakes tests, although they believed the tests were educationally indefensible, damaging to students self-respect, and racist, because the consequences of failure (especially for low-income African American children) were so grave. A number of African American teachers saw preparing their students for yet another racist hurdle as an act of solidarity. Ms. Hawkins, a middle grades teacher at Westview, talked about standardized tests and retention as social control enacted by those in power against "us":

> I think it's a farce. Some of their [CPS] policies. You know I explain them to the students and I want them to be aware of the promotion policy, for example, if they don't score a certain amount. . . . I talk to them the way I would like to be talked to. "Look, we're going to get ready for this test." Because that's how they are grading us from this standardized test. That's how they determine if we pass or not. So I'm going to teach you everything you need to know. (January 2001).

Patterns of opposition suggest some of the conditions and dispositions that may allow teachers to stand against the tide of accountability. These patterns also suggest that the difficulty of resisting in the most centrally controlled contexts contributes to greater inequities in the quality of teaching between the lowest-scoring schools and others. Three categories of teachers were more likely to contest accountability-driven teaching: (1) teachers with confidence in their professional competence; (2) teachers with a strong, social justice orientation; and (3) those who did not teach benchmark grades.

There were perhaps four teachers at each of the schools whose confidence in their own professional knowledge was the basis for exercising their own judgment in the face of the pressures of accountability. They had a strong grasp of content and teaching strategies and a clear educational philosophy. They reflected critically on their own teaching, kept abreast of relevant research, and believed their methods, curricula, and forms of assessment were superior to those being pushed by the board. Often they were recognized as among the "best" teachers in their school. Ms. Jaeger, who taught fourth grade at Westview, was an example: "I guess a lot of my ideas I get from reading. I read a lot of professional books, a lot of whole language type books. . . . I'm at the point now where I'm really reassessing what I'm doing and I'm asking myself, 'Is this the best way? How else could I do this?'" She won special permission from the principal to use a literature-based curriculum in place of the required basal reader, which she described as "contrived and skill oriented" and "butchering the literature." In my observations, her students were focused and motivated (rarely requiring a reprimand from her), listened to each other, wrote richly descriptive autobiographies and classroom newsletters, read independently, and had thoughtful conversations about novels and mathematics. The classroom matched the democratic learning communities that some commentators believe are not feasible in urban schools (Ladson-Billings, 1994). Ms. Jaeger: "It's a democratic classroom. The kids are part of the rule-making and problem solving. They have lots of discussions and work out problems together. They help choose what to read and write" (December 1998).

Second, a handful of teachers at Grover were explicitly committed to aspects of critical pedagogy and/or culturally relevant teaching. They wanted students to develop critical dispositions toward knowledge in the face of policies that encouraged them to consume information passively. Ms. Kopke, a primary level teacher, exemplified this group. She had an advanced degree in curriculum and participated in thoughtful, university-based reading and mathematics projects. She described her pedagogical aims: "to be critical, to know that you can't believe everything you read and that we have to look deep inside of language and messages that we read in order to use our own personal experience to critique them" (Interview, December 1998). In the same interview, she defined her educational priorities: "to have every classroom teaching children to think critically and to have their curriculum and education include, if not lead by, but at least to include the children's own lives and interest in community issues within the curriculum." Hers was a pedagogy committed to helping students examine knowledge and their own lived experiences, consider their experiences in social–political context, and develop a sense of agency against injustice, even at a young age (Freire, 1970/1994). This included helping her students see their strengths despite the message of high stakes tests:

> I talk very openly with my students that this test is not going to be fun, it's not going to be like when you get to pick your favorite book off the shelf and sit in the corner with your best friend. . . . And, you know, this test isn't exactly fair because you take this one test and you might have a bad day and then everybody is going to think that is how you read. Whereas if they came out and they sat next to you and they read with you they would see you can do these things . . . there are some things that we have to do, but we don't necessarily have to agree with them or think that they are the best things in the world. (December 1998)

Ms. Kopke's young students wrote intensively, discussed books in literature circles, examined U.S. history critically with a focus on the perspective and history of African Americans. She integrated arts and dance into her curriculum and used students' concerns about racism, poverty, and their family's hopes and struggles as a point of departure. Her classroom was filled with books and posters related to social justice, student investigations, and important questions students were grappling with, such as "Why are there gangs?" Ms. DuPree was another example. Her main goal for her students was "to give something back to the world instead of just surviving and existing" (Interview, March 2000). She refused to be driven by accountability policies. She believed that if students were taught well, they would do well on the tests. During one of my observations, her class was reading *Roll of Thunder, Hear My Cry* (Taylor, 1991), a challenging novel about racial oppression in the South during the Depression. The novel was part of the class's analysis of African American struggles against racism.

Third, in both schools, teachers of nonbenchmark grades spent less time preparing for standardized tests because the stakes were lower at these grades.[6] Ms. Washington at Westview transferred from third to fourth grade in 2000 to escape the intense pressure of the benchmark grade. "That's one reason I went to fourth grade. Because I just couldn't deal with the third grade benchmark grade. I needed a break from it" (Interview, December 2000). As a fourth grade teacher, she reported using more holistic literacy strategies, a more conceptual approach to math, more group work, and more integration of writing with reading. Ms. Jaeger, Ms. DuPree, and Ms. Kopke also taught nonbenchmark grades. Even Ms. Kopke remarked that if she taught a benchmark grade, she "probably would have to spend more time" on the tests.

In short, teacher resistance was grounded in specific intellectual, situational, and ideological conditions. Indeed, given the consequences of failing the ITBS, resistance was at odds with commitment to one's students *unless* one had sufficient confidence in one's pedagogical knowledge, a counterhegemonic ideological framework, and ameliorating circumstances, *and* unless one assumed that if students were taught well, they would do fairly well on the standardized tests. Thus, teachers' positions on accountability cannot simply be read off from their actions. They are also a reflection of their ideological and intellectual grounding as well as the room they have to maneuver. This is important because it is yet another indication of how accountability and centralized regulation maintain existing disparities. Whereas the strongest teachers in the least restrictive contexts and those who held critical perspectives were able, to some extent, to create intellectually rich, critical learning experiences in spite of the constraints of accountability, other teachers were more likely to succumb to the schools' routinized, skills-oriented agenda. There was little in the sanctions that helped weaker teachers become more like the stronger teachers.

Social Control and Powerlessness

Reframing equity in the language of standards and accountability ideologically deflects responsibility for educational failure from the state to individuals, yet gives them less room to act. On the one hand, the state abrogates its responsibility for righting social, economic, and educational injustices and inequitable education. On the other, it tightens control through processes of public punishment, intense monitoring, and normalizing discourses of accountability. The ideological and emotional consequences for teachers and students can be devastating. A Grover teacher described formerly motivated students who were struggling academically, "just having their whole lives shattered because of their Iowa test scores. And suddenly they are getting suspended and they are getting sent out into the hallway . . . because it is too much pressure on a kid" (Interview, March 2000). Another teacher described certain teachers' telling students, "This was your score and it is really horrible and so you're not worthy, you can't go to third grade, you can't read, you can't write, you can't do math." This culture of blame also affected teachers, who described it as a principal cause of the high rate of teacher exodus at Grover:

> Teacher: We have lost a lot of great teachers over the last two years who just couldn't take it anymore.
> Interviewer: What couldn't they take?
> Teacher: The pressure. The test pressure. They hated being told they are not doing enough when they were fabulous teachers and they couldn't take it that their kids weren't passing. (November 2000)

Although teachers were held responsible for their students' test scores, at Grover, a probation school, they not only lacked resources to improve teaching, but had less authority over their work. In addition to oversight by BCS, in 1999, two weeks before the start of the school year, without consulting teachers or administrators, the board imposed a second external oversight agency with a new instructional program. The program required much additional paperwork by teachers and was universally opposed by administrators and teachers, who said it bore little relation to the realities of teaching. Nevertheless they were required to follow it on top of BCS mandates. The next year, the board dropped it. An administrator described the program's disdain for teachers. "She may think that she can do the best that she possibly can with another method, and has felt that she's been very successful . . . with that method. But they have now said, 'You must use this method for reading, period'" (Interview, March 2000).

Social Control as Spectacle and Surveillance

Under accountability, individual success or failure is highly public. At Grover, the teacher with the highest test scores received a public award. Some teachers posted students' test scores from the previous year, and some school personnel threatened to embarrass children who were misbehaving by telling everyone their scores. Although policies that label children "failures" are supposedly race-neutral, concretely, this label is primarily attached to African American and Latino/a students. Publishing school test scores has become a way of shaming teachers and schools in African American and Latino/a communities, part of what Ball (1990) has called the "discourse of derision" aimed at urban public schools to justify their centralized regulation and, ultimately, privatization. Teachers at Grover were keenly aware of this public derision. Ms. Cannon, a Grover teacher:

> He [Vallas] started the name-calling by calling teachers names. Saying we were incompetent, saying that because we work in a low-income area. And now I know that the things that he said have directly affected people throughout the system, because I've gone to schools where people don't want to shake my hand because I work at [Grover]. (November 2000)

This is social control as spectacle (Foucault, 1995/1977)—public labeling and punishment of specific students, schools, and communities as a way to discipline the majority. It is relevant that the language of "probation" is associated with the criminal justice system. A Grover teacher said, "The administration keeps this probation climate going so strongly that I think the parents feel like they are on probation, their kids are on probation and the whole community is on probation, and so you can't resist that,

that is the law and that is how it is." This was a message heard by the students as well. Ms. Kopke:

> The kids know "probation" because several of the kids know through the jail system what probation means. . . . So you are connecting the jail system with the school and them hearing this word "probation" and it becomes like a hammer just knocking them down, knocking them down.

Although probation targets specific schools for punishment, it is also a public display of what will happen to others if they also "fail." Westview's furious effort to raise its test scores in 1997–98 was intended to prevent the humiliation of probation. The spectacle of Grover hung over Westview as an impending threat.

At the same moment, accountability is a panoptic order of surveillance, an exercise of power that works through constant and universal monitoring to ensure that people conform to required behaviors, teaching them to discipline themselves. Foucault (1995/1977) describes the mechanisms of surveillance as hierarchical observation, normalizing discourses, and the examination. (See also Gillbourn & Youdell, 2000; Vinson & Ross, 2001.) Chicago fits this pattern with its high stakes tests, probation, rankings of students and schools, competition for high scores, and educational triage. Through these mechanisms, central office staff monitor principals, principals monitor teachers, and teachers and staff monitor students and parents—engulfed in a system that has become normal, routine, and all-encompassing, people learn to police themselves.

Probation schools are the ones subject to the most intense oversight and inspection.[7] Grover was under the direct oversight of central office monitors, BCS, and, for one year, a third external agency. BCS and district office authorities observed classes unannounced and cited teachers for noncompliance with mandated practices, and BCS required teachers to post lesson plans on their classroom doors. Teachers described this intense scrutiny as intrusive, omnipresent, and punitive:

> A middle grades teacher said, "You know and sometimes, it's restrictive too, when people tell me that, say between 10:00 and 10:20, I should be doing this." (Interview, November 1999)

A primary teacher described her experience as

> abusive, especially when you get into the Targeted Assistance program [for probation schools]. . . . I got written up for having scribble on the board.[8]. . . They kind of walk in and see what we are doing. They come anytime. And she [Targeted Assistance person] wanted to take me down to the Board. I was not doing reading during the scheduled reading hour. (Teacher interview, December 2000)

That surveillance teaches powerlessness is evidenced in teacher interviews. As a Grover teacher put it: "I don't think we have too much [control over what we can do in the classroom] because when you're on probation, it seems everybody wants to help you, everybody to tell you how to do things. You really don't have too much power or say-so in what goes on" (Interview, March 2000). This is reinforced by the capricious authoritarianism of district officials who continually issue new mandates and paperwork, summon teachers and principals to meetings at central office without notice, reschedule meetings at the last minute, and inspect classrooms at will—reminding teachers that their work is not important and is not in their control. Teachers and school administrators internalize the discourse and police themselves and each other by competing for the highest test scores. The night after the teacher was observed with "scribble" on the board, she spent hours organizing her grade book in the order the supervisors required, "in case they come back." Schools also become part of the state's surveillance apparatus. Grover and Westview administrators were required to report student absences and tardiness to the Chicago Housing Authority, which could evict parents on grounds of their children's truancy. At a time when people are being turned out of the projects, this record can also be used to deny them public housing. Another offshoot of the regime of surveillance is that critical, culturally relevant curriculum (not part of Standards or posted lesson plans) is more vulnerable to censorship. In one instance, a Grover intern was discharged after a monitor observed that her students were studying the death penalty and had written letters to the governor of Pennsylvania about Mumia Abu Jamal,[9] a political activist on death row.

Because most low-scoring schools and schools on probation serve African American and Latino/a communities, these policies help to shape the representation of race and ethnicity in the city. The "necessity" for centralized intervention and supervision signifies the delinquency of these communities and their incompetence to act in their own interests. Thus, racialized school policies contribute to the demonization of African Americans and some Latinos/as and provide fodder for their social exclusion, containment, and removal through antigang laws, police occupation, dismantling of public housing, and displacement. Concretely, accountability policies help clear the land for developers and white upper-middle-class gentrifiers who wish to claim the city as their own.

The Discourse of Inevitability

Accountability has been woven into classroom practices and school routines and has permeated professional conversation, normalized by a discourse of inevitability. Each grade has to focus on test preparation, because students must be prepared for testing in the grade to come. Students will always face tests so they might as well get started. As a Grover first grade teacher put it, "I don't really like it [test preparation], but I can also see it as being good since they're gonna start really being important when they're in third grade. They might as well get the practice in now" (April 2000). Some teachers described test taking as "a lifelong learning skill" and defined their own agency as the ability to determine how to meet the goals prescribed by the board. A Westview teacher said: "I don't like it but that's life. Paul Vallas and the powers that be like the test results" (Interview, June 1998). As the policies became routinized, most people at Grover & Westview seemed to adapt to the inevitable. "So long as such controls are new and in the press, they remain problematic and debatable. Over time, however, overt controls tend to become imbedded in the structure and taken for granted once they are in place" (McNeil, 2000, p. 169). As Gramsci (1971) argues, accommodation to the status quo is an indication of the power of dominant policies to organize consciousness.

The hegemony of the accountability discourse, its normalization, as well as the consequences of noncompliance and the lack of organized resistance silenced debate and critique at Grover and Westview. When a Grover teacher told her colleagues that she was honest with her students and told them standardized tests are unfair: "Everybody looked at me like I was just insane. They said, 'You talk to the kids about the test and say the test won't be fun and the test isn't fair, how could you do that? The kids are not going to do their best now they heard you saying that the test stinks'" (Teacher interview, December 2000). When the same teacher challenged the ethics of a district supervisor's advice to practice educational triage, she got no support from other teachers. Despite widespread anger at BCS's teacher workshops, I found no evidence of anyone openly criticizing them (though teachers passed nasty notes). At the same time, teachers described students' sense of powerless and fatalism in the face of an immutable regime of testing, sorting, labeling, and exclusion. "There is this sense that the test scores are who you are and that it determines your future and so I have seen former students of mine just feel like they are done. They did not pass the 3rd grade or the 6th grade Iowa test and so they are not worth it anymore" (Teacher interview, April 2000).

However, there has been some public resistance. In 1998 and 1999, high school students boycotted the CASE exam (Chicago Academic Standards Exam) and demonstrated at the board. The same year African American eighth graders also revolted in their school cafeteria when they were told many of them had failed the ITBS. In 1999, Latino/a parents and their children picketed the CPS central office, petitioning for waivers for students who were failed because of their ITBS scores. In spring 2002, the Chicago teachers' union held a public forum on high stakes testing, and in the fall, twelve teachers at Curie High School announced they would not administer the high school CASE exam. Some teachers in other schools signed petitions of support and wore "Erase the CASE" buttons. This protest pushed the board to drop the CASE (although the Board promised to substitute a new, better test). And a coalition of school reform groups has proposed an alternative to the district's high stakes assessment.[10] Especially since the bold action of the "Curie 12," cracks have begun to appear, yet, overall, the accountability regime has been a powerful means of controlling students and teachers.

Teacher Despair

At Grover, voices of anger, demoralization, and despair became increasingly insistent in my teacher interviews and observations and in the steady exodus of teachers, including some of the most committed and intellectually engaged. Between 1996–97 and 2000–01, at least twenty-six teachers chose to leave (in a staff of about thirty-five classroom teachers in 1997 down to twenty by 2000). This included six very competent young teachers, several highly respected veterans, and a winner of a prestigious statewide teaching award. Most of those I talked with said they could no longer live with the contradictions the current CPS policies posed for them. They were replaced by a succession of inexperienced teachers and interns and uncertified and/or substitute teachers.

In 1998–99, Grover had been on probation for three years with little improvement, and rumors about the school's being reconstituted (taken over by central office and all staff replaced) circulated all year. An administrator described teachers' demoralization: "And so what I sometimes don't see is when that flame is flickering in people and it doesn't seem to be able to be relit too easily." An administrator told me that the principal was considering bringing in a counselor for the teachers. When I asked Grover teachers whom they would name as a school leader, everyone I interviewed that year named Ms. Jones, a seventeen-year veteran African American teacher who grew up in the Grover neighborhood and returned to "give something back" to the community. For her, teaching was a mission. She was famous for taking her students home on weekends and raising money in her church to take them on bus trips. She exemplified Ladson-Billings's (1994) notion of culturally relevant teaching. She built on students' experiences and allegiance to collective identity to help them succeed academically and critique injustice. Her pedagogy was anchored in her relationships with students and their families. But 1998–99 was her last year at Grover. In a long interview, Ms. Jones described how CPS's high stakes accountability and regulatory climate eroded her relationships with her students, her health, and her sense of worth and purpose. She said this was the worst year for her since she began teaching, "because this is the first time in a long, long time since I was a child that I really feel I'm compromising my beliefs" (Interview, February 1999). In the following excerpts, she testifies to the deep contradictions and despair experienced by teachers whose commitment to teaching as an ethical pursuit is undermined by deprofessionalization, surveillance, and standardization:

> I had a class last year that I had for three years, for 6th, 7th, and 8th grade and these were wonderful, wonderful kids. One time last year, one of my kids said, "you know, you're really mean now." And I knew she was telling the truth, because we had that kind of rapport. I had gotten that way because I was so afraid. And these kids had been producing since maybe fourth, really producing well. And I was just so intent on teaching test material that I finally said, "Forget it, I'm going to be me and do what I normally do and go wherever." And I had 26 students and 25 of them graduated. I only had one that came back [failed]. But I had to ease back, and I was out sick, and the kids said, "was it because of your surgery that you changed?" But it wasn't that and I told them, I was honest with them, you know; there's so much pressure on the school system, there's so much pressure on the teachers. And some people should be pressured to a certain degree because in any job you go into, everybody's not doing their job. But I internalized that pressure, and I externalized it by putting it on them. And it wasn't fair. . . . And I was putting my stress and my pressure for these standardized tests on them, and I did it the wrong way, maybe I went about it the wrong way, and they were acting out at home and they didn't want to tell their parents Mrs. [Jones] is getting on my nerves, and we talked about it and I said, "I know you all work hard and you always give me your best, and we'll just take it from there." I had never taught like I had taught last year, and that really bothered me, because I didn't even see it as being me. . . . And then I thought about that and I said, "These are my kids. I know them better than anyone who walks in off the street. I know who I have to sit next to at certain times of the day, and I know who I need to encourage and who needs what. And I'm not going to let them dictate my teaching style to that point. I don't care how many times they observe me, and I never see what they write anyway." I don't care anymore, because I lost focus, and I don't want to lose focus and if I do, it's time for me to leave this system. (December 1998)

Teachers were bitter because they were blamed for the school's failure but were denied a role in analyzing problems and developing solutions. Ms. Capella, a primary teacher, said, "No one has ever asked the teachers what we want." Again Ms. Jones:

> You're [Vallas] going to colleges for the sole purpose of, because you want better teachers for the City of Chicago. What do you think that's doing to the morale of the teachers who have been on the front lines who have acted as nurses, doctors, and family mediators, and you know, whatever, parents and guardians and whatever? And I just think—it's bothering me because it's hard for me to believe that you're saying succeed but you're not asking the people that are there, "What do you need in order to succeed?" (Interview, December 1998)

At the same time, it was painful for teachers to see students struggling with consequences of low test scores. Ms. DuPree, a fifth grade teacher, talked about this:

> Ms. DuPree: And I think it's very devastating when you're in eighth grade and you don't make a score and they said you can't pass
> Interviewer: Have you seen that here?
> Ms. DuPree: [pause] I've seen it here, and I saw it firsthand with my daughter with some of the students that didn't make it with her. I saw students break down. They didn't even know what their score was. You know they gave them an envelope and they had to, their scores were in the envelope, and the girl broke down before she even opened it. . . . I heard students [pause] one committed suicide. [crying] (Interview, March 2000)

In 1999, Ms. Jones left Grover to teach special education at another school. She thought she could "really teach there" because special ed students are exempt from accountability measures. In 2000, Ms. Kopke left to teach at a teacher-led charter school. It is not only incompetent or uncommitted teachers who are being weeded out. It is also culturally relevant, critical teachers who are being driven out because they find the ethos of the current policies intolerable. This is important because these teachers exemplify the sort of education most crucial for African American, Latino/a, and other students of color in particular.

Westview had a somewhat different experience. Teachers did not face the intense surveillance of schools on probation, and their culture of collective support, as well as some teachers' relatively stronger professional knowledge, seemed to buffer them somewhat. From 1997 through 2002, the school lost few teachers. However, the coercive power of accountability channeled teachers' commitment and mutual support toward raising test scores. Higher scores were achieved at a great cost to students and teachers alike. One teacher said: "It's like a family here to be honest. Everyone is so close. . . . I just know that [Westview] has really worked together, we've worked hard and long. I mean all these after school hours take a toll on our bodies, but I guess they're helping the kids" (Interview, May 1998). By test time, the stress on students and teachers was palpable. A third grade teacher:

> It's just so much pressure on the teachers, it's like, and the school and the principal and everyone knows how important it is. The kids know how important it is. I had three kids start crying during the test. I mean, they know if they mess it up [pause] everyone's like super high pressure on these tests. (May 1998)

Ms. Washington said, "When they see that test prep book they're like 'ugh God.' You know and I think they need a break from that. They're third graders. This is their first time with all this pressure" (Interview, January 2000). Although exhausted, teachers went above and beyond the parameters of their jobs, working in the after-school program (even without pay during a temporary budget snafu) and serving on multiple committees. One veteran teacher, Ms. Waller, said, "With all the sick days and things I have, I can be off any time and any day but I come every day. It's the commitment I guess to the school and the children and to our administrator." (Interview, May 1998)

Conclusion

There are several inferences to be drawn from the study of Grover and Westview. First, on balance, the constraints posed by accountability did not promote equity. They did not narrow disparities in curriculum, quality of teaching, or educational opportunities. Rather than enrich teaching and learning, the accountability policies promoted a narrow focus on high stakes tests. The dispositions and identities produced by this sort of schooling prepare students for low-skill, low-paid jobs in the growing service economy. Rather than make the knowledge of the strongest teachers a basis for improving teaching, the policies seemed to drive out some of them without substantively altering the teaching of weaker teachers. The disciplinary power of accountability pressed weaker teachers and those in more punitive contexts into routinized teaching and test preparation as the norm.

Second, accountability redefines a "good school" solely as a high-scoring school. Paradoxically what makes a school "good" can also make it "bad," as these determinations rest on the characteristics of institutions that are valued (Ball, 1997a). The discourse of accountability redefines a good school in technical and narrowly instrumental terms. This is a message given to the students and one deployed widely to teachers, parents, and the general public. In this discourse, Grover became a somewhat "better" school as its test scores inched up and as instruction became more systematic and standardized across the school. Westview became quite a "good" school as its test scores approached 50 percent of students at or above grade level on the ITBS. In fall 2002, Westview was one of sixty schools given a ten-thousand-dollar award by CPS for improvement based on ITBS scores. But both schools also became more test driven, and Grover lost its strongest teachers.

Westview's "improvement" was the product of teachers' extraordinary effort and weeks of test prep. At Grover, monitoring and regulation produced more systematic but also mechanical and slow-paced instruction and a culture of individual blame. Although a few incompetent teachers were pushed out, so were some of the strongest. These teachers had a different vision of a good school—one that was critical, antiracist, culturally relevant, and humane.

Third, the regime of inspection, testing, and marking of failing schools and students individualizes failure and places the blame on principals, teachers, students, and parents, negating the state's responsibility for the structural roots of the problem. "There is a very real sense in which participants on both sides of the school desk feel trapped within a system where the rules are made by others and where external forces, much bigger than any individual school, teacher or pupil, are setting the pace that all must follow" (Gillborn & Youdell, 2000, p. 43). This process also contributes to disempowering urban communities of color.

Fourth, policies that regulate and punish schools in African American communities contribute to the representation of these communities, and especially of Black youth, as undisciplined and pathological. In this way education policy contributes to the construction of consciousness about race and the city, making reasonable the dispersal and containment of African American communities. Education policies that support the dislocation of African American communities, like those of Grover and Westview, support a hegemonic reconstruction of the city as a space of rationality, order, stability, and whiteness (Haymes, 1995; Sassen, 1998).

Finally, educational issues at Grover and Westview cannot be separated from the reality of living in some of the most impoverished neighborhoods in the United States. Nor can they be understood out of the context of the documented history of inequality and racism that have permeated the city and the school system. Not only is there a failure to concentrate significant human and material resources in these schools, they are embedded in an economic system and racial order that have bred impoverishment, social crises, and profoundly contrasting futures. Color-blind policies (i.e., everyone is held to the same standards and tests) leave no space for discussion of these issues. It should be noted that Grover and Westview were working with woefully inadequate resources, and until the demolition of the projects drastically reduced enrollment, they had more than thirty students per class. Both schools were in communities with an average annual family income of about seven thousand dollars and an unemployment rate above 90 percent. As one Grover teacher pointedly summed up: "If you look at where most of the probation schools are, the environments are about the same. I think something needs to be done about that."

CHAPTER 5

The Policies and Politics of Cultural Assimilation

Coauthored with Eric Gutstein

I think that they, the system [pause] I think that Hispanics are becoming
a little more powerful. We're not a minority anymore, we're becoming a majority.
They have to find a way to stop it. They feel threatened. So in my opinion,
I feel like they're taking that away and just making everybody the same.

(Ms. Guzmán, Brewer teacher)

In 1994, Brewer Elementary School was on the cusp of a promising new direction. The same year, one of us (Gutstein) began working with the teachers and the principal, Mr. Rodríguez, who had just been chosen by the Local School Council as the school's first Mexican American principal. Rodríguez had a vision for the school as a vital community educational and cultural center. In his first few years at Brewer, he pursued this goal boldly and tenaciously. He was intent on remolding the anti-Spanish and deficit assumptions of some of the staff and creating a school that upheld bilingualism and biculturalism. One of his opening salvos was to hang a large banner in the school proclaiming, *Es Bonito Ser Bilingue,"* and its English translation, "It's beautiful to be bilingual." Although the school's bilingual program was transitional to English, under Mr. Rodríguez's principalship, Spanish achieved equal status as a public language. Public announcements were made in Spanish and English, administrators conversed with each other openly in Spanish, and Spanish reverberated in the halls and cafeteria. Rodríguez also had an educational vision of student-centered, multicultural teaching and a curriculum that emphasized problem solving, multiple perspectives, and construction of knowledge. He encouraged student leadership and involvement in the community. Rodríguez had been a bilingual education teacher and community activist, and in the first few years he also supported and recruited teachers whose educational goals were explicitly political and critical. A central task for him was to nurture greater initiative, collaboration, dialogue, and shared learning among teachers. In the first month at his new job, Mr. Rodríguez organized a faculty retreat over three weekends to forge collectively a new vision for the school.

In this chapter, we examine the implications of CPS policies for the progress of this educational agenda. We begin by describing Brewer and its community context. Then we explore implications of CPS policies for critical approaches to knowledge, bilingualism and biculturalism, and the school change process as a whole. We describe how teachers and administrators negotiated the dominant agenda, the contradictions it posed, and the compromises they were forced to make. We examine the larger implications of Brewer's story in the context of struggles over culture and representation in the city, the control of urban space, and the stratified labor market. Finally, we consider what is at stake in the context of potential Latino/a political power and labor insurgency and the challenges this insurgency is posing to processes of globalization and inequality in the United States. Brewer also illustrates the possibility of an alternative path for transforming urban schools in culturally relevant, socially critical, thoughtful directions.

Brewer Elementary School and Its Community

> And they risked their lives as they crossed the river or as they were smuggled into this country. Not only did they risk their life, but they risked the fact that they may be deported or caught on the way. So they put too much at stake to just sit and wait. Coming here for a better life means we're coming here to get a better life like what the Anglos have. (Ms. Ortiz, Marion Park activist and Brewer home–school liaison, June 1998)

Brewer Elementary School is located in Marion Park, a dense, vibrant, economically struggling working-class neighborhood of packed apartments, *taquerias,* small stores and restaurants, schools, churches, and pushcarts selling *elotes, churros,* and *paletas.* Marion Park is still a "port of entry" for immigrants. Its Mexican identity is nourished by a steady stream of new immigrants dislocated by the workings of global capital and by the constant movement of family members between Mexico and the United States. Unable to sustain themselves economically on either side of the border, families engage in "strategic mitosis," creating transnational households and a transnational family economy (Davis, 2001) and new, complex transnational identities. Many extended families reside across permeable borders that link Chicago with Guanajuato, Michoacán and other Mexican states.

Marion Park has a long and continuing history of organizing against oppression of undocumented workers and for social justice. Recently it has also been a center of worker organizing. Ms. Ortiz described this history:

> We call it the incubator where a lot of causes are born, where a lot of issues are born. A lot of organizations, not only in social service but in the way people stand up for what they believe is right. People in this community have stood up to the Board of Ed., have stood up to the city of Chicago. . . . And we said, "Wait a minute, you made a decision with our lives that affects our lives and you didn't include us—we have an alternate plan . . . we fought for our school and never took no for an answer—five years. It was a five year fight. That is because, the people in this community are very determined. (June 1998)

Today, Marion Park residents are threatened with displacement by new condo developments and rehabbed buildings already popping up at the community's boundaries. For decades Marion Park was not even on the radar screen for city investment in infrastructure improvements. It was one of the low-income neighborhoods whose city services were curtailed in the mid-1990s. The community's crumbling streets and sidewalks were the butt of jokes about disappearing cars and people. Once we returned to our car parked in front of a friend's house in the neighborhood to find it half-buried in a four-foot-deep hole. The pavement had just collapsed beneath it. But these days, the sidewalks are being redone. Artists and students—"pioneers" of gentrification—are beginning to move in, tempted by the still-low rents and the ambiance of the community. Community residents tell stories about realtors who warn them about rising taxes and offer them cash for their homes without even stepping inside the buildings. While the city alderperson, allied with Mayor Daley, hails these changes as signs of progress, a longtime community organization has been leading the fight against gentrification. Through direct action and community mobilization, it succeeded in slowing down a city-sponsored development scheme that would have forced out some homeowners and renters and funneled money to developers.

Marion Park is home to literally thousands of low-wage workers, many of whom are undocumented. The low income of Latino/a workers in general is linked to historical discrimination and to immigration policies that tied them to low-wage labor sectors, particularly in manufacturing. Betancur, Cordova, and Torres (1993) observe, "[L]acking the resources to carry them through difficult times, and having no or weak political or institutional ties and jobs, Latino workers [in Chicago] were the least prepared for economic restructuring, and indeed, have suffered the most from it" (p.

125). Many Mexican workers were absorbed into low-wage hotel, landscaping, restaurant, and construction work and downgraded manufacturing, industries in which they are now concentrated. Indeed, restaurants across the city run on the labor of Latino/a (primarily Mexican) table bussers, cooks, and dishwashers. One staff person at Brewer joked that when he ate in Chinatown he went into the kitchen and asked the Mexican cooks to make his favorite dishes. Marion Park residents also work in nonunion sweatshops that pay minimum wage with virtually no benefits or safety regulations. According to the 2000 census, median Latino/a household income in Chicago was 74.2 percent that of whites (Mendel & Little, 2002). These low-wage workers are the parents of Brewer students.

Brewer is a kindergarten to eighth grade school. The student body is more than 90 percent Latino/a, mainly Mexican.[1] About 90 percent of the students receive free or reduced-price lunch, and at least half are immigrants themselves; almost all other students are the first generation in their family to be born in the United States. The faculty is about 35 percent Latino/a (Mexican, Central or South American, Puerto Rican), about 50 percent white, and about 15 percent African American. Brewer's scores on the ITBS tend to be above the CPS average, and in 2001 about 50 percent of the students scored at or above national norms. The attendance rate is significantly higher than that of the district and state, and student mobility and chronic truancy rates are far lower. The school has both bilingual and monolingual English classes and an honors track and a "regular" academic track.

Brewer is in a modern two-story red brick structure surrounded by neighborhood stores and apartments. The school has many visible expressions of Mexican cultural identity—art, displays of Mexican history, and artifacts from Mexico adorn the walls. According to Ms. Ortiz, a community activist and Brewer's home-school coordinator, the cultural programs, art, and student uniform policy were developed to make Brewer more like schools in Mexico. She said the parents' goal was "to soak them with so much of their culture that they would feel proud of who they are." The teacher aides are all mothers who live in the community. The principal also invested a lot of the school's discretionary funds and grant monies in providing the school with state-of-the art computers and computer software.

Undermining Critical Approaches to Knowledge

> I want to make kids humans who question and ask why? why? why? Again and again. . . . I want them to give their own opinions and know their rights, not just know their rights but act on them, act on their rights. (Ms. Díaz, primary teacher, November 1996)

District policies influenced teachers' attempts to assist students in developing two types of critical dispositions to knowledge. In the first place, the policies interfered with teachers' efforts to develop *critical literacy*—the ability to examine knowledge critically and see relationships between ideas and their social–historical contexts so as to understand and act on oppressive social relations (Freire, 1970/1994). Accountability pressures also affected the school's use of an innovative, inquiry-based mathematics curriculum, *Meaningful Mathematics* (MM).[2] MM is based on the standards developed by the National Council of Teachers of Mathematics (NCTM) (1989, 1991, 1995, 2000) and supports multiple approaches to problem solving, real-world connections, students' constructions of knowledge, and elaborated communication of mathematical ideas.

Challenges to Critical Literacy

Freire (1970/1994; Freire & Macedo, 1987) describes critical literacy as a process, a set of cultural practices toward liberation. For Freire, literacy never is limited to simply decoding text (reading the *word*, in his terms) but implies a deep understanding of the social, political, historical, cultural, and economic reality of the reader (reading the *world*). Furthermore, in his view, there is an inextricable relationship between the two; one learns to read the world as a precondition to reading the word, and the two work together dialectically throughout the process of gaining literacy and understanding: "Reading the world always precedes reading the word, and reading the word implies continually reading the world" (Freire & Macedo, 1987, p. 35).

At Brewer, there were a number of teachers who embraced aspects of Freire's ideas, and their practices reflected elements of his pedagogy and philosophy. Some of these teachers explicitly defined their goals as preparing students to examine critically and question authorized sources of knowledge (teachers, texts, media) and consider them from multiple perspectives. Here we focus on four who taught the benchmark grades three, six, and eight because the influence of accountability was strongest at these grades: Mr. Falcón, Ms. Guzmán, Ms. Pantoja, and Ms. Rossman. We do not mean to suggest that these teachers exemplified Freirian pedagogy or were explicitly committed to critical literacy as a focus of their teaching. In fact, there were other teachers who perhaps were more so. However, their practice and their perspectives reflected aspects of teaching for critical literacy, and Ms. Rossman, an eighth grade teacher, was explicit about this goal. In her class, students critiqued popular culture, examined social inequality, and questioned dominant ideologies so they could develop their own perspectives. Ms. Rossman described her goals for her English class:

> I feel like having a command of the language that you're going to be using and knowing how to express yourself in that language and to critically evaluate writing in terms of propaganda. It's in the newspapers and advertising. That's what I feel like they have to be prepared for. (June 1999)

Mr. Rodriguez actively recruited and supported these teachers. He made a distinction between critical thinking (e.g., inquiry-based curriculum) and critical literacy, and he named the subversive nature of the latter:

> The bureaucracy . . . they say that's what they want to do, I mean, everybody, critical thinkers . . . they even have workshops on how to develop critical thinking. But that's a very superficial . . . If you're talking critical thinking, and you open up a textbook and you figure out this problem or what have you, it's not being a critical thinker like one who actually questions and challenges. I mean, that's the last thing they want. (June 1999)

CPS policies, particularly the intrusion of standardized-test preparation, presented significant obstacles to these teachers. Practically, the time required for test preparation ate away at their educational goals, and ideologically, the tests ran counter to critical literacy. Time is always a factor when teachers want to go beyond the standard curriculum; Brewer teachers, like their counterparts at Grover and Westview, were caught between their educational goals and the enormous consequences of failing the ITBS. Those who embraced aspects of critical literacy agonized over this dilemma. Mr. Falcón:

> I know we have to prepare the students from day one for that test. I understand why we have to do that because we want the students to score [well]. I want all of my kids to go on to seventh grade . . . it affects us in a lot of ways. . . . Everybody's worried about the test and everybody's trying to drill these kids too long to do well. (June 1999)

Ms. Guzmán, a third grade teacher, also perceived this contradiction: "The activities that you used to do before, it's like, okay, now I gotta stop doing that . . . I know that I won't have time to prepare them for what real-life situations are out there."

Committed teachers do what is needed to maximize their children's chance of passing tests that are both the primary promotion barrier and a significant gatekeeper to greater educational opportunities. Especially for children of color who face racial barriers throughout their education, the consequences of these tests are very serious. Ms. Rossman was devastated when several students failed the 1998 ITBS, and thus, eighth grade, despite doing well in her class. The next year she felt compelled to spend more time practicing ITBS-like questions and topics. She describes what she did and what she gave up in the process. For the first two quarters, her students wrote intensively and read sophisticated literature; then, she shifted to test prep:

> Ms. Rossman: I wanted them to get used to the format of a short, mediocre selection of writing. I had some questions on different levels. I tried to get them to recognize this type of question is asking you for some really basic information you can go back and look for. This kind of question is asking you to evaluate. This kind of question is asking you to relate or "what would you do if you were . . ." so I used those for the entire quarter.
> Interviewer: The entire quarter? Is that what you did every day for a quarter?
> Ms. Rossman: Most days, yes.
> Interviewer: What quarter did you do it?
> Ms. Rossman: Third quarter, right before the test.
> Interviewer: So for two quarters they read literature and they did these writing logs and they wrote them, and then for a quarter they did the SRA kit [a skill-oriented program]?
> Ms. Rossman. Right . . . the third quarter, we did test preparation.

That district mandates interfere with teachers' goals is not news, but for these teachers, it was not just lack of time that undermined critical literacy. The ideological influence of standardized test preparation teaches students that they are neither creators nor arbitrators of knowledge. At the very least, the conflicting pedagogies of test preparation and critical literacy send students contradictory messages and ideologically impact teachers' efforts to foster critical literacy. This manifests itself in different ways. The speed required by the ITBS works against an environment in which students air views and listen to others before making up their mind. Taking the time to develop one's own ideas is incompatible with racing to find the correct answer in forty-five seconds. The emphasis of standardized tests on finding the right answer contradicts multiple perspectives and development of one's own interpretation of texts. For example, Ms. Rossman wanted her students to understand that all history is written from a particular perspective and to confront dominant historical myths:

> There's a section from Columbus' diary where he's landed on the island and the natives approach him . . . his first thought was that "I could enslave all of them with 50 men." . . . That informs the entire, as far as I'm concerned, true history of European conquest of this continent in a way that is just absolutely opposite of what the kids get from the history book. (June 1999)

Questioning and challenging teachers, texts, and official sources of knowledge are incompatible with the ideological messages perpetrated by incessant test preparation. Mr. Falcón: "You tell them there's a million answers for this [a discussion question], but there's one answer for this test." Ms. Pantoja acknowledged the ideological impact of test preparation but hoped that what she had done in the classroom would overcome it:

> What I tried to talk about in class when we were getting ready for the Iowas was that they were going to be given four answers and then they have to choose whichever one is closest . . . the big emphasis [in my class is] that there is not

just one right answer. So what they thought and what the Iowa test might present may not be similar. (June 1999)

Developing critical literacy is obviously difficult given the standard curricula and pedagogies in U.S. schools that inhibit independent thought and critical analysis (Macedo, 1994). However, high stakes testing creates new barriers. Reverberating through our interviews are the contradictions and conflicts teachers experienced between their efforts to help students see knowledge as a tool to analyze the world and the process and practice of preparing for standardized tests. We are not arguing that teachers cannot negotiate the conceptions of knowledge and stifling of voice promoted by test preparation. However, accountability policies have become an additional, powerful, publicly sanctioned obstacle. Mr. Falcón summed up the struggles he and others faced: "And I don't know if you're preparing the kids for life in that way. . . . [W]e're all trying to do two things at the same time: preparing the kids for life and preparing the kids for a test. . . . [I]t's difficult to juggle those two things" (June 1999). Two of the four teachers are no longer teaching. Ms. Rossman left at the end of 2000; she said she felt the system's demands and pressure interfered too strongly with her educational goals and philosophy. Mr. Falcón left after 2002. Ms. Pantoja stayed at Brewer but said she had to make compromises and that she worried, "I am losing my idealism" (June 2002). Ms. Guzmán continued at Brewer but said she felt constrained by CPS policies.

For low-income children of color who compose most urban school districts, critical literacy is essential for personal and community survival in contexts of race, gender, and class oppression as well as an important tool to transform these conditions (Ladson-Billings, 1994). A number of Brewer teachers wanted their students to learn the standard curriculum beyond what was necessary for the tests—and critique it as well. They wanted students to be fluent writers, thoughtful readers, critical thinkers, questioners. As Freire (Freire & Macedo, 1987) suggests:

> To acquire the . . . knowledge contained in the dominant curriculum should be a goal attained by subordinate students in the process of self and group empowerment. They can use the dominant knowledge effectively in their struggle to change the material and historical conditions that have enslaved them. . . . The dominant knowledge must gradually become dominated by the . . . students so as to help them in their struggle for social equity and justice. (p. 128)

But critical literacy is more than reading the world; in Freire's terms it is also *writing* or *rewriting* the world, developing a sense of agency and acting against social injustices (Freire & Macedo, 1987). Ms. Díaz, a primary teacher, described this goal: "One contribution we can make is to help make individuals who question, who do not just accept, who are fighters, who can help to change society" (January 1996). Mr. Rodríguez shared this goal and even encouraged students to challenge unjust school rules and practices. But accountability, particularly the promotion/retention policy, undermined students' sense of agency by leading them to blame themselves for their own failure.

In a series of interviews with former Brewer students conducted in 1999 and 2000, and in many conversations from 1997 to 2002 with current and former students, students frequently blamed themselves for failure. Failure in Chicago schools is extremely visible, especially in eighth grade, because students who do not pass the ITBS do not graduate with their peers.[3] Brewer students consistently said that graduating "on stage" with their peers at the end of eighth grade was exceedingly important to them. For about half, it would be their only graduation—in fact, Brewer's neighborhood high school graduated *less* than 50 percent of the entering 1998 class. The fear and the pain of failing the ITBS were visible. Ms. Rossman described everyone in her classroom crying as ITBS scores were released and the collective sense of failure that ensued: "I feel like a failure. We all feel like a big, fat, failure." When asked how they felt when they found out that they had failed the ITBS, the responses of Zulma and Olivia, both eighth grade students, were typical: Zulma said: "I was angry at myself, 'cause I didn't, probably didn't do my best. And probably because I didn't pay attention in school. And I don't know. I was disappointed" (March 2000). Olivia said: "I felt like I was stupid. Like I don't know anything, thinking I was dumb" (March 2000). Margarita, who attended transition school, did not pass the eighth grade ITBS until her fourth try in May of what would have been her freshman year of high school. She said: "I felt bad. I felt good 'cause I tried my best and I got more scores. But at the same time I felt bad because I didn't pass. And I tried my best. . . . Yeah. I took it like three times and I was like, I took it three times and I'm not gonna pass it" (April 2000). In a school culture permeated with the ideology of individual achievement in which success and failure are publicly displayed, it is difficult for students (and thoughtful, committed teachers) *not* to blame themselves.

However, seeds of deeper understanding overlapped with self-blame, just as teachers had contradictory responses. Sometimes they understood the political dimension of education and looked beyond their perceived deficiencies. Mónica and Raquel, two sisters who went through the transition school, ended their interview with the following provocative question and analysis:

> Raquel: Do the white people take it [ITBS] the same?
> Interviewer: Ah, that's a really good question. White people take the test, black people take the test, Latinos take the test.
> Raquel: But I don't think we should take it all together. There should be a different test for each one.

Interviewer: Why?
Raquel: Because white people, they already like, they know. I mean, they're not smarter than us, 'cause they're not. I mean, but they, they know already their language and while we're trying to learn our language, we're trying to study and learn the language.
Mónica: Yeah, because. . . .
Raquel: And trying not to forget our own language. And they, they just, they, the only problem they have is learning what they need to learn. We have trouble learning the language, but we need to learn mathematics, everything and plus, trying not to forget our language. . . . I don't think it's fair for, I think there should be um, different tests for um, Mexicans, different tests for Americans. (April 2000)

Olivia blamed herself and "felt stupid" when she failed, but she was also angry and made a political analysis. At the time of this interview, she was a high school junior on a college-bound track but was still angry about being failed because of her ITBS score:

Because it does not . . . test my knowledge, because I'm getting all these honors classes and A.P. [Advanced Placement] . . . it does not say who I am or what is my strength, it just doesn't say anything about me. . . . It's just a stupid number that they put on your forehead. . . . It's injustice. . . . It's a stupid way to . . . decide whether a student should pass or stay. (March 2000)

Thus, Brewer students faced a double injustice: First, they received a substandard education—the school system devalued their language, culture, identities; pushed them to take high stakes tests in English before they were ready; and provided them with underprepared teachers[4] and insufficient resources. CPS policies undermined teachers' efforts to enable students to develop critical approaches to knowledge by privileging ITBS scores over inquiry-based, culturally relevant curriculum. Second, students received the unrelenting message that they were responsible for their own educational shortcomings—and they often blamed themselves for the system's failures. Despite this obfuscation, however, some students—like teachers—were able to develop their own analyses and demonstrated signs of transformational resistance.

Challenges to Constructing Meaningful Mathematical Knowledge
From 1995 to 1999, a group of ten mathematics teachers began using a new, NCTM Standards–based curriculum in grades four to eight. They wanted students to engage in thoughtful learning activities involving problem solving and knowledge construction. This group participated in professional development focused on the NCTM Standards led by one of us (Gutstein) during 1994–95. Their mathematics knowledge and teaching experiences varied greatly. The contexts for this fairly diverse group were Mr. Rodríguez's support for student-centered, inquiry-based curricula; his

encouragement for them to experiment; and his commitment of resources for teachers to participate in professional development and work collaboratively. Here we examine how accountability policies influenced efforts to support inquiry-based curricula as illustrated by the school's experience with the mathematics curriculum. We focus on three middle grades teachers because they had strong content knowledge and were Brewer's lead, and most experienced, mathematics teachers: Ms. Cárdenas, Ms. Dawson, and Mr. Hibarro.

The three NCTM Standards documents (1989, 1991, 1995) on curriculum, teaching, and assessment together present a unified and cohesive view of school mathematics. A central idea is that students should learn mathematics with understanding and construct their own knowledge (Hiebert & Carpenter, 1992) rather than memorize and regurgitate decontextualized procedures.[5] Students are encouraged to develop their own modes of thinking about and expressing mathematical ideas and strategies, and teachers are guides and facilitators, rather than didactic "tellers," in the knowledge-construction process. *Meaningful Mathematics* (MM) is one of many curricula developed to exemplify and instantiate the standards; Brewer teachers gradually started piloting it in 1995.

The NCTM calls for the type of knowledge that is privileged in a post-industrial, information-based society and is essential cultural capital for upper-strata workers. In such an environment, data are ubiquitous and many knowledge workers need to make independent decisions and reason and communicate mathematically about sophisticated, real-world problems. But low-income students and students of color have historically had less access to mathematics curricula, like MM, that provide students with these skills, dispositions, and knowledge (Oakes, 1985, 1990; Secada, 1992). These students have usually been taught low-skill, "basic" curricula in which they repeatedly apply rote procedures to contrived problems—in short, an education for subordination. Thus it is significant that Brewer was one of the first CPS schools to use an NCTM Standards–based curriculum. Mr. Rodríguez saw use of MM as essentially an equity issue and believed that Brewer students should have the same access to a world-class, twenty-first-century education as those in well-off and highly educated communities.

Teachers were initially optimistic because MM encouraged students to think deeply about mathematics and learn with understanding. Some of its goals were in sync with the child-centered, holistic Brewer vision, for example, that students should develop their own problem-solving methods and that teachers should listen closely to students' thinking to respond to and build on their ideas. As teachers began to use MM, they reflected on differences from the traditional curriculum, MM's strengths, what they were learning, and the changes needed in their own teaching and in students' dispositions and orientations. They discovered from listening to students that they were capable of developing their own problem-solving strategies. Mr Hibarro:

> You have 30 different minds working on one problem [with MM]. You have to adapt to each one of them. . . . They ask things that you never thought about. . . . There will always be . . . another approach or . . . solution to the problems. . . . Sometimes I . . . am amazed at the approaches. . . . They solve the problems in a way that I had never thought of. (December 1996)

Ms. Dawson added: "I've learned to listen to the students. I have been surprised at some of the ways they've approached a problem" (December 1996).

MM also focused on applying mathematics to daily life and real-world problems, as opposed to traditional mathematics curricula, which tend to emphasize decontextualized computation problems. Brewer teachers liked this emphasis. Mr. Hibarro's reaction was representative:

> What I'm saying is that this is more like a real life. . . . When they go to the outside world, they won't say, "Here, do these 30 problems." There is a situation. They will have to talk to a lot of people and listen and have to make conclusions, and then they will apply math. This is a good step. (December 1996)

Though teachers initially supported MM, they also found it very challenging. As they began using MM, it became apparent to them that the demands were different from those of the traditional curriculum and pedagogy with which teachers and students were familiar. They were not used to students' being arbitrators of knowledge or to the level of reading, writing, explanation, and justification required. For example, in the "stories" in the curriculum, the "characters" sometimes have arguments with each other that are mathematically based. Students not only have to decide which character is correct (and sometimes all are), they have to justify their reasoning. Teachers found that students' dispositions toward knowledge, established over years, made it harder to use MM than traditional curricula, and they therefore had to reorient both themselves and students to think in new and different ways. Ms. Cárdenas commented: "I mean, sometimes, there is no right or wrong answer, so students get confused with that because they have been always exposed to math as only right and wrong answers. So students need to be introduced to those ideas" (March 1998).

At the same time that teachers were struggling with MM's challenges, the district began to ramp up accountability. The ITBS began to loom much larger. Under increasing pressure to increase scores, several teachers were concerned that MM was not aligned closely enough with the ITBS, even though it was closely aligned with both the NCTM Standards and the Illinois State Goals for Learning.[6] This meant that they could not just follow MM but had to supplement it with specific ITBS preparation. Ms. Cárdenas:

> Well, the [district] constraints are that there is a lot of stuff that needs to be covered in one school year in order for this program to work, like I said, to be really well correlated with . . . the Iowa. . . . If we find some stuff that is not addressed by Meaningful Mathematics, we have to somehow cover that. (March 1998)

Teachers felt that the ITBS was what really mattered to the district, and this priority had a tremendous impact on schools and students. By spring of 1997, promotion and high school placement depended largely on ITBS scores, and teachers felt powerlessness. Mr. Hibarro:

> As the office [school administration] emphasizes, we will be graded on those tests and how the kids do. It's like, "I don't care what you do. All I care is the Iowa. I don't care if you are using [MM], or if you are doing nothing, or if you are using a regular math book. All I care is about how the kids do in the Iowa." I don't agree, but I don't have power in that. (December 1996)

Ms. Dawson:

> My tests mean something on a report card, but the [ITBS] tests mean something as far as their future, are they going to go to seventh grade, and where are they going to place in high school based on the Iowa. So which one weighs more heavily right now? The Iowa. I'm glad that they understand one problem conceptually, but the problem is, can you perform 25 of them in a short period of time? I don't have an answer for that. (March 1998)

Accountability became increasingly salient in teachers' reluctance to use MM. Gradually, teachers began to "supplement" MM with "skills and drills," especially as May (testing time) approached. Although MM might encourage students to solve a problem in three different ways and to understand deeper mathematical commonalities and larger principles, teachers, fearful of time constraints and test results, pushed students to practice by rote the "quick" way. Some of the less mathematically prepared teachers stopped using it entirely. Also, Brewer lacked the resources to continue paying for professional development, as often happens with curricular innovations in urban school systems. Curricula like MM are so challenging that teachers need multiple years of professional development even without ITBS pressures (Franke, Fennema, & Carpenter, 1997). By 1999, only a few teachers were using MM, and only one consistently. The fear that ITBS scores might drop was the principal reason, and even though Brewer's scores slowly rose during this period, most teachers attributed this increase to their specific skill-based preparation of the students rather than to MM.

Eventually, Brewer stopped using MM altogether, except a couple of teachers who occasionally use it. In its place, Mr. Rodríguez found an external partner that provided free ongoing multiyear on-site professional development with a different mathematics curriculum. This was also based on the NCTM Standards, but teachers unanimously considered it more like what they and students were used to. Most teachers preferred it because they believed that they would have to supplement it less and that its problems were more similar to those on the ITBS.[7] Nonetheless, teachers continued to supplement the new curriculum with "skills" as test time rolled around.

We contrast this experience with Brewer's science curriculum. In 1999, when mathematics teachers were pulling back from MM, science teachers were embracing a new curriculum that emphasized similar dispositions to knowledge. Ms. Pantoja, a science teacher, commented that the "very conservative" sixth grade science department wanted the new curriculum. However, in Chicago, the two subjects that "matter" are language arts and mathematics, and students' scores on the ITBS science section are irrelevant to promotion decisions—that is, there are no stakes attached. In fact, schools can choose whether or not to give the ITBS science exam. So science teachers have the freedom and luxury to experiment, and in the climate at Brewer, even "conservative" science teachers, without a guillotine over their heads, could, and did, try out new ideas and curricula.

Thus, the opportunities for low-income students of color to develop critical thinking in mathematics were curtailed in part as a result of the actual and ideological constraints of district policies on testing, promotion, and retention. These are the very students who historically have had less access to high-powered, challenging academic curricula (Oakes, 1985, 1990). That Brewer did not revert to a traditional, skill-oriented basic mathematics curriculum was a tribute to Mr. Rodríguez's perseverance and leadership—he was not willing to give up his vision of what Brewer students needed. But just as with developing critical literacy, the opportunities were diminished for Brewer students to cultivate critical dispositions and approaches to knowledge—precisely what they need to challenge the injustices of society. Teacher resistance to the dominant policies continued at Brewer, in a variety of forms, but overall the district's emphasis on high stakes accountability measures had a chilling impact.

Education for Assimilation: The Assault on Language, Culture, and Identity

> I can imagine feeling inadequate and thinking, "God, if I want to be recognized or be anything, I'd better get rid of the Spanish and start getting on with the English. I mean that's what counts." So, again, a feeling of inadequacy and what you have is not good enough, or what you have is not worth [pause] it's not what counts. Who cares what you have. It's like, we don't want that. We want something else. (Mr. Rodríguez, June 1999)

CPS's policies have important implications for linguistic and cultural assimilation. Bilingual education in Chicago has become effectively a curriculum of English acquisition, squeezing out support for literacy in students' first language and delegitimating that language in favor of English. We see this policy as part of a cultural politics of assimilation. The message conveyed by the policy and the pressures it creates for teachers and students mark English the preferred/superior language and signify that "success" requires adopting English and "American" norms. Standardized tests also undermine the efforts of some teachers to link curricula to students' cultural identities. We argue that these CPS policies are implicated in the contention over representation and power in the city.

"Being Bilingual Isn't Important Anymore"

For Brewer students, Spanish is central to family relationships and to the cultural connections that tie the community together. Language is a central aspect of identity and "a substantive part of a well-functioning social network in which knowledge is embedded" (Garcia, 1995, p. 383). Language is also the means through which people make sense of their own experience, produce meaning, and act on the world. In this sense, Macedo (1994) argues that bilingual education is fundamentally political. To ignore the role of language as a major force in shaping human identity is to ignore "the way language may either confirm or deny the life histories and experiences of the people who use it" (p. 131). The issue here is not to restrict students to Spanish; to deny students fluency in English would deny them tools to participate fully in the broader society. Rather it is to support the development of fluent bilingualism/biliteracy.

However, beginning with the 1998–99 school year, CPS mandated a three-year limit on bilingual education for most students.[8] According to CPS, the policy is to strengthen and standardize bilingual education programs to speed up the transition to English through new measures of accountability (Language and Cultural Education Initiatives, 1998). Regardless of English proficiency, at the end of the third year in bilingual education, students take the ITBS with the same consequences as monolingual English students (summer school, grade retention, transition high school). There is no language support for students transitioned into the regular program, and although principals can request a fourth or fifth year in bilingual education for individual students, funds for a teacher may not be available. As part of the accountability system, schools must also show an upward trend in transition rates to English: that is, each year a higher percentage of students completing the third year in bilingual education must pass the ITBS in English. This policy is counter to substantial research indicating that students take a minimum of five years to catch up to native speakers in academic use of a second language and that high-quality bilingual, biliteracy programs show better academic outcomes than English-only or quick-exit transitional programs (like Chicago's) that do not aspire to develop bilingualism and biliteracy (Cummins, 2000). Under the

CPS policy, bilingual education students at Brewer were pulled out of their classes and instructed in English (a standard English as Second Language [ESL] model). In this Chicago mirrors the national backlash against bilingual education, exemplified by California's Proposition 227 and now national policy under the federal *No Child Left Behind* Act (2001). In the guise of equity, these policies are part of the antiimmigrant campaign that gathered steam in the 1990s, targeting Latinos/as in particular.

Chicago's quick-exit bilingual policy presses teachers to teach in English at the expense of students' first language. In the rush to transition students to English, in the spring of 1998, thousands of students in bilingual education classrooms who were making good academic progress, working hard, and attending regularly suddenly were required to spend eight weeks in an intensive ESL summer school because of their ITBS scores. According to Mr. Rodríguez, as a result of this dramatic experience, teachers felt compelled to sacrifice a rich bilingual-education curriculum: "We're not doing it justice. So it's sort of like, you know, again, let's put our beliefs aside, let's not think about 'it's great to be bilingual.' We can't practice what we believe" (June 1999). Ms. Guzmán talked about this issue in spring of 1999:

> Ms. Guzmán: It's just that word "English, English, English. Let's get to more English," you know, that gets me a little bit nervous.
> Interviewer: Do you feel like you're sacrificing their Spanish in the meantime?
> Ms. Guzmán: Yes. yes. And I feel like I'm trying to work them toward English, but I'm not working as much with the other language, which makes them what they are—bilingual. So just working toward the English, what's gonna happen to that Spanish? I know that by the time they get to me, they have to be totally bilingual, so their Spanish skills are up there, but by the time I finish the year I feel like the Spanish seems to be decreasing and decreasing even more, because now the survival language is English, because now they're going to take a test, and if they don't score what they're supposed to score, they're gonna be held back.

The pressures against biliteracy and biculturalism were compounded by high stakes tests when students moved to the English program. Ms. Guzmán:

> By the time they reach eighth grade, it's completely English. So, even when we say "Why don't we at least give them forty minutes of Spanish, that would be really good," and then the teacher says "No! Look at all this stuff we have to do because of the tests." So you hear it even from the upper grades. (June 1999)

Standardized testing concretely and symbolically authorizes English as the superior language, the language of power. The lesson is clear—the price of success in mainstream institutions is the delegitimization of one's language, identity, and sense of self. The ideological force of this policy is directed to the public as well. The cultural politics of delegitimizing Spanish is to devalue Latino/a identities and specifically to devalue immigrants, whose use of Spanish marks them as "other." It signifies the supremacy of English (read, white) and indicates that to be "American" is to be like Anglos, to speak white, standard English. Ms. Guzmán:

> So now I think that they're seeing that message like being bilingual isn't impor-
> tant anymore. It's not . . . *you're not seen as something important* [emphasis
> added]; you're just seen as trying to get the English and if you don't get it, that's
> it. So I think that the message that they're getting is just like "oh well, I guess
> Spanish is not important." (June 1999)

In fact, an explicit aspect of the CPS *English as a Second Language Goals and Standards* (1998) is promotion of culturally assimilationist behavior. According to the Standards, instruction should "focus on the cultural setting of the United States" and promote "the use of English to succeed in all academic areas and in all social and personal contexts." Although some of the standards seem generic for learning a second language (e.g., "Recognize differences between formal and informal language"), others are linked to a normative notion of appropriate "American" behaviors (e.g., "Establish and maintain appropriate eye contact"). These standards specifically valorize dominant, white, middle-class norms in everyday activities that sixth graders are certainly competent in within their own cultural frame of reference. These include, according to Ms. Pantoja, "how to make a telephone call and conversation, how to initiate play and games." This curriculum teaches Mexican students that their ways of interacting and behaving are deficient, diminishing who they are. Ms. Guzmán: "They're erasing that Mexican-American image of that child. Because now Spanish is not important anymore. Now it's the English."

The contradictions this posed for teachers were pedagogical and personal. Teachers, as well as students, were caught between two worlds. Ms. Guzmán was an example. Over the nine years we have known her, she has consistently demonstrated her dedication to helping her students develop confidence to think for themselves. For her, teaching is a way to contribute to her community. In 1996, she described how she felt about teaching in the community where she grew up:

> These kids, I see myself as them. So I think coming back and just being offered
> that opportunity [to teach here] is like a great gift to me. There's a lot of times
> where they're [dominant society] not taking us seriously, and I want to change
> that, because they should be taking us seriously. They're [Mexican students]
> something; they're the future. We need to take them as seriously as any other
> person. (October 1996)

Yet, in the face of accountability policies, she found that her commitments were pitted against the necessity she felt to privilege English. Even with her own children, she said she had begun to emphasize English over Spanish:

> So I feel like sometimes that Spanish is like taken away, and I even see it some-
> times in my children, my own children, when I have to move them towards
> English. That I want them to be just as prepared because that's what's gonna be
> all on the school tests. And if you don't test at your grade level, you're gonna be
> held back. (June 1999)

Suppression of Spanish is a way of asserting cultural dominance over Mexicans and other politically marginalized Spanish-speaking Latinos/as
(Macedo, 1994). It is also a political act of silencing and subordinating
those students (Macedo, 1994). Because language is an inextricable part of
social identity, collective experience, and community, an education that
validates students' first language confirms their lived experiences and the
meaning they make of the world. It confirms their agency as subjects
(Freire in Macedo, 1994). Giroux draws this connection between language
and voice: "Language represents a central force in the struggle for voice . . .
language is able to shape the way various individuals and groups encode
and thereby engage the world" (Giroux quoted in Ruiz, 1997, p. 320). Fluent bilingualism/ biliteracy gives students access to the common linguistic
code and the use of their own language to "make themselves 'heard' and to
define themselves as active authors of their worlds" (Giroux quoted in
Macedo, 1994, p. 133).

CPS's bilingual education policy is yet another example of using the historical inequalities and failure of urban schools to construct a new common sense around a dominant agenda. Across the system, there are
students who have spent years in bilingual education without learning
English and are significantly below grade level. Antiimmigrant political
forces, such as those behind Proposition 227 in California, identify bilingual education as the root of economic and academic failure. CPS press releases and comments in the media refer to students in bilingual programs
as "institutionalized," discursively linking bilingual education with con-
finement, punishment, and remedial programs. This ignores the failure of
CPS to create sufficient high-quality bilingual education programs (programs that provide qualified bilingual teachers, excellent curricula, and
sufficient and current texts). It also negates sociopolitical explanations that
point to economic, political, and cultural subordination of specific groups,
including many Latino/a groups, who do poorly in school regardless of
access to bilingual education. In short, CPS is using language as an explanation for inequality, negating the racism and class oppression and educational inequality that have influenced the academic performance and
produced the grinding poverty of Latinos/as and other immigrant students (Cummins, 1996; Garcia, 1995; National Council of La Raza, 1990;
Ruiz, 1997). In place of assimilationist policies, the situation urgently demands an array of affirmative education policies that begin with students'

culture and language as resources, not problems,[9] and that challenge coercive power relations. Cummins (2000) provides this framework:

> Students' identities are affirmed and academic achievement promoted when teachers express respect for the language and culture students bring to the classroom and when the instruction is focused on helping students generate new knowledge, create literature and art, and act on social realities that affect their lives. (p 34)

A compelling argument for high-quality bilingual/biliteracy education is the success of Inter-American Magnet School in Chicago, a national model, dual-language school (Spanish and English) staffed by highly qualified teachers (including several winners of a prestigious state teaching award) based on a rigorous program that promotes dual language literacy, critical approaches to knowledge, and a multicultural curriculum. Admission is by lottery (Urow & Sontag, 2001). (The school is also one of the highest-scoring in the city on the ITBS.)

Decentering Students' Cultural Identities

Brewer students are a diverse, multifaceted group, their identities shaped by urban and rural experiences, gender, sexual orientation, family situation, transnational and immigration experiences, popular culture, and other influences. Brewer's school dances display these varied identities. The disc jockey alternates between free-style, hip-hop, and disco for first-generation students and *banda, merengue, la musica norteña*, and *la quebradita* for recent immigrant students—sometimes the same students listen to both. Yet through common family experiences and a common language; through living together in an insular, supportive urban neighborhood; and through common experiences of racism and oppression, the students also develop aspects of a shared identity (Darder, 1995).

CPS standards and accountability constrained the efforts of some teachers to center curriculum in these shared experiences and sense of identity. Although the Standards contain general language supporting "multiculturalism," in a climate that validates whatever is tested and measured, they carry little weight. Ms. Pantoja: "I haven't seen anything put out by CPS that encourages teachers to use the students' culture. They say we should celebrate it by suggesting sporadic mini-lessons on multiculturalism" (June 1999). In the face of pressure to practice for standardized tests and to teach specific information that is tested, socially and culturally centered curricula were pushed aside. And in a school context where there were ideological differences over language, representation, and cultural assimilation, attempts by some teachers and administrators to persuade other faculty to explore more culturally responsive curricula were undermined by the systemwide legitimation of the dominant Eurocentric knowledge at the core of the ITBS and ISAT. This process was similar to the way that the press for test preparation drove out critical literacy. Ms. Guzmán: "a lot of the strategies that teachers were using, you know to maintain their culture, it's being taken away because now that time has to be consumed in preparing for the tests" (June 1999).

Ms. Pantoja's sixth-grade language arts class was an example.

> Ms. Pantoja: I'd like to [use] a lot more Chicano literature, and it's not in the curriculum, and I'm sure there's a way to go around it and stick it in there, but I don't have the time to develop a whole new Chicano literature curriculum to fit into it because I've got all these other things going on. I've got testing [in English]. I've got the Prueba [standardized test in Spanish]. So that's one of the big things that I would love to be able to include a lot more.

Moreover, teachers talked about how test items legitimated dominant knowledge and experience and negated Brewer students' knowledge and experiences. Mr. Falcón talked about the vocabulary tested by the ITBS: "Dandelion. If these kids don't have a yard where they're pulling these weeds, they won't know that dandelion is a weed. These words come from a white perspective" (June 1999).

Our interviews suggest that the pressures and tensions were great, and especially for teachers who were just beginning to consider these issues, the force of the CPS agenda worked against transforming the curriculum or even altering it. Darder (1995) argues that if Latino/a students are to develop bicultural identities and social agency, they need teachers

> who understand the dynamic of cultural subordination and the impact that this has upon students, their families, and their cultural communities. Latino students also need critically conscious teachers who come from their own cultural communities, can speak and instruct them in their native language, can serve as translators of the bicultural experience, and can reinforce an identity grounded in the cultural integrity of their own people. (p. 328)

This is precisely what was in danger of being driven further to the margins at Brewer. In a school with competing agendas and ideologies, the system of accountability favored the dominant knowledge and ways of learning sanctioned by standardized tests and worked against critical, culturally relevant pedagogies.

CPS Policies and Educational Change at Brewer

When the LSC selected Mr. Rodríguez as principal in 1994, Brewer was similar to many other CPS schools. Teachers reported that they worked in relative isolation and focused primarily on their own classrooms with little input in important decisions. The majority maintained a daily routine of traditional, teacher-centered, skill-based teaching. They were used to a strong principal who had built up the school, had a traditional educational philosophy, and did not speak Spanish. Under the terms of the 1988 reform, parents in the local school council seized the opportunity to choose one of their own to lead the school.

Between 1995 and 1999 we observed, and participated in, an effort, led by Mr. Rodríguez, to promote student-centered, inquiry-based teaching and to connect the curriculum with students' cultural backgrounds and experiences. Over time, this process generated the seeds of a critical examination of assumptions about the community, culture, and student "abilities." To help fulfill his educational aims, Mr. Rodríguez recruited several teachers from his previous school and hired others who supported this agenda. Together with several Brewer teachers, they formed a small core of potential teacher leadership for this new direction. This group was loosely, and variously, committed to a set of goals that included inquiry-based instruction, bilingual/bicultural education, critical literacy, culturally relevant teaching, and community involvement. In addition, Ms. Ortiz, the home–school coordinator, contributed her experiences and perspective as a respected community activist. Between 1995 and 1999, the struggle for the direction of Brewer unfolded within the dynamic tensions between the established culture and routine of the school and the new principal's educational goals, and between teachers with diverse ideological and educational perspectives. Most important, from our point of view, the change process began simultaneously with CPS accountability. The tensions at Brewer played out in relation to the material and ideological consolidation of CPS's centralized regulation and accountability, a context that was to create new contradictions and pressures.

Opening up Dangerous Dialogues

Mr. Rodríguez hoped to change the culture of the school through infusing new ideas and opening up dialogue about unspoken beliefs and assumptions. His first act was to convene a series of retreats in which administrators and teachers collectively hammered out a vision of holistic, progressive education and acknowledgment of the strengths of the students' cultural background and community. He also organized professional development focused on problem-solving curricula and multifaceted forms of assessment. Perhaps most important, he initiated a sustained process of inquiry and discussion among the entire school staff to explore their own ideologies and beliefs about the students and their families and the values embedded in the school's routine practices.

In 1996 the Illinois State Board of Education mandated a Quality Review process in all public schools. External teams of teachers, principals, and other outside experts visited schools to observe classes, examine student work, and interview teachers, students, and parents. On the basis of a week of data gathering, they presented their reflections to the school as a whole. The school was to use the external team's findings to help guide its school-improvement process. This process was to be preceded by a similar internal self-study involving teachers, community members, and administrators. The state provided funds for each school to conduct this self-study. From our conversations with CPS teachers and principals, observations in other schools, and the reflections of a team of researchers working in schools across the city, our impression is that most schools treated the Quality Review as just another bureaucratically mandated evaluation. Typically it sent school personnel scurrying to compile materials and put together a performance that would satisfy the evaluators.[10]

But Mr. Rodríguez seized on the Quality Review as an opportunity for schoolwide critical reflection and dialogue on how well the school was fulfilling its stated vision. He formed an inquiry team composed of a diverse cross section of teachers and staff (both of us participated as external "reflective colleagues"). The team observed classes, interviewed students and adults, and facilitated schoolwide discussions on key issues that emerged from the data. (When one of us told a researcher involved in a number of CPS schools about the Brewer process, she was astonished because it was such an aberration from the typical pro forma response to the Quality Review.) Half-day meetings of the whole staff (faculty, teacher aides, professional staff) were devoted to this process throughout most of the 1996–97 school year.

From an initial analysis of teachers' written responses, the internal self-study team identified three critical issues: conflicting views of the place of Mexican culture and community experiences in the curriculum, differing perceptions of parents' involvement in their children's education, and divisions among teachers. Led by the principal, the team put these differences on the table for discussion. The discussions were framed by thought-provoking readings and grounded in the data that had been collected. This process sparked conversation about deficit notions of families, Latino/a-centered curriculum versus multiculturalism, and Latino/a teachers' privileged knowledge about the students and families.[11] In the spring, the team presented a synthesis of interviews of Brewer students. That discussion focused on student perceptions that regular track students were "second class" at Brewer and that some students saw bilingualism as "dumb." This report, based on students' own words, evoked a riveting two-hour discussion on tracking as a "self-fulfilling prophesy," on the value of bilingualism and biculturalism, and on the proactive role the school could play in mobilizing the community around gentrification. At this amazing meeting, some teachers suggested Brewer should become a dual-language school and others proposed organizing joint parent–student–teacher meetings on important community issues.

The self-study process provoked what we came to call "dangerous dialogues" about race, culture, power, language, and the privileging of middle-class perspectives—core issues at Brewer, from our perspective, and in urban schools in general. These kinds of frank discussions are rare in schools yet essential to school change (Lipman, 1998). By opening up these dialogues and selecting a team composed of people with different perspectives, Mr. Rodríguez created the conditions for teachers, in painful and halting steps, to begin openly to question deficit theories that privileged dominant cultural norms and acquisition of English at the expense of Spanish. These dialogues also created conditions for Latino/a teachers to share their own experiences as immigrants and begin to challenge assimilationist practices and perspectives. Our field notes capture the first tentative steps toward revisioning a school that would be bilingual/bicultural, less stratified, and more rooted in the community and its struggles.

Although the official self-study was completed in June 1997, Mr. Rodríguez continued it in the following years. During the second year, CPS administrators ramped up accountability, and the self-study focused for a time on contradictions between the school vision and the CPS agenda. Teachers were split. Some seized on accountability to challenge the school's new direction, arguing that didactic instruction and standardized tests should be in the forefront; others firmly opposed the narrowness and prescriptiveness of CPS's agenda; others were uncertain. Mr. Rodríguez used the self-study and the team to generate open debate on these perspectives. In a system that was imposing centralized control of teachers and defining education by achievement on standardized tests, Brewer was struggling to chart its own direction.

Negotiating the CPS Agenda

In the next few years, teachers and administrators were caught between these educational agendas and had conflicting and contradictory responses. Even some of the most critical teachers saw some value in CPS's accountability measures. They responded to the "good sense" of a policy that spoke to righting obvious wrongs in the system. The bilingual policy and the equity supposedly created by the ITBS made sense to some, given the problems with some CPS bilingual programs and the general failure of schools to educate students of color. But, as teachers, they also saw the policies as being coercive and as undermining bilingualism and critical literacy. Ms. Guzmán, a parent as well as a bilingual teacher, articulated this conflicting perspective. Immediately after talking about the unfairness of testing bilingual students in English and the pressure she felt as a third grade teacher, she said:

> But now seeing both ways, like as a parent and as a teacher . . . so as a parent I feel more at ease cause now I know that these kids are gonna be held just as responsible as any other student. So as a parent I feel like "good"! Because I feel like if that English support is not given, then that child is not gonna be able to survive in the outer world. (June 1999)

She resolved this contradiction by using CPS's argument: some teachers are not doing their job and need the pressure of accountability to ensure that all students get the same education:

> It puts a lot of pressure, puts a lot of stress, but only if you're not doing a good job from the beginning. But, if you're doing a good job, and you're doing what you're supposed to, then you shouldn't feel threatened. . . . Any child, bilingual or not, should be given the opportunity and the skills that they need to survive, and I think that's the way I see [that] Paul Vallas sees it. (June 1999)

However, in practice, the teachers and administrators struggled to negotiate their educational goals and the demands of the tests. Initially, teachers committed to a broader educational vision were determined to prevent the ITBS from driving their curriculum. However, as CPS intensified accountability and pressured the school to increase its scores, this became increasingly difficult. Meanwhile, other teachers who had resisted the school's new direction were bolstered by the accountability policies. As the school grappled with these tensions, teachers attempted to reconcile the serious consequences of standardized test scores and their educational philosophy. Minutes from a faculty dialogue session:

> In keeping with our school vision, in order for our students to be "well rounded students," preparing them to take standardized tests should not be seen as being contrary to our vision. Nor should it be seen that our school philosophy has changed or will change because we must address these tests. Our students are being judged on their IOWA scores and are being accepted or denied to certain high schools because of them. . . . Instead the solution is to ensure that our teaching strategies are well rounded. (January 1998)

Teachers negotiated competing claims in a variety of ways. Some tried to integrate them. Ms. Rossman spent one quarter on test preparation. Others expressed frustration at a conflict they found unresolvable. Mr. Falcón:

> Interviewer: How do you deal with the contradiction between the standardized tests that are these multiple choice answers, one right answer, and then you're trying to get them to think, to question, to see it from more than one point of view? Mr. Falcón: I don't know. To be honest with you it's hard. . . . I try to downplay everything that's standardized. It's hard to do to be honest with you. I don't have an answer for you in that I can't do it. (June 1999)

Perhaps no one wrestled with this tension more than Mr. Rodríguez, whose dream for Brewer was increasingly challenged by the accountability policies that he was required to implement. In 1998–99, even though Brewer's test scores were relatively high CPS central authorities threatened to impose a standardized curriculum if the scores did not increase each year. Even more devastating, a substantial number of eighth graders were retained because they failed the ITBS. The constraints and costs of accountability were simply too great. Mr. Rodríguez insisted that teachers spend more time on test prep:

> A lot of times it sounds like I'm talking out of both sides of my mouth, because on the one hand, I'm pushing for it to be a child centered, enriching experience for these kids to find who they really are besides getting the academics, and it's like, "But you know what, guys? But you still got to get them ready for the Iowa." So it's sort of like I think with my faculty it was like a tug because I think we really flipped the other way in terms of the Iowa's not [being] important. And I really had to tighten it up this year, and I think the faculty felt it, too, and really said, "You know what? It's not a matter of what we believe . . . but the reality is, if we don't get these kids ready for the Iowa, we're slamming the door. We're helping the door be slammed in their face." So that's a real big contradiction. (June 1999)

He also had to compromise his bilingual/biliteracy agenda. "[P]eople that believe in dual-language acquisition, it's like you're talking out of both sides of your mouth, and that's another great contradiction that I'm having because I believe in it. Am I practicing it? No. Can my teachers that believe in it practice it? No. We had to come to grips with that." At the same time, he took a stand and refused to implement the educational triage that was practiced at Grover and Westview and many other schools across the city to raise test scores.

"It Gets under Your Skin": The Ideological Power of the Dominant Agenda

Over time, accountability imposed practical and ideological constraints. Gradually, the ideological impact was reflected in talk and in practice. In the first place, CPS's framework shaped the issues and monopolized public discourse so that no viable alternative could be easily considered. What other solution was there, for example, for so many bilingual students' failing the ITBS, as Ms. Guzmán said? Second, accountability worked as a hierarchical and all-encompassing system of surveillance as each level was forced to implement policies foisted on it by the level above. And those who were rewarded were those who most taught to the tests. It was this logic that drove Ms. Rossman to spend the third quarter on Iowa test preparation.

> I know these tests are [poor assessments] yet I know I'm going to be judged on them. I know my principal in his heart doesn't believe in it, yet he's going to be judged on it so he has to judge me on it. Of course, the kids. It was like, I'm not fulfilling my responsibility by not preparing them. So there's this teacher at school . . . she does exactly the same thing every day from the book . . . do the spelling words before you read, read the story together, ask all the questions as you go through them. Do the questions at the end. She had the most kids pass . . . I just thought about that. That's so cruel. (June 1999)

This was the power of the "pecking order," as Mr. Rodríguez called it:

> I feel that in my heart I know what I want for kids and how I want the teachers to feel, to empower them, but on the other hand, it's sort of like it's a pecking order. It's like my evaluation is based on how close we are to the 50th percentile. . . . I keep seeing more and more that the actual evaluation of the teacher is going to be tied up to how their kids [score]. (June 1999)

Third, as accountability became all-encompassing, it left less space for resistance. Two themes ran through our interviews—powerlessness and the fear that students would suffer. Ms. Guzmán: "If we keep griping about it, if we keep complaining, then who's gonna be affected? The kids" (June 1999). Ms. Rossman: "I feel like we're all wearing these handicaps because of these policies and that if we take them off, we'll be shot. . . . It's really stifling and depressing. If I knew something to do to change it, if there was a way I could do to change it without getting fired or jeopardizing my career, then I would" (June 1999). In a context in which the faculty had only begun to forge a common perspective, collective resistance was elusive Mr. Rodríguez:

> I mean, we would really have to make a commitment to each other, and like you said, in other places, teachers refuse to give the test and say "We're all going down on this one. We're gonna take a stand." That's the type of [pause] to have an impact, that's what you would need. . . . Are people going to do that? Again, it's only a handful, because they end up getting slapped in the face. (June 1999)

Over time, for all of the reasons indicated, teachers and administrators absorbed aspects of the accountability discourse, shaping their practice and language to the dominant framework. In 1998, Mr. Rodríguez decided to retain seventh graders with low ITBS scores (even though this was not a benchmark grade) in the hope of preventing them from being retained in eighth grade. He believed this was more humane than not allowing them to graduate with their peers or sending them to the transition high school. "Because I just think it's devastating to have to go through what some of these kids have gone through this year, especially when they're [CPS] getting that tight about it that a [tenth of a] point will keep you from graduating. . . . I would never have thought in the past that I would be keeping 29 kids and not passing them on. . . ." The necessity to compromise took hold.

For example, in 2001, he ordered expensive test-prep books for every grade in anticipation that the district would require them. And Ms. Rossman described how teachers had absorbed, and finally internalized, the rationale and discourse of accountability, reproducing it in their own practices:

> We look at their Iowa scores and we judge them like that. . . . A self-fulfilling prophecy because we look at that and we think, "Oh, my God, what am I going to do with this kid who's got a 5.0 [ITBS score] in eighth grade?" I think it affects teachers on this really subtle level on the surface and then it really gets under your skin. You start just kind of going with it. . . . But if you don't have that very strong basis, you know we're rooted in this progressive education and it's kind of wishy-washy, you know what I mean? (June 1999)

In the end, people felt forced to compromise, negotiate, and give up part of what they believed in—or leave teaching altogether, as Ms. Rossman did. Ms. Guzmán relinquished some of her commitment to bilingualism and put pressure on the second grade bilingual teacher to push the kids in English. Mr. Falcón gave up part of his critical literacy curriculum. In 2001–2, Ms. Pantoja tacked between her inquiry-based science and a boxed curriculum with multiple choice tests that would yield the data to assign a grade in "listening" now required by CPS. Mr. Rodríguez struggled to maintain part of his vision, but increasingly he said he was "forced to play the game," in order to do what he could to improve the school within the constraints imposed:

> I affects me, I mean, in a personal way because it's sort of like [pause] it doesn't let me be how I really want to be. It doesn't allow for, you know, to provide the type of leadership that I really would like to be providing because the minute I do that, forget it. You know? So basically, I feel like [pause] I've sold out to a certain point. But then I figure if I don't negotiate, or try to justify what I'm doing, so what? As little as the changes [have been] at Brewer . . . the conditions are much greater for kids than they have been, you know? (June 1999)

Techniques of surveillance teach people to discipline themselves (Foucault, 1977). Concretely, this process succeeds in the absence of a strong alternative ideology and organized opposition that can counter the dominant trend. It is important to note that Ms. Rossman recognized that the school had not coalesced around a strong enough counterhegemonic perspective to stand up, ideologically, to the district's mandates. Perhaps it was the seeming impossibility of organized resistance that also led Mr. Rodríguez to compromise in the interest of accomplishing what he could. Brewer illustrates the constraints that accountability and centralized regulation put on a thoughtful, sustained process of change. It also illustrates the critical need for a counter-hegemoniec discourse and practice that can crystallize resistance. However, Brewer also provides a glimpse, although short-circuited by these constraints, of democratic possibilities for transforming urban schools.

"It's All Linked"—Education Policy and the Cultural Politics of Race and Ethnicity

We have argued that CPS policies that promote assimilation and devalue the home language of Mexican and other immigrant students and students of color are linked with nativist, white supremacist movements against cultural diversity, multiculturalism, and immigrants. But the policies are also part of the cultural politics of race and ethnicity in the city. Several Brewer teachers drew this connection. They saw the school system's bilingual education policy as part of a broader campaign to suppress the political power of Latinos/as, and the Marion Park community specifically.

Whose City Is It?

Education policies that effectively suppress students' language and cultural identities take on particular significance in the struggle for representation, place, and power in the city. This struggle is rooted in the intense political, economic, and cultural contradictions of cities that bring together the immense power and wealth of international corporations and masses of disempowered and impoverished people of color, immigrants, and women. Global cities are international not only because they concentrate transnational firms and telecommunications, but because they have a racially and ethnically diverse working class:

> The large Western city of today concentrates diversity. Its spaces are inscribed with the dominant corporate culture but also with a multiplicity of other cultures and identities. The slippage is evident: the dominant culture can encompass only part of the city. And while corporate power inscribes these cultures and identifies them with "otherness" thereby devaluing them, they are present everywhere. (Sassen, 1998, p. xxxi)

Latinos/as in Chicago exemplify displaced immigrant populations seeking a new home in the city. Marion Park, like other immigrant communities, establishes continuity with life in the home country and is a space of collective identity, support, and resistance in the United States. "For years we have had to fight for almost every—just to live here—just to keep this place, just to say that we want to live on [Allen Street] the rest of our lives" (Ms. Ortiz, Feburary 1996). The residents of Marion Park are an important part of the low-wage labor force that is integral to global production processes and the lifestyles of the powerful but whose cultural norms, racialized identity, and linguistic visibility—its "place making practices" (Haymes, 1996)—represent a challenge to the cultural appropriation of the city by (mostly white) elites. They emerge as subjects despite efforts to marginalize and ghettoize them (Sassen, 1998). Their presence is felt in the dense profusion of Mexican, Puerto Rican, and Central American religious, commercial, gastronomic, and cultural life centered in Marion Park and other Latino/a barrios and spilling over to other parts of the city, in *banda* and *salsa* rhythms emanating from stores around the city, in the growing presence of Spanish in public spaces, and in the inability of white, anglophone elites to decode fully this linguistic–cultural scene and thus manage and control it.

The state and sectors of capital isolate and marginalize communities such as Marion Park through segregated housing markets, racial discrimination, and disinvestment in public services and infrastructure. But this isolation also becomes a basis of community cohesion and strength. Low-income immigrant communities establish networks of mutual assistance in migration, form supportive social networks of households, and mobilize for collective action (Smith & Tarallo, 1993). This is evident in the support for newly arrived families from Mexico and elsewhere, the exchange of knowledge and skills that facilitate day-to-day survival (Moll, Amanti, Neff, & Gonzalez, 1992), and the history of struggles in Marion Park. Goldberg (1993) argues that in such communities people turn spatial containment into affirmative resistance. "It is on, and from these sites, the social margins, that the battles of resistance will be waged, the fights for full recognition of rights, for registered voices, and for the insistence on fully integrated social institutions, resources, and space" (p. 57). As Ms. Ortiz said when recounting the history of struggle around education in Marion Park: "I cannot fight for my son alone. If this school is going to be good for my son, it has to be good for 250 others. We are always part of the others."

Because language is key to community cohesion and a means of cultural contention for space and place in the city, education policies that undermine the community's linguistic and cultural integrity weaken the community and its presence in the city. These policies are tied to a constellation of Daley administration efforts to constrict Latinos'/as' claims to public space. Among these is the city's attempt to close down street food vendors on grounds of sanitation (an irony not lost on Chicagoans wise to the lore of a well-worn tradition of paying off city health inspectors). Many of the vendors are Mexicans and Puerto Ricans who have turned street corners in neighborhoods like Marion Park and multiracial neighborhoods in other parts of the city into mini-*mercados* with their pushcarts of *elotes, piraguas, tamales, churros,* mangos, and *paletas* and pickup trucks selling fruit and vegetables. These Chicago pushcart wars are emblematic of wider contests over the definition of urban public space. "Across the vast pan-American range of cultural nuance, the social reproduction of *latinidad,* however defined, presupposes a rich proliferation of public space" that challenges the "frozen geometries of the old spatial order" (Davis, 2001, p. 65).

Marketing Ethnicity—Marion Park as an Urban Theme Park

Paradoxically, while the city works to contain the insertion of the heterogeneous cultural expressions of African Americans, Latinos/as, and other immigrant working-class people of color into its corporate, gentrified image, it also seeks to market a romanticized and sanitized version of diversity. A folkloric multiculturalism is part of the "exotic" appeal of the city, the urban cultural magnetism that is a draw for tourists and the cosmopolitan new upper-middle-class city dwellers. The markteting of diversity is quickly evident in the "multicultural" murals that greet travelers at Chicago's O'Hare Airport. But its sharpest expression is in the packaging of certain ethnic neighborhoods as new urban theme parks for middle-class consumption (Haymes, 1995). Chinatown and Pilsen on the South Side are billed as tourist attractions, as is Devon Avenue on the North, home to a rich mix of East Indians, Pakistanis, Jews, Russians, and Eastern Europeans. Marion Park is becoming another one of these tourist designations. As Marion Park is being constructed in a "Latino/a" image, tour groups are beginning to appear along the main street. These carefully controlled sightseeing junkets allow visitors to "view" the neighborhood without coming in contact with the realities of daily life in an immigrant community.

In the white imagination, Marion Park and Latinos/as are objectified and romanticized in Day of the Dead performances, Latin dance, and murals emptied of their race and class content. The grown daughter of a Brewer teacher's aide described being besieged by picture-snapping tourists while she was buying *pan de muerte* at a local bakery during the Mexican Day of the Dead holidays. This commodification of Marion Park as an "ethnic" attraction transforms a community of working-class people in all their complexity, diversity, struggles, and accomplishments into a folkloric stereotype. Integral to this stereotype is the necessary process of writing out the low wages, crowded living conditions, lack of health care, racism, and daily humiliations in the city, as well as working-class and ethnic social history and social movements, which together form the warp on which daily life is woven. Packaging Marion Park this way serves a fraction of the local business owners as well as powerful financial interests and city leaders eager to boost a tourist industry that is central to the global city. With the encroachment of gentrification at its borders, Marion Park is also headed toward becoming one of the next "hot" neighborhoods. Paradoxically, its "charm" and growing tourism also open up the area to real estate developers and the new "urban pioneers" they aim to attract. At some point, the interests of different sectors of capital may collide if gentrification erases the area's appeal for tourists, or merely the trappings of a Mexican–Latino/a community, for instance, restaurants, may be left, with the people pushed out. As Neal Smith (1996) points out: "The new urban pioneers seek to scrub the city clean of its working-class geography and history. By remaking the geography of the city they simultaneously rewrite its social history as a preemptive justification for a new urban future" (pp. 26–27).

Remaining intact—spatially, culturally, and linguistically—is a necessary condition for the community to continue to struggle against these incursions. Mr. Rodríguez identified the link between school policies that weakened community cohesion and the political project of powerful interests outside the community to define and exploit Marion Park:

> This whole issue of pushing them out and not graduating them, dropping them out, not acknowledging their bilingualism . . . has to have a negative impact on the community. And it's all linked. It seems to me that there's a link through a lot, and the link is mainly to get rid of that community. . . You tie all that into what's happening in the education . . . you know, if you really analyzed it, it's [pause] they're going out 100 plus to really force that community out of there, and they're gonna do it. (Interview, June 1999).

Conclusion: What's at Stake

In 1995, Brewer was a school poised for change. Certainly, there were multiple and competing educational philosophies and ideologies at work, but the school had a core of critical, culturally relevant teachers and a bold new principal committed to the community and to a humanistic educational vision and high-quality bilingual education. Under his leadership, the school began an extraordinary process of reflection, self-study, and dialogue that involved the participation of teachers, administrators, school staff at all levels; students; and supportive university faculty. The process began openly to address issues of race, culture, and power that are central to the inequalities and injustices in urban schools but largely absent from educators' public discussions (Lipman, 1998). This beginning process contrasted sharply with intensified centralized regulation and surveillance and the incentives and punishments that characterize CPS's accountability system and *No Child Left Behind* (2001). In this chapter, we have described how this process and the seeds of liberatory education—critical approaches to knowledge, culturally relevant teaching, and support for bilingual education—were undermined by the dominant CPS policies. The case of Brewer Elementary School counters those who argue that there is no alternative to top-down accountability and surveillance as the way to improve urban schools. It also speaks to the destructive effect of these policies on a genuine attempt to challenge entrenched, middle-class assumptions and racist ideologies and practices in schools—and to the damage to the spirit of teachers and students alike these policies produce.

There are broader social implications as well. Education policies that work against the political strength of the community are part of the process of containing a Latino/a social movement for social and economic justice. Latinos/as are now 26 percent of Chicago's population, more than three-quarters of a million people, the third largest after those of New York and Los Angeles (*Census 2000*, 2000). Their rapid expansion positions them to be a powerful political force in their own interests (Bonilla & Morales, 1993). The growing political power of Latinos/as in Chicago became apparent in the 1982 mayoral election, when the Latino/a vote was a key element in electing Harold Washington. Today, Latinos/as are a much larger portion of the population and a potentially powerful force in opposition to the Daley administration and its growth machine–global city agenda. This point is not lost on Daley, who has promoted his own Latino/a political representatives and strategically placed Latino/a public officials, including in the top CPS administration.

There is another dimension, as well, related to the major role of Latino/a labor in Chicago's low-wage economy:

> The availability of a large, subordinated, low-wage Latino work force has facilitated the development of the so-called service sector and has kept in business many manufacturing firms with low profit margins. As an employer in the West Side of Chicago pointed out to us: "I don't need to move to Mexico to get cheap labor. We have plenty of them here. By staying in Chicago I have the best of both worlds." (Betancur et al., 1993, p. 132)

In the 1998 policy paper *Chicago Metropolis 2020* (Johnson, 1998), Chicago's business and financial leaders stressed the need to improve the basic educational performance (as measured by standardized tests) of schools serving "minorities" "for the economy to prosper." The report specifically highlights "Hispanics," whose "student population [in the Chicago metro region] is expected to increase by 120 percent, to 272,000 students, between 1990 and 2020" (Johnson, 1998, p. 6). School accountability policies that discipline, sort, and teach students they are responsible for their own failure serve as a powerful form of ideological preparation for integration into a stratified and compliant workforce. As Mr. Rodgríguez put it, "In the name of better education or higher standards or better expectations . . . that's just a cover for, I think, the racism and the tracking that they want to do."

Although the relationship between school accountability policies and labor discipline is important in general, it has specific meaning in the context of the growing militancy of Latino/a workers in particular. Davis (2000) notes:

> Over the last decade, Latino rank-and-file workers have made the Los Angeles area the major R&D center for 21st-century trade unionism. The defiant and

exuberant spirit of the *huelgas* of the 1960s and early 1970s has reemerged in one sweatshop industry and low-paid service sector after another. (p. 170)

In L.A. the support of Latino workers for the African American bus drivers' strike in 2000 (Davis, 2000) gave a taste of the potential impact of multiracial worker solidarity. The same phenomenon has begun to surface in Chicago, where Latino/a workers have been in the forefront of several sweatshop struggles. In the summer of 2002, Chicago hotel workers, overwhelmingly immigrants and people of color, won an important victory to improve their substandard wages and meager health care plan. The climax was a traffic-stopping march of several thousand Chinese, Filipino, Vietnamese, African American, Polish, Bosnian, Mexican, Puerto Rican, and Central American hotel workers through the streets of downtown Chicago during rush hour chanting together *Si Se Puede!* (It can be done!). Davis argues that Latino/a worker militancy has been an important element of the multiracial national campaign of low-wage workers for a "living wage"—a campaign that is not simply reactive, but injects "an alternative political economy of the working class" into the debate about the future of L.A. (p. 174) and, we add, U.S. cities in general.

In part, CPS policies should be gauged in relation to this emergent Latino/a labor uprising and its potential role in catalyzing a multiracial labor movement. Indirectly, we believe it is this threat to capital of a mobilized low-wage population that has spurred Chicago Metropolis 2020 (which includes the Commercial Club of Chicago) to name poverty and lack of affordable housing and health care as serious threats to the Chicago metro region's development (Regional Realities, 2001). The stakes are high. We should not underestimate the centrality of education policy to labor discipline in a global economy that demands an uninterrupted flow of low-wage labor.

CHAPTER **6**

"It's Us versus the Board—The Enemy"

Race, Class, and the Power to Oppose

[Farley] has always been a school where the faculty has taken teaching seriously
and the community is very serious about kids being well-educated,
not about test scores. Well-educated isn't synonymous with test scores.
(Farley teacher, December, 2000)

Farley Elementary School provides an interesting contrast with Brewer, Grover, and Westview, one that illustrates the different consequences of CPS policies in relation to race and class and the power of the school community. Although teaching approaches are diverse, the school has generally managed to cultivate a culture of literacy and sustain a group of thoughtful, knowledgeable teachers who see themselves as professionals and intellectuals. Farley illustrates that the regime of accountability and regulation of teachers and schools can widen the gap between schools that struggle with curriculum and teaching and schools that cultivate rich literacies and support the work of competent teachers. As I have argued in other chapters, the implications of this widening gap are particularly significant in an economy that places a premium on the creation and manipulation of knowledge. Farley also illustrates the quite obvious point that the complexity of nurturing thoughtful teaching and learning is unlikely to be addressed by regulatory and punitive policies. On the other hand, Farley's challenges point to another potential consequence of accountability measures that has not been generally discussed. Policies that hold teachers, administrators, and students accountable for test scores as a pathway to equity do little to address deep-seated ideological and structural issues of race and class in even the seemingly best urban schools. Farley's strengths and its weaknesses put in focus some of the fundamental challenges facing urban schools and the unlikelihood that a national education policy agenda rooted in accountability will address them. Indeed, Farley strengthens the argument that these policies are a means of disciplining students and teachers and sorting students for a highly stratified labor force and society. When viewed through a wider, more critical, lens, Farley also demonstrates the limits of "good" schools that operate within the dominant paradigm and the need for fundamental change.

In this chapter, I begin by describing Farley and its politically powerful community, its culture of literacy, and its relatively wider space for teacher and student agency. This provides a context for interpreting teachers' and administrators' generally oppositional responses to accountability and centralized regulation, their struggle to negotiate these tensions, and some of the conditions that seem to support their resistance. However, persistent issues of race, class, and equity also confound the school. I propose that accountability policies may further obscure the roots of these issues and construct another barrier to addressing them openly. My observations at Farley suggest that all-encompassing systems of accountability may make educators act more conservatively by further discouraging them from examining and challenging the race and class inequality and marginalization that are at the center of the crisis in urban education.

Farley Elementary School and Its Community

Farley Elementary School is one of the highest-scoring schools on the ITBS in the city. In the year I studied the school (2000–1) about 75 percent of students scored at or above national norms in reading and math, and this level has remained fairly constant. Students also do very well in citywide academic competitions such as science fairs. The student body is about 60 percent African American with the remainder whites, Asians, and Latinos/as, in that order. About 30 percent of students are classified as low-income in a district in which 85 percent are classified as low-income. The size of the school's enrollment is comparable to that of the other three schools in this study. There are also a sizable number of special education students, most of whom are included in regular classes. About a third of the teachers are African American, and most of the rest are white. Farley has a solid core of veteran teachers, including some who have been at the school for more than twenty years and a large percentage who have taught there at least seven years. Repeatedly teachers told me that Farley is such a good place to teach that they would not dream of going elsewhere. For a new teacher, a job at Farley is considered a real plum. Most teachers have advanced degrees, and some have participated in developing and piloting research-based curricula. There are a core of teachers who remain abreast of their field and make complicated, nuanced judgments about curriculum, assessment, and education policies. The principal, Mr. Underwood, had been at Farley for ten years when I began my study. During our first meeting he effortlessly walked me through the curriculum at all grade levels and provided the rationale for each assigned text and his perceptions of the strengths and weaknesses of each subject area. He was also quite critical of accountability policies and the endless and evolving mandates issued by the central office that ended up in the receiving tray of his fax machine.

Farley is a big old brick structure with huge windows and artful stonework, all recently refurbished. It is surrounded by trees, small flower gardens, a large enclosed playground with extensive playground equipment, and a large play yard. Inside, there is little that has been modernized since the school opened in the 1930s. The building has high ceilings; wide stairways, old irregular, scuffed wood floors; and somewhat outmoded, but clean bathrooms. It is clean, freshly painted, and decorated with student work, art posters, student projects, quilts, and artifacts from various countries. Classrooms are huge by the standards of a modern school. They are still outfitted with original floor-to-ceiling wood cabinets with seemingly endless drawers and cupboards. The windows are so tall that each room is equipped with a special long-handled tool to raise and lower shades and windows. The teachers' lounge is a spacious, but unmodernized room on the ground floor with long tables, an old kitchen annex, a couple of comfortable chairs, a refrigerator, and several telephones. The school office is equally outdated but also cramped and cluttered. Although there is one computer lab and there are a couple of computers in each classroom, Farley has none of the up-to-date technology that Brewer has.

I observed less overt restriction of students at this school than any school I have visited in Chicago. Kids did carry hall passes, but there was none of the heavy-duty monitoring, policing, walkie-talkie crackling that pervades many urban schools. I never observed an adult demand to see a student's pass, although this may have happened. The occasional first grader skipping and humming in the hallways was likely to be greeted by a smile and friendly word or a laugh rather than a reprimand. (Although some teachers said it depended on *who* the student was—a topic I take up later when I talk about issues of race and class.) Teachers strolled through the halls, stopped to chat with students, and were typically courteous and friendly. Although there were two security guards, I rarely saw any walkie-talkies in use and heard much less yelling at kids than is typical in the public schools I visit, including the three others in this study. I did observe much mentoring of students and some one-on-one intense conversations between teachers and students that were definitely about student behaviors. Kids lined up for lunch or other activities, but these lines were invariably somewhat loose, and there was little effort to demand complete silence. I would describe the school environment as overall relaxed, calm, orderly, humorous, nurturing, and much less rigid and controlled than the other three schools. Three short field note vignettes are illustrative.

> The kids are on their way to lunch. A third grade African American girl is standing in the hall, crying. Mr. Marks (not her teacher) goes over to her. Putting his hand on her shoulder he asks gently, "What's the matter honey? Did you lose something? Someone hit you?" She shakes her head, keeps crying. Ms. Carter, an older African American resource teacher, comes up and puts her arm around her. "She'll tell me because I'm a twin too. She can talk to me. We feel the same way."

> The second graders are in the hall in their costumes for the annual Halloween parade of primary kids through the school. They are a noisy, squealing, excited bunch. I'm struck that the teachers are laughing. No one is shushing them. Passing teachers comment on costumes and laugh too. This noisy excitement seems to be expected.

> The seventh and eighth graders have just gotten out of class. It's noisy. Groups of kids talking, laughing, playing around—most are African American, a few white. Lots of growing, awkward bodies jostling each other, but there is no threatening or fighting, and no teachers in the hall yelling at kids. Some teachers are in their classrooms talking with groups of students. Ms. Townsend and Ms. Wright, both African American teachers, are in the hallway, corralling small groups of students in intense conversations. One is about attitudes toward a particular student, the other about a project the kids are planning excitedly. I have a sense the teachers "know" these kids.

Farley is in a mixed-income mixed-race area known as North River (a pseudonym). North River has a history of juggling race and class demographics that has resulted in a racially stable integrated area of middle- and upper-middle-class whites and working-class and middle-class African Americans. North River has historically had a lot of political clout in the city. About five hundred of Farley's students live in the neighborhood and about three hundred are bused in from one of the most impoverished African American communities in the city. The school has gone through a series of enrollment plans since the 1970s, each designed to maintain racial integration while ensuring that neighborhood kids remain the majority. Tensions over race and class are still felt today in achievement gaps between white and African American students, in perceptions of behavior problems and deficiencies of some African American students, and in skewed enrollment patterns in the upper grades. As it turns out, the upper grades are more African American and low-income than the lower grades.

This seems to be explained by several factors: Neighborhood families take their children out of Farley in sixth or seventh grade to enroll them in one of CPS's accelerated Academic Centers located in select high schools or to enroll them in a private school. A parent told me that the private and selective schools are not more academically challenging than Farley but admission to these schools in seventh grade guarantees a student's enrollment in high school, and this is the main reason for the seventh grade exodus. At the same time, more African American students from surrounding areas take advantage of the openings created in these grades to enroll in Farley because it is perceived as superior to many neighborhood schools.

An Engaged Academic Culture

> The rest falls into place once you develop literacy. It changes the kids' outlook on the world; they're less insular. (Ms. Clemens, November 2000)

Farley students were generally immersed in a rich culture of literacy that, in many classes, involved engagement in meaningful reading, writing, and discussion. There was direct teaching as well as constructivist pedagogy, but overall teachers and administrators shared the value that education involves sharing ideas, disagreeing, and developing one's own perspective. This was reflected in classes in which even very young children engaged in sustained discussion of concepts, texts, and classroom social relations and were encouraged to construct their own knowledge and be creative. This did not hold for all classes I observed. Some were routinized, dull, and textbook-driven. But in many of the classes I observed, students actively shared their ideas, raised questions, and participated in discussions. They seemed accustomed to having their thoughts taken seriously. In this sense, the school cultivated a sense of individual agency. Perhaps this was carried over from teachers who tended to be actively engaged in their profession and the pursuit of professional knowledge. This group of teachers was prepared to make careful, informed judgments about curriculum and pedagogy.

A Culture of Literacy

One of my first reactions to Farley was that the children really seemed to be immersed in reading. I began to check this out by randomly stopping students in the halls or classes I was observing and asking whether they were reading a book right now, which one, and what it was about. Every child I asked began to talk, usually quite articulately and sometimes voluminously, about the book she or he was reading. In my classroom observations, nearly all students were in the midst of a novel or nonfiction book, stealing a chance to read a page or two whenever they had finished their work or they had free reading time. From first graders to eighth graders, kids walked through the halls with a novel or book of nonfiction under their arms, and some read in the lunch line. Teachers explained that in part this occurs because the school has adopted the *Dive into Reading* (DIR) program. Every student from second through eighth grade was required to read five additional books each quarter and to take a short, factual computerized quiz on the book. These books had become the backbone of schoolwide recreational reading. Some teachers also used the DIR records to ascertain students' interests, direct them to new authors or titles, encourage them to take up more challenging titles, or engage in discussions with them about the books they had read.[1] There were also after-school book clubs run by volunteers from local colleges. Many teachers expressed a passion for reading and writing as the heart of the curriculum. Despite the possible coerciveness of DIR, most kids seemed to want to read.

Beyond this, in most of the classes I observed, children were involved in thoughtful reading and writing activities and discussions about books. Field notes from two of these classes are illustrative. The first is Ms. Contini's intermediate grades class.[2] Her classroom library contained hundreds of high-quality paperback books, which she had purchased over the years she taught at Farley. They were carefully catalogued, and children could check them out at any time. Her students did a lot of creative, expository, and persuasive writing as well. On this day, they were discussing books written and illustrated by students in the class as part of the Young Authors contest. She asked permission of the authors to read four aloud and began with Carl's book:

> Ms. Contini: "There are incredibly beautiful illustrations also." [She holds up the book for everyone to see.] Carl's story is about the death of his grandmother. Ms C. says she cried when she read the book and she warns them she may cry again. She says, "I don't cry easily when I read books, but this shows how well Carl has captured the feelings." All the students are rapt throughout her reading. At each page she shows the illustrations. At one point Carl has written something derogatory toward women.
> Ms. C.: "Carl, I want to encourage you to rethink your opinion of females. Women will appreciate you more also." When she finishes, she asks for comments from the class. [I think this is an astoundingly well written story by a fourth grader.]
> A girl: "Carl, it was well-written and a great story."
> Second girl: "I know how it feels. My grandfather died three weeks ago."
> Ms. Contini: "People are making these comments because you write how you feel; that's why it connects for them. That's a great gift." (Field notes January 2001)

The second is Mr. Marks's primary class:

> The kids have just come in from lunch. He begins reading aloud a story. Some kids seem to be listening while others are reading their own books or writing in their journals. [It's interesting that he lets them do this in a very comfortable way. There's a sense of all these literacy activities going on, almost like in a fam-

ily without the "school" thing that everybody has to focus on the teacher and all do the same thing at the same time.] When he finishes, they talk about the moral of the story, about generosity. . . .
Mr. Marks: "What feeling do you have when you're jealous?"
A boy: "Mad."
Mr. Marks: "Anger is not a cause of jealousy, it's an effect." He draws on the board:

? ——> anger   cause ——> effect.

There is an extended discussion of jealousy, anger, sharing your feelings, working out differences, with kids jockeying for space to give their opinions. (Field notes, February 2001)

The school also had a new constructivist science curriculum centered on inquiry and experiments. In Mr. Marks's class students were studying anatomy and examined parts of a complete skeleton, a cranium, and a rubber heart. Later in the day, a parent who is a computational neurologist demonstrated through student role playing how neural responses work and then showed how to graph them electronically. In mathematics, primary teachers piloted a NCTM Standards–based curriculum that focused on developing conceptual mathematics knowledge. The primary grades language arts curriculum had a strong phonics component as well as opportunities to read good literature and to engage in multiple literacy activities (reading, writing, discussing, drama). The phonics was part of a reading series supposedly proved to raise test scores. Teachers said this was the principal's response to the school's less than satisfactory third grade ITBS scores. A number disapproved of this reading program, saying that it was too formulaic and that it diluted the school's strong literature-based orientation to literacy instruction.

Thinking and the Sense that One's Ideas Matter
In a number of classes, there was also an emphasis on students' thinking for themselves and on sustained classroom conversations. Ms. Winston, a veteran teacher, described goals similar to those of many teachers I interviewed: "[My goal is] they are learning to think. 'What does this information mean to me? What is its relevance to my life? How can I use it?' That's what education is about." I observed thoughtful student discussions about the meaning of a story, a character's motivations, opinions about a new school that was planned for the area and would siphon off students from Farley, a conflict between two groups of girls, the process of seed germination, and interpretations of a series of abstract paintings by Kandinsky—to name a few topics. In these discussions adults took children's ideas seriously and students disagreed with each other but listened to each other and developed arguments and analyses. This process began in the primary

grades so that by the time children reached upper grades they had developed the dispositions to engage in these discussions in productive ways. Two teachers who were team teaching explained their decision to make thoughtful discussions part of their second grade class so that students would articulate and become more aware of the strategies they were using in math and reading. In an interview they talked excitedly about children running their own discussion. The students did something called "handing off" the discussion to the next student. Ms. Trask: "Their ideas were flying. . . . It puts the responsibility on the kids, and they respond to that. They went on for ten minutes and we had nothing to do with it. We just sat back and watched!" They described how at first they were skeptical and scared. Ms. Stewart: "Oh my God. Can we do this? Are we going to try it?" But then they decided to risk it. Ms. Trask: "Discussing is a skill: You can't expect kids to be good discussion group leaders in seventh grade if they don't learn to do it earlier" (November 2000).

Preparing children and trusting them to lead their own activities are aspects of confirming they are responsible, trustworthy people who can do meaningful things. Although I do not want to generalize, I did observe a relatively relaxed attitude toward hall passes and tardiness. For example, when two girls walked into Mr. Marks's class a couple of minutes late, he ignored them. They quickly took their seats and picked up the lesson in progress. Later he explained that he assumed they were late for a good reason and generally does not divert classroom time to unnecessary disciplining. Ms. Contini's class was also illustrative. Every Friday afternoon Ms. Contini's intermediate grade students had free time to play games, read, or do art projects. Her enormous wooden cupboard was filled with a huge array of interesting math and word games, complicated puzzles, art activities, blocks, board games, chess sets, and so on. Field notes from an observation of one of these free periods:

> The kids quickly talk to each other about what they want to do, run to her cupboard all along one wall which is filled with board games, interesting blocks, chess, checkers, etc. The rest of the afternoon, about an hour or more, they play games (2 girls draw; 8 kids on the floor in two groups build models out of small wood blocks, one is the Eiffel Tower; 4 kids play checkers—two to play and two to kibbitz; three boys are working on a construction set; some kids are playing board games.) It's noisy but it's all engagement in interesting and complex and fun games and projects. I don't see anyone disengaged, even Shaun, who has been estranged from the class and in trouble with Ms. Contini most of the day. She does not interrupt other than to talk with kids a bit about what they are doing. She says she rarely intervenes during game time because she thinks it's important for the kids to work things out themselves. . . . A special education teacher, a visiting consultant, and the principal stop in. All the adults seem completely unfazed by the noisy energy and sprawling kids. [I am struck

by how impossible it would be for this to happen at Grover or Westview or even Brewer outside the honors program. The kids are so used to being tightly regulated they would be shocked in this situation, and the adults would never let anything so "out of control" happen.] . . . When she announces "Four minutes for clean up," they all do it. There's not a big fight over this. (October 2000)

These children were learning to organize and regulate their own activities in ways that are collectively productive. This is a pedagogy in which one is more likely to see oneself as subject and actor. It creates a structure within which children can develop dispositions for leadership and self-actualization that are very different from those that generally prevailed at the other three schools and in repressive school contexts that practice a pedagogy of authoritarianism and regimented learning. "The privilege" to be self-regulating is located within a larger set of class privileges that characterize this secure confortable community. This comparison should not be confused with structure versus the freedom to do whatever one wants, or as Delpit (1988) describes it: "that to make any rules or expectations explicit is to act against liberal principles" (p. 284). There were clearly established boundaries, but there was self-control within those parameters toward productive goals. As a whole, these practices constitute a discourse that teaches students ways of "talking, acting, interacting, and valuing" that constitute certain social identities (Gee et al., 1996, p. 104). These ways of being are aligned with flexible, collaborative problem-solving, knowledge-constructing roles in the upper strata of the new workforce and leadership roles in society. These children are being schooled in the grammar of personal efficacy and the worth of their own opinions as *actors* in society.

Teachers' Professional Efficacy—"We Teach"

Teachers also had relatively more professional efficacy than the teachers at the other schools I studied. They were able to take risks, make nuanced judgments about teaching and learning, and act on them. In part this was because many teachers at Farley were recognized as highly competent, seasoned veterans who were confident in their professional judgments. Ms. Trask had been teaching for more than twenty years and led teacher professional development in mathematics education at a local university. Ms. Stewart had taught for over more than fifteen and had a master's degree in special education. These teachers did not believe they had to simply accept existing arrangements or district mandates. They initiated programs and curriculum. For example, Ms. Stewart was involved in an advocacy group for total inclusion of disabled students in regular classes, and she wanted to see that happen at Farley. She and Ms. Trask proposed to the principal combining a special education class and a regular class that they would team teach and follow through two grades. Ms. Stewart: "We argued that the disabled kids need the independence with people in the real world." Ms. Trask: "It's important for them if they are going to make it in the world, but my kids need this too [to be with the disabled students]." Ms. Stewart: "I was so excited to work with [Ms. Trask]. She's so progressive and open. We're on the same page. She's on the cutting edge" (November 2000).

Teachers' confidence in their own professional judgment resulted in a diversity of pedagogical approaches and sometimes unorthodox practices. Ms. Parker, a veteran teacher, described working with a Bulgarian student. "A wonderful child. He built intricate paper structures and did excellent thinking, but he didn't speak English. He did not do well on paper and pencil activities." So she had him work in groups with other children and copy their answers. The other kids said he was cheating. "But I explained to them that he was simply adopting some of their answers and this was a way for him to learn; he was benefiting from cross-learning. He had a wonderful imagination and a wealth of knowledge but it didn't transfer to test-taking." She simply exempted him from classroom tests. "By the end of the year he was one of the best students in the class" (November 2000).

We should recall that there were highly competent, thoughtful teachers at the other three schools as well, but they were working under, to varying degrees, quite different conditions. Farley teachers generally enjoyed Mr. Underwood's support. He described the teaching staff as the core of the school's excellence and said he often deferred to their judgment. He also involved teachers in resolving curricular disagreements and other differences. Farley adopted a data-driven inquiry process that the staff learned through working with a local university. To resolve disagreements over substantive issues, they set up a committee to study the topic and to put disparate opinions on the table in the context of data. Although some teachers said they were not always informed about this process or specific issues, one of the nonteaching professionals said, the philosophy was, "If there's a problem, we should do something about it. That's Mr. Underwood's big contribution" (November 2000).

Many of the teachers I talked with described their educational goals in holistic terms—developing sophisticated literacies and a love of reading, promoting the ability to think independently, nurturing children's creativity, encouraging humane values—never raising test scores. Ms. Townsend, an upper grades teacher, said the goal of schooling should be to develop "*good* [her emphasis], smart people who have awareness and kindness toward their peers. Kids who think about the right thing to do." Teachers also talked about their concern for children's all-around development. This orientation cut across teachers' race, age, and years of teaching. Although these goals are not uncommon, at the three other schools in this study, teachers often lamented the necessity to give up aspects of a broader agenda to meet district and school mandates. In practice, at Farley, teachers seemed to interpret these goals in multiple ways. Some classes, like those of Ms. Stewart and Ms. Trask, were activity-centered and constructivist; others were more traditional but steeped in reading and writing, thoughtful and challenging assignments, and the production of meaningful work. Still others seemed textbook-driven, mundane, and task-oriented. Yet many classes provided opportunities for students to create art work, play brain-teasing games, read for enjoyment, play chess, do creative work, discuss, analyze experiments, and read, read, read.

Despite pedagogical differences, there was a schoolwide ethos of teaching children well. This is, of course, also a goal in other schools. But at Farley, teachers faced fewer dictates, mandates, directives, and pressures, and thus they seemed to have greater freedom to teach, in the full sense of the term. This was apparent in the many instances of adults' taking time to engage with students. In the upper grades, Ms. Connor had 170 language arts students, yet she managed to maintain a regular journal correspondence with all of them because she considered this a critical part of her job. Ms. Townsend, the upper grades science teacher, used part of her class time to address issues of sexuality and identity that the young teenagers in her classes were grappling with. These were the sorts of activities some teachers at Grover and Westview, in particular, said they had to give up to focus extra attention on testing. Most days, Mr. Marks ate lunch in his room with a few of his primary students who were finishing up a project or wanted to spend time writing or reading or playing chess. André was a regular. He explained to me, "Sometimes me and Thomas stay in the room and talk to Mr. [Marks] at lunch because we don't have dads at home and he didn't have a dad when he was growing up" (February 2001).

This holistic approach was nurtured by a discourse of professional efficacy and respect for the complexity of teachers' work. This discourse was embedded in the school's culture and history and made possible by the school's power to remain somewhat flexible in the face of accountability policies. I observed ISAT and ITBS practice; however, teachers worked in a context not defined by the need to spend every classroom moment on the skills to be tested on the ITBS or ISAT. Because teachers felt less external pressure, they were less drained by test prep and more able to expend their energy in directions to which they were truly committed. Ms. Clemens said, at Farley teachers "have the ability to be independent thinkers and to make a difference." Contrasting Farley with other CPS schools that are "so rigid" and "test driven," she said the difference at Farley is "We teach." Teachers at Farley were not burned out and despairing, although many were discouraged by the district's emphasis on standardized tests, as I describe later. Ms. Stewart explained: "The reason we have the emotion in us to care is we're not sapped. We're energized by the kids." This did not mean that teachers were not overworked (a topic I return to later). In addition to the many committees they were on, most teachers stayed after school for at least one to two hours every day planning and meeting with other teachers. Ms. Clemens, a veteran teacher, told me that anyone not willing to make this sort of commitment did not last at Farley. But their hard work was less directed to meeting ITBS goals and more intrinsically driven by their own larger purposes.

Trying to Follow Their Own Course

Teachers and administrators at Farley had a variety of perspectives on CPS accountability, standards, and centralized regulation. The policies affected teaching to varying degrees, but not to the extent they did at Grover, West-view, and Brewer. In this section I try to capture some of the complexity, nuances, and variety of views as well as convey the general effort to maintain the school's independent direction.

Multiple and Contradictory Views on Accountability

Teachers' responses to accountability were mixed and contradictory, reflecting different interests and ideologies, but the majority of the teachers I talked with, across age and race and years of teaching, opposed the board's accountability system, which they saw as narrowing the curriculum, undermining teachers' professional judgment, and imposing a limited form of assessment. A few representative comments give a flavor of this view. Ms. Stewart: "The problem with the tests is that they test skills, but a lot of the kids' strengths don't show up on that. It's a very limited assessment. It also puts a lot of pressure on teachers and schools" (November 2000). Ms. Trask: "Reading is being beaten into them and kids can get turned off to school. There are parents who are panicked and spend kids' time at home drilling them with flash cards. In second grade some kids are calling out words but don't know how to think" (November 2000). Mr. Marks said summer school "is aimed solely at test-taking. It's self-serving for the Board. If they really want to help the kids they should spend money on kids during the year, not fail them" (October 2001). Ms. Winston and Ms. Brown, veteran and new teachers, respectively, were both particularly critical of standardized tests that did not mirror the curriculum. Ms. Winston: "Writing in class should be a place for practice, but it's truncated [on the ISAT] and parts of the process are missing. They do peer editing, collaboration, etc., and then they take the Iowas. The tests don't mirror the classroom. In math they get partial credit for their thinking, but that's not the Iowa either" (February 2001). Ms. Brown: "Kindergarten through fourth grade science is hands-on in the classroom, but what they are tested on [on the ISAT] may not be what the book we are using covers. . . . They may get it right but that doesn't mean they know what it means" (February 2001).

One of the most interesting perspectives was that high stakes tests undermined Farley's rigorous academic standards. Because for many students at Farley scoring well on these tests was not difficult, teachers in the upper grades in particular echoed Ms. Townsend's view that "the tests have affected kids' work ethic because they only have to pass the tests. They don't think they have to do more" (February 2001). This is an interesting insight into what high stakes tests that demand a minimal level of proficiency may mean for schools at the top end of the test-score spectrum. It is another example of the long-term implications of an education agenda that reduces schools and teaching to standardized mediocrity (see also Mc-Neil, 2000).

Nevertheless, the policies also resonated with a few teachers as a means of enforcing educational equity. Ms. Clemens, a veteran African American teacher, was perhaps the strongest proponent of the view that accountability policies were necessary because they forced the school system to uphold its obligations to educate African American and Latino/a students. For her, the policies made sense as a way to ensure that all students were being taught and held to high standards:

> I look at the policies as an African American citizen. Either you measure up or you don't. There is something wrong with the system when African American students are not learning. We should be able to hold our own. African Americans and Latinos ought to be able to hold their own. . . . If you haven't mastered 5th grade, then you need to be retained because social promotion is not doing them a favor. [There should be other things to factor in besides the tests] but they are justified in making the tests a major part. That's the way the world is. Throughout your life you will be looked at in the context of "Do you measure up?" (November 2000).

However, support for accountability as a necessary system reform did not translate into support for a curriculum centered on preparing for standardized tests. Ms. Clemens, for example, spent little time on explicit test preparation. In my reading, teachers who supported accountability saw it as a reasonable *systemwide* strategy to promote academic achievement, in the absence of any other alternative, although not one they necessarily needed at *Farley*. I think this attitude reflected the idea that if other schools did what Farley did, their students would do well on the tests. Ms. Clemens taught for fifteen years in a low-income African American school on the West Side of Chicago that lacked basic resources, so she spent several thousand dollars creating a really good classroom library. She said she immersed her students in literacy: they wrote journals, did lots of sustained silent reading, and "I read them wonderful books. It was contagious." Some teachers also expressed the idea that a system of accountability might be needed to improve other schools, but it was not needed at Farley, where children had valued cultural capital. In this view, Farley was different from most other schools, and it was successful. This "Farley exceptionalism" was an underlying theme in my data, one I take up later. Echoing this theme, Ms. Clemens commented that a critical need is for [other] "schools to enrich poor kids' experiences."

Walking a Tight Rope in the Face of Accountability

The influence of high stakes tests and Standards varied, but in general teaching and learning were not driven by test preparation in the same way as at Grover and Westview or even Brewer. I did not hear any classroom conversation that centered on tests or learning aligned with standardized tests as I did at Grover and Westview. Preparation for the ISAT and ITBS was set off from the regular curriculum and geared to promoting familiarity with the kinds of questions on the ITBS and ISAT. Ms. Clemens said she did not use the test-prep books, but two weeks before the standardized tests she prepared her students for the format. Ms. Winston had her students practice test-taking procedures so they would "develop confidence and not be so stressed." She encouraged them to approach the tests by using all their "critical thinking" skills. She did test prep with her students about thirty minutes a day in the three weeks before the test, but she was very clear on its limited function. "They aren't learning anything. It's teaching them to take a test" (November 2000). Upper grades teachers mainly focused on practicing timed tests since they did not generally use these kinds of tests in their classes. Nevertheless, the stress the ITBS and ISAT seemed to take a toll on students, especially eighth graders. Ms. Connor said they worked with the kids on "having a positive attitude" because "the kids are so scared." Ms. Kraft, a member of the professional staff, described the eighth graders as "a wreck."

Although not immune to it, Farley maintained a certain independence in the face of increasing centralized control. An example was prekindergarten. New state mandates required teachers to assess students on 135 measures and maintain a journal of anecdotal records according to a prescribed protocol. Farley was in a cluster with other elementary schools, and this mandate was monitored by the cluster supervisor. A prekindergarten teacher described this paperwork load for her forty students as "totally impossible." "The principal would never expect me to do this." So she did not. Her noncompliance was possible because "the district doesn't mess with [Farley] because it's one of the best schools." The school also did not use the board report cards and lesson plans. Mr. Underwood said, "We just don't use them."

Because teachers approached the Standards critically, those Standards did not necessarily drive the curriculum. Instead, teachers developed their own schoolwide educational objectives. Mr. Underwood claimed the school was "following its own course." Third grade teachers followed the ISAT prep book for writing for one year, but after discussions they decided to drop its formulaic approach in favor of their own writing curriculum. A third grade teacher said, "It was horrible. The kids just get a blueprint, a boiler plate. Everybody sounds the same and is writing the same. Now we're doing a more creative process. We want the creativity from the kids first" (November 2000). Similarly, fourth grade teachers said they used the CPS Standards for science selectively because they disagreed with them from disciplinary and developmental standpoints. Ms. Winston's approach was fairly typical. When she did her lesson plan, she went through the Standards and asked, "What do they want me to do?" But she also said, "Teachers have to be reflective. They can use the Standards to reflect on what they are teaching." This was just one example of how some teachers used CPS Standards thoughtfully and critically to inform their teaching because they had the space and professional knowledge to do so. This example points to the contextual mediation of standards. In the more typical CPS context, they became simply another top-down mandate to be managed, as at Grover and Brewer.

However, accountability impinged on Farley's curriculum to some extent, although teachers with a more traditional, textbook-centered approach seemed to be least affected. Even when they chose not to allow the tests to define their curriculum, as in the case of third grade writing, concerns about test scores were always present. Ms. Trask said conditions had "changed a lot. . . . The third grade teachers feel so much pressure. For the first time in my career I have had to deal with the tests as a threat." Second grade teachers used to spend two months studying all subjects through the history of Native American nations. "The kids would learn everything they could about Native American history. We went into depth." But now, they no longer had that "luxury." "It's coverage over depth." They also used to spend a lot of time on art projects. Now they could not do so much of that. She said she had to "selectively abandon things" she did in the past, and "I'm not sure I'm a better teacher for it."

Mr. Underwood was opposed to the accountability regime and said he tried to buffer the school from it as much as possible. For example, at one faculty meeting he informed teachers of a new CPS policy, expressed his disagreement with it, and then let them know they could do whatever they wanted. At the same time, some mandates could not be ignored. Before 1995, the LSC wanted to boycott the ITBS, which at that point was not a high stakes test. But he said some parents had become concerned about the scores, especially for African American students, because their future is more tightly linked to them. And some parents, across race and class, wanted more test preparation because ITBS scores are a criterion for admission to selective public high schools. Moreover, a noticeable drop in scores could lead to tighter supervision and regulation of Farley. At the same time, there were other parents who did not want their children to take the ITBS at all. Mr. Underwood said he feared a boycott would certainly draw unwanted attention from central administrators. So he was in the stressful position of "managing" these tensions. "That's half of what I do," he said. "Some of the things that come down [from the central office] the teachers don't even see." But one teacher said test pressures were creating conflicts between teachers and administrators. The hierarchy of surveillance at the core of accountability meant that the principal was forced to transfer a certain amount of regulation from the central office onto teachers. Despite some acts of resistance, he said, in some matters, "You can't buck the system." The contradictions and stress Mr. Underwood faced mirrored Mr. Rodriguez's experience at Brewer.

In sum, teachers and administrators were walking a tightrope, balancing their own professional judgments about good teaching against the pressures of the dominant regime. They resisted within the constraints imposed on them. Underlying this stance was a desire to protect what they had at Farley, while maintaining high test scores to ward off surveillance. Mr. Marks described the school, despite some dissension, as "a coalition, a defense against the Board—the enemy." Despite concessions and limitations, they had more control of their own destiny and faced a less colonial model of education (Carlson, 1997) than Grover and Westview and perhaps Brewer.

Race, Class, and the Power to Be Oppositional

The school's ability to maintain some distance from centralized mandates was rooted in the sedimented race and class power of the North River community and a portion of the Farley parents and the resulting quality of education they had secured for their children. A teacher who had been at Farley more than twenty years described it as

> very much the same school [as twenty years ago]. [Of course] there are more minorities; it's more integrated, [but] we've been blessed with good administrators and influential parents [who] are not afraid of the Board. The parents *know people* [his emphasis]. (October 2000)

He described a succession of influential and independent principals, including one who "always said, 'As a principal, you have to be ready to be fired.' We've always had that kind of principal. And the community won't stand for the Board dictating to them." Underlying this resistance was a powerful sense of class and race entitlement.

Farley had a record of opposing CPS directives and a long history of parent activism. When the board mandated Mastery Learning[3] in the

1980s, Farley refused to implement it and obtained a waiver. According to Mr. Underwood, the parent teachers association (PTA) functioned as an LSC, that is, with power and authority, even before the 1988 reform established LSCs. The current LSC met once a week, and sometimes there were four different subcommittee meetings going on at once. "There are subcommittees, task forces, and task forces of task forces," he said. These were made up of not only LSC members, but other parents and teachers as well. Mr. Underwood said he was trying to prevent the LSC from going to board meetings to complain. "You can't be a thorn in their side or they'll start paying attention to you." The integral role that activist (and perhaps powerful) parents played in core aspects of the school is illustrated by the first preplanning meeting for the annual School Improvement Plan (SIP). From a summary of field notes (February 2001):

> There are two teachers, Ms. [Jones] an LSC parent representative, the principal, and me at the meeting. Ms. Jones, the parent, takes the official notes. The principal outlines the process of reviewing this year's SIP and developing the new SIP. . . . They take turns listing the school's accomplishments over the past year [part of the SIP]. Ms. Jones adds as much as the teachers and principal. [She's obviously intricately familiar with what is going on at Farley.] . . . Mr. Underwood describes the work of curriculum committees, made up of teachers at every grade level, that will make recommendations for the SIP. They schedule the next meeting. Looking at Ms. Jones, he says, "I don't have to be here [for the next meeting]."

The school's ability to maintain a degree of independence was also related to the strength of the faculty. This too was also linked to the community's race and class power. A well-run school, in a middle-class community, with a strong culture of support for teachers' professionalism attracts and retains highly qualified teachers, as defined by dominant indicators of quality (e.g., advanced degrees, innovation, professional knowledge, recognition for piloting curricula), as well as teachers who are simply looking for support for actual teaching and a context that upholds their professional judgment and expertise. Their professional confidence was reinforced by the principal and was collectively confirmed. (Teachers repeatedly talked about how strong the staff was as a whole.) Moreover their professional status was enhanced by their affiliation with the prestigious North River community, a base whose support they could also potentially rely on to resist external mandates. Thus, the ability of a school like Farley to attract and retain a group of highly qualified teachers is a self-replicating result of the community's race and class advantages. The sense of efficacy fostered by these conditions was quite different from the demoralization and belittlement of teachers at schools like Grover, for example, who are under probation and intense surveillance and are relentlessly reminded of their own "deficiency" and the perceived deficiencies of their school's community.

Farley was also a school in which students' cultural capital positioned them to succeed with the dominant curriculum and on traditional measures of academic success, including standardized tests. Many of Farley's students fit normalized (white, middle-class, Eurocentric) notions of intelligence, "good" behavior, valuable life experiences, and "appropriate" dispositions to knowledge (Oakes, Wells, Jones, & Datnow, 1997). Some teachers, both white and African American, were quick to point to the "broad" experiences of the children of highly successful professionals—Asian, white, and African American—who attended Farley, contrasting them to children in other schools who were supposedly "lacking" this cultural capital. (I consider this topic later.) Moreover, since Farley had the sort of students CPS is trying to attract and retain with enticements such as magnet and IB programs, the central school administration was perhaps less likely to push them out of the public schools with a distasteful, regimented curriculum. Thus, Farley illustrates how sedimented advantages position schools like it to resist centralized regulation in contrast with schools in low-income communities of color.

Farley also illustrates that entrenched advantages are compounded by accountability and centralized regulation to produce even greater disparities in teaching and learning and intellectual and social dispositions. Teacher turnover at Farley was very minimal and vastly different from that of Grover, for example, where as much as three-quarters of the staff left and was replaced in the three years I spent there and where the principal scrambled every fall to fill teaching positions. So, while Farley was maintaining its highly qualified staff, Grover was losing some of its strongest teachers, including teachers with solid ties to the community who were committed to teaching African American students and to culturally relevant and critical pedagogies. These teachers were being replaced by teaching interns, long-term substitutes, and uncertified teachers in a revolving door of teacher hiring. Whereas Farley teachers with a broader educational vision were able to maintain a multifaceted curriculum, those at Grover and Westview, and, to some extent, Brewer, were becoming more defined by the constraints of accountability discourses. This finding mirrors McNeil's (2000) study of the role of accountability in the reproduction of inequality in Texas schools.

Some North River parents' opposition to central mandates also has to be understood in relation to the school's privileged location within a stratified unban education system. Farley was working for their children. Why would they want to diminish their education with a narrowed curriculum that was driven by CPS accountability and designed for "failing" schools? Accountability reforms made little sense to these parents. Thus, Farley is like magnet and specialty schools and programs that avoid some of the standardization imposed by CPS because of their "specialness."[4] These schools are able to escape, to some extent, the regimentation of accountability, as Farley had hoped to do, as well. In a nutshell, opposition to CPS policies was grounded in the privilege to hold onto the status quo. This does not mean teachers were not constantly striving to improve; many of them were and were working incredibly hard. Nor am I suggesting that Farley's opposition was unwarranted or that Farley would be a better school if it succumbed to a test-driven, circumscribed, and narrowly instrumental notion of education. But I am suggesting that in the context of an urban school system that has largely failed to educate its students, opposition to change in a middle-class school that is "working" can reinforce a sense of (race and class) entitlement to a different kind of education and perhaps different policies from those reserved for the masses of students in failing schools. It can justify an official dual curriculum, as in New York City, where the top 208 schools were exempted from a new mandated curriculum instituted in 2003. Farley's exceptionalism can undermine a critique of what is wrong with the Chicago Public Schools as a whole, shifting responsibility to the children and parents who do not make it in that system. And it can mask ways in which supposedly successful schools like Farley may not work for students whose cultural capital is not valued. In this context, accountability regimes may subvert a more radical critique of the nature of schooling in even the "best" schools.

Silences and Comfort Zones

Farley's strengths, in comparison with those of many other schools, also obscured ways in which race and class operated to produce educational inequality and narrow the educational experiences of all the students in the school. I want to suggest that as accountability measures reinforced Farley's "success," just as they highlighted Grover's "failure," they may have contributed to Farley's inability to get to the bottom of academic and discipline disparities between African American students, on one hand, and white and Asian students, on the other. The school's success, relative to that of other schools, also masked its very real need for more faculty and support staff, time, and material resources. Finally, there is a more fundamental issue. By ranking schools like Grover, Westview, and Brewer against schools like Farley, systems of accountability, with their narrow measures of what constitutes "good" and "bad schools," construct a very restricted notion of what we might hope to achieve in schools. Put another way, in the end, is Farley educating its students for purposes that are fundamentally different from those that govern Grover, Westview, and Brewer? Or is it simply disciplining its students to *different* dispositions that prepare them for more powerful positions in the existing social order?

Running through my interviews was the theme of Farley's exceptionalism, its freedom and flexibility, its professional conditions compared with those of other CPS schools, its meaningful learning experiences. Although this perception seemed in some ways warranted, it was also problematic. Teachers defined Farley by a language of juxtaposition and difference from "other" public schools in the city. For example, Ms. Dingal, a primary teacher, said she "couldn't imagine the stress" of teaching in a school that is on probation. "It wouldn't make teaching fun or meaningful" (November 2000). Ms. Winston said, "A lot of CPS teachers have a *different* experience," but Farley "allows creativity compared with *other* schools I've visited that are much more restrictive" [my emphases] (November 2000). Ms. Parker said: "[Farley] is not a direct instruction school. In *those* schools, teachers are on a treadmill. They are more test-driven than we are. We can focus more on knowledge for the sake of knowledge, and we can be child-oriented and teach to different learning styles" [my emphasis] (November 2000). Ms. Trask talked about visiting a Chicago school where it seemed the main goal was "keeping the lid on." "Everything was lockstep, rote, an emphasis on order instead of creativity. When they're noisy, that's when they're learning. How can you be an intellectual in a situation like *that* [my emphasis]?" Teachers I talked with said that if Farley became like "*other*" schools, they would leave Farley or leave teaching altogether. This appreciation for Farley's advantages was grounded in awareness of real deprofessionalization and dehumanization elsewhere, but it also veiled Farley's weaknesses.

Race and Academic Achievement—Whose School Is It, Anyway?

> There are too many people at [Farley] who work too hard. . . . When you're good you say, "If we could only do this we'd be so much better." When you're already so good you look for being a little bit better. (Teacher interview, June 2001)

But was Farley "good" for all students? Popkewitz (2000) argues:

> When pedagogical practices focus on innovative strategies . . . to effect "good" teaching, the distinctions embodied in the "good teaching" are not universal and stable concepts. The concepts of "good," "successful," and "expert" are related to particular capabilities drawn from particular groups who have the power to sanctify and consecrate their dispositions as those appropriate for the whole society. (p. 24)

A school that is good for middle-class white and African American students may not be good in all ways for low-income African American students and may neither value nor support dispositions and ways of being that are important to them (Delpit, 1988; Lipman, 1998). In my brief time at Farley, there were clearly-marked signposts that race was a submerged but potent issue and that race and class intersected in complex ways. I was not able to plumb these issues with teachers, parents, administrators, and students, but I suggest that the signposts point to a problematic conjuncture of race and class marginalization and subordination that typifies urban schools in the United States. This issue was woven through the vexed history of a school that espoused a liberal commitment to racial integration but had isolated low-income African American students from *both* black and white middle-class children through a variety of organizational measures over the years. During my participation in the school, these issues surfaced in several ways.

First, a number of teachers told me that African American parents had raised concerns about the decline in African American student achievement, particularly that of males, beginning in fourth grade. The LSC commissioned a study to investigate, produce a report, and make recommendations. The study was led by several teachers and parents. The teachers used the school's inquiry process to gather data and analyze the problem. The study's findings were that, in general, Farley's ITBS scores tended to drop in third grade,[5] but white students' scores recovered whereas African Americans', especially males', did not. The outcome of the report was that teachers were to identify students who needed special help and establish after-school tutoring and mentoring for those students, particularly in the third grade, when the problem first emerged. Some teachers I talked with said this was a race-neutral issue. It did not, in their view, reflect the marginalization or subordination of African American students. The school's way of dealing with race, they said, was not at the root of the problem, but perhaps home environment and students' lack of important cultural capital were.

Second, some teachers noted that African American parents who could afford to tended to remove their male children from Farley after fourth or fifth grade and enroll them in a nearby parochial school because there was an achievement gap, but also because some teachers "stereotyped" African American male students. A parent said some African American parents thought these children were treated "unfairly." In my own anecdoted observations, African American students were more often in the office for discipline violations, and this impression was confirmed by teachers. Also in my observations, there seemed to be disproportionate disciplining of African American and some Latino boys and other children of color for actions that I observed white and/or female students do without reprimand, such as talking too loudly, turning around in line, playing with other children in line. The pattern was subtle, it did not pervade all classes, and punishments were quite mild compared with those of other schools, for instance, denial of classroom privileges. Nevertheless, patterns of identifying specific postures and actions of African American males as disruptive have been noted in other studies (e.g., Gilmore, 1985; Irvine, 1991; Ferguson, 2000). In her powerful analysis of the construction of African American male elementary school students as "bad" through racialized systems of discipline and control, Ann Arnett Ferguson (2000) describes how race is used as a filter to (mis)interpret the behavior of Black boys. She argues that this pattern is rooted in deeply entrenched assumptions about the danger and deficiency of African American males. "This apprehension of Black boys as inherently different both in terms of character and of their place in the social order is a crucial factor in teacher disciplinary practices" (p. 88). In this racialized system, specific body language, ways of talking, and styles of dress are interpreted as defiance of the normalized white standard. Disciplining Black students, particularly males, to this standard through techniques of regulation and surveillance is part of the process of exercising domination over them. Ferguson writes, "The outer limit is the black child: the closer to whiteness, to the norm of bodies, language, emotion, the more these children *are* self disciplined and acceptable members of the institution" (p. 72). This pattern is a lens through which to contextualize the fourth grade African American male "slump" at Farley.

Third, there was a recurring discourse of deficits in relation to low-income African American students' families, "culture," and community. Most frequently this discourse was used in relation to students in "other" schools to explain their educational failure as the product of deficient homes and lack of cultural capital. For example, a teacher said: "There are deeper issues. Kids have deficits. They have so many social problems, and it's not fair to put that on the teachers. [Instead of the tests] they should invest more time and money in parent education and parenting skills" (November 2000). But this discourse was also used to refer to specific "problem" African American children at Farley, as when a teacher argued that it was unjust to hold teachers accountable for student performance because "teachers can't change the conditions or the culture they're coming to school with even if they care about the kids." Another teacher referred to an African American male student she was having problems with as "probably LD [learning disabled]," although he had never been evaluated for a disability. Much has been written on the pervasiveness of this discourse in schools and its potency to construct definitions of African American children, to assign them to lower tracks and special education, and to obscure an examination of both school-based and social roots of their academic failure (e.g., Delpit, 1992b; Ferguson, 2000; Lipman, 1998; Oakes et al., 1997). This was coupled with the pervasive presence of whiteness as a norm and a curriculum that generally contained little of the knowledge, experiences, histories, and cultural meanings of African American and other children of color. Farley felt as if it were a white middle-class school.

These signals point to the need to hold up to collective scrutiny the ways in which race is built into the structure of social institutions and what Joyce King (1992) has termed "dysconscious racism"—an uncritical acceptance of white dominance. The embedded racialization of schooling is central to the overdisciplining of African American students, their academic underachievement, and assumptions about their language, culture, home environment, and ways of being in the world (King, 1991). Because structural and cultural racism permeates white-dominated society, uncovering and transforming it require conscious, critical reflection. Ladson-Billings (2001) argues that for teachers the starting point is looking at their collective practices, norms, and school organization rather than trying to fix students (or their families). For schools as a whole, this project involves looking at practice and organization in relation to issues that have been established as central to the marginalization and failure of African American students, such as hostile discipline practices, deficit discourses, devaluation of African American students' language and cultural capital, tracking, Eurocentric curricula largely disconnected from students' lived experience, literacy practices disconnected from personal and social agency, and race and class power differentials among parents (see Delpit, 1988; Fine, 1993; Irvine, 1991; King, 1991; Ladson-Billings, 1994, 2001). Such a critical self-examination demands political will that is rare in any social arena in the United States. The attempt of Brewer's principal to begin such an examination and the pitfalls and constraints of the CPS policy context illustrate some of the difficulties.

I am not suggesting that Farley teachers were generally complacent. I have described them as hardworking and reflective. Nor could teachers and administrators be accused of simply ignoring racial disparities. When pressed, they set up a mechanism to study the issue and implemented a plan of action to address it. But the response was to locate the problem primarily in the children and find ways to remediate them individually. While institutional norms and societal racism work against schools' examining their assumptions and practices and dealing seriously with the sociopolitical nature of race and racism, accountability may make this process even more difficult, and unlikely.

For Farley, accountability was another obstacle to (or rationale to avoid) a reflective and public engagement about racial disparities of which everyone seemed to be aware. In the first place, trying to maintain the school's relative insulation from accountability-driven practices was the focus. The coercive, authoritarian context of Chicago's policies meant that public controversy or acknowledgment of problems (i.e., public discussion of lower achievement of African American students, racial disparities in discipline, disagreements among teachers or parents) might generate scrutiny and monitoring by central administrators.[6] This could take away whatever autonomy the school had. Thus, accountability was a conservative factor compounding an established belief in the "goodness" of the school. As one teacher said, critically, "We're the elite and we don't want to shake things up by talking about these things." Policies that put tremendous pressure on teachers to improve test scores also generate a culture of blame and resentment that pits teachers against parents, reinforcing notions that parents are the source of problems that teachers are expected to "fix." As one Farley teacher put it, referring to high stakes tests, "Teachers feel like their job is on the line, but it really goes back to the home and the kids' environment and teachers and schools are being punished because parents don't know how to read to their kids" (November, 2000).

Defining schools by test scores and using them to identify the few "successful" schools compared with the majority of failing schools mask ways in which supposedly successful schools may be failing some students, particularly students of color, immigrant students, and language minority students marginalized by the schools' norms, practices, and dominant assumptions. This is the case *even if data are disaggregated by race (as with NCLB)*, because there is nothing in the policies to provoke an examination of underlying ideologies, structures, and discourses at the root of the problem. In fact, if the school "works," disaggregating test scores by race can reinforce the idea that those for whom the school is not working have something wrong with them. The policies support exactly what Farley did—focus on improving individuals—since the school's overall high rating suggested it was doing well. As accountability narrows the definition of what constitutes a good school, it obscures these complex and critical issues. Thus, accountability may make a critical examination of the structural and ideological process of racism even less likely and, perhaps, make it seem less relevant.

Making Do

Farley provides a concrete example of the consequences of a policy discourse that substitutes standards-based outcomes and high stakes tests for equitable distribution of resources and increased public funding for education. Farley's accomplishments, in terms of both test scores and teachers' broader pedagogical goals, obscured its lack of resources. Although Farley was in better shape than some CPS schools, the interior required renovation, the school needed upgraded technology, and teachers faced the usual lack of professional support (telephones, offices, clerical support, teacher aides—the latter were eliminated midway through 2000–1). Teachers made do with extra funds raised by the PTA (one hundred to two hundred dollars for each teacher for supplies) and materials and services donated by parents (e.g., a skeleton in one classroom, guest lectures, arts activities). A series of parent fundraising activities generated the money to replace the gym ceiling in 2002. It was the relative affluence of some parents that filled a few of the gaps left by inadequate public funding. As in most public schools, instructional materials were also paid for by teachers. Some rented copy machines and spent hundreds of dollars of their own money to build classroom libraries and buy classroom materials.

Most important, Farley, as did virtually all Chicago public schools except those undergoing dramatic contraction of enrollment caused by neighborhood gentrificatioin or the demolition of public housing, as at Grover, had class sizes that were too large[7]—thirty-seven to thirty-nine students in upper grade classes and thirty to thirty-seven in primary and intermediate grades. (By 2002 the lower grades were up to thirty-eight, as well.) When I revisited teachers at the end of the 2001–2 year and asked them what they needed to improve teaching and learning, smaller class size was the universal, emphatic response, as reflected in the comments of just two of the teachers I talked with:

> Class size, class size, class size! My goal is to *educate* [emphasis original], to treat each kid as an individual. I need to sit with each child. Why are you having trouble solving this problem? Let's solve it together. We need time to touch base with each kid during the day. [I wish it was like this] so I could enjoy my job, so teaching isn't a tug of war and you leave school exhausted. For me the pay is less important, and I need money. But I would work for the same salary if there was reduced class size. (Ms. Clemens, June 2001)

> I had 37 in Language Arts and 30 in my homeroom. That's the main reason why portfolio assessments are unreasonable. . . . You need to do conferences with kids about their reading and writing . . . you have to have time and fewer students. (Ms. Contini, June 2001)

Large classes, coupled with lack of professional resources, meant an enormous burden of work for teachers. Ms. Connor gave up her lunch hour four days a week to work with a group of students to whom she could not give individual attention during class time, and she read 170 student journals a week. The upper grades teachers had four parent conferences every morning before school started, and they said they met "constantly" about individual students. Team teaching, new mathematics curricula, art exhibits, and science projects all demanded extra time. All teachers worked after school, in their classroom or in one of many committees and task forces they shouldered. As in the other schools, what was accomplished was largely due to the extraordinary effort of many if not most of the teachers in the face of inadequate working conditions and enormous pressures. The infusion of significant human and material resources and support for teachers is absent from the discourse of accountability. At high-scoring schools, such as Farley, high test scores obscure this need, whereas at "failing" schools additional resources may be diverted to test-prep materials and after-school test-prep programs, as they were at Grover and Westview.

Stepping outside the Dominant Paradigm: Education for What?

In many ways Farley provides a contrast with Grover, Westview, and Brewer. Yet, the school's progressive educational practices and strong culture of literacy also need to be interrogated for their meanings for the African American students who are not thriving in this context, and for their implications for all the students. Was the purpose of literacy at Farley fundamentally different from that of the other three schools? Was the system of ideas that organized curriculum, pedagogy, and social relations in the school one that bends toward social agency and social justice or toward high-status knowledge within a dominant system of social relations? Was there a relationship between Farley's exclusionary practices in relation to some African American students and what it was educating all its students for?

Popkewitz (2000) reminds us, "The systems of ideas that order pedagogy, childhood, achievement, participation, and educational policy are social constructions and effects of power" (p. 27). Assumptions about what constituted legitimate knowledge and the parameters of classroom inquiry at Farley, although different from those at Grover and Westview, for example, were nevertheless bounded by a rather unquetioning acceptance of the social order. Returning to the theme of schools as settings for the construction of social identities, and literacy as a set of social practices that apprentice students to particular social identities, Farley's literacy practices were geared to the production of specific kinds of learners, workers, and citizens. As Gee, Hull, and Lankshear (1996) argue, "the Discourse creates social positions . . . from which people are 'invited' . . . to speak, listen, act, read and write, think, feel, believe and value in certain characteristic, historically recognizable ways" (p. 10). To the extent that these are directed to the development of "strategic intelligence," problem solving, and nonhierarchical learning, they cultivate intellectual and social dispositions for the privileged knowledge production strata of the new capitalism (Gee et al., 1996). However, these practices do not necessarily create space for reflection and critique of the social order they prepare students for, a social order that relegates the vast majority to the periphery of the economy and society. Reflection and critique, in this sense, are not part of the "core values" of the discourse (p. 68).

The kinds of literacies cultivated at Farley (at least for some students) can position students more successfully, but uncritically, to participate in an increasingly hierarchical economy and social structure. This may be important to their economic survival in the new economy, but children need strong literacy skills *and* the ability to critique social inequality and challenge various forms of oppression (critical literacy). A curriculum that develops facility with the dominant discourse *and* thinking and problem solving can facilitate critical literacy, but only with specific conditions and orientations (Gutstein, 2003).

A more thoroughgoing critique of urban schools and the accountability policies that dominate them demands a paradigmatic shift that refocuses on the central question, "Education for what?" This is an urgent and practical problem as well as a philosophical concern, one that is related to Farley's challenges as well. In the dominant discourse, ameliorating race and class disparities is framed as "closing the achievement gap," but the bigger question is, "Achievement for what?" What kind of world and what kind of participation in it are the school preparing students for? Race and class disparities demand rethinking the curriculum and one's orientation as a teacher, not only to question dominant narratives of progress and Eurocentric official knowledge, but to examine critically relations of power and injustice as they are lived. Race and class differences in schools open up possibilities to examine culture as a complex concept that affects every aspect of life (Ladson-Billings, 2001) and to think about what it means to negotiate multicultural contexts, such as Chicago, democratically. Schools such as Farley could take advantage of the experiences and perspectives of all the children in the school, centering and building on them to complicate and deepen all students' thinking about inequality and injustice and about what it might mean to live in multicultural, diverse democratic public spheres.

Conclusion

More than those of the other three schools, Farley's classrooms prepared students to develop their own ideas, to engage with texts, to write in multiple voices for multiple audiences, and to think. In general, the students were being apprenticed to values, knowledge, and intellectual dispositions oriented to the upper tiers of a knowledge-driven economy and a highly stratified social structure. They were immersed in social practices that taught them that their views mattered; that they were actors, not simply acted upon, as is the case with highly regimented forms of instruction. Whether this "message" resonated with all students in the school needs further investigation in light of the racial disparities and racialized practices described. Indeed, Farley's seeming success may obscure these issues just as the apparent failures of a less-successful school may expose them.

But Farley demonstrates that a school that is backed up by an economically and socially powerful community and that enjoys sedimented race and class advantages experiences and shapes accountability quite differently than working-class and low-income schools in communities with far less power do. It further illustrates how accountability policies can heighten already huge disparities in educational experiences and opportunities. At the same time, even Farley was not immune to the pressures of accountability, which threatened its professional culture and rich literacy practices. Some of the key elements of Farley's strength—its knowledgeable and active teaching staff, literacy instruction, holistic educational goals, and independence—are unlikely to be cultivated at other schools by top-down directives, prescriptive pedagogies, and pressures to raise test scores through endless test-preparation drills. The centralized regulation that has driven some of the most thoughtful teachers out of Grover, Westview, and Brewer is the very condition Farley has been able to resist, at least to some extent. Nor can schools simply compensate for Farley's race and class advantages by raising standards and holding everyone to them. In short, we will not be able to get from Grover to Farley by using the dominant policies. In fact, I have argued in chapters 4 and 5 that accountability and centralized regulation drove out highly competent teachers whose classrooms paralleled and exceeded the literacy practices I observed at Farley. Moreover, some of the strengths of teachers at Grover, Westview, and Brewer—culturally relevant teaching, efforts at developing critical literacy, a deep commitment to the education of low-income children of color, and integration of students' identities and lived experiences—might well benefit teachers at Farley. But in a system that simplistically ranks "successful" schools, these textured practices have little currency. Indeed, they are under siege and made irrelevant in the current context.

Farley demonstrates some of what is lacking in many Chicago public schools. But the danger in simply positioning Farley as an alternative to test-driven schools is not only that it oversimplifies and occludes the school's challenges. To do so would be to leave unchallenged the dominant framework of what constitutes literacy, legitimate classroom knowledge, and the purpose of education. This negates a vision of education that builds on the cultures and knowledge of all students and fosters critique and possibility. As Gee, Hull, and Lankshear (1996) suggest:

> At the very least we need to develop sociocultural approaches to language and literacy that construct as well as deconstruct, that synthesize as well as analyze, that frame ideal "possible worlds," and that enable readers to unveil textual representations of reality and their interest-serving consequences. (p. 131)

As I have argued throughout, such an education is not an illusory ideal but an urgent necessity if students are to survive and challenge deepening global social chasms of class, gender, race and ethnicity, increasing militarization of U.S. society, and the politics of racial exclusion and demonization.

CHAPTER 7

Beyond Accountability
Toward Schools that Create New People for a New Way of Life

In February 2003, I was having dinner with several friends, all CPS teachers. As I looked around the table, I saw stress etched into everyone's face. One friend, who teaches sixth grade, described going to the opera for the first time and being shocked at her own lack of analytical keenness. "And that's something I'm really good at, literary analysis." With all the constant monitoring and test preparation, she said, she just has no time to think. "I want to do those creative things in the classroom, but there's just no space. What happened to the intellectual excitement? I feel like I'm operating on a low 6th grade level." Another teacher talked about feeling schizophrenic. She is active in Teachers for Social Justice, but in her school she finds herself doing things against her beliefs in order to manage a situation in which the pressures of accountability are worse than ever and the social stress on kids rebounds on the classroom. A new high school teacher, also a social activist, with two master's degrees, said, "If it's going to be like this, more mandates every day and no time, I don't think I can do this job for more than three or four years. And this is what I want to do." These are some of the most thoughtful, committed, critically minded teachers I know.

January 2003: At a meeting of CPS students and teachers, a student at one of the city's regular high schools (I'll call him Manuel) described his school. It is so overcrowded they are on double shifts. There are forty kids in a class, and his math class shares a classroom with an English class. It is hard to concentrate on math with the English teacher right next to him. There are lockers for only one third of the students, and the students are not allowed to wear coats and backpacks in school (CPS discipline policy).

It is winter, so lots of kids just do not go to school because they do not have lockers. He missed school for two weeks in the fall for this reason. Finally he found a friend who let him share his locker. There are three kids and all their stuff in one narrow locker. Half of his chemistry lab is roped off because there is a big hole in the floor. Some of his teachers are not teaching in their subject area, and the curriculum provides no space for his voice; nor is it relevant to the serious issues he and his friends grapple with in their lives. Manuel is a senior, and he has been bombarded by military recruiters promising him training, job skills, free college tuition. That is the only recruitment he has seen. He has received no college counseling and does not think he has a future in college. There are few true college prep classes in his high school except for the small, selective IB program. Manuel is a leader of a citywide student activist organization.

These stories capture a slice of life in Chicago's mostly nonselective public schools eight years after the introduction of a regime of accountability that, in many respects, has become national policy with George W. Bush's *No Child Left Behind* (NCLB) (2001). NCLB crystallizes neoliberal, business-oriented education policy.[1] Business rhetoric of efficiency, accountability, and performance standards and the redefinition of education to serve the labor market have become the common vocabulary of educational policies across the United States, and increasingly, globally. Chicago embodies this agenda in action, with its high stakes testing and penalties for failure and its differentiated schools (a variant of neoliberal school choice). Under NCLB, every school district and every school will be measured, driven, and sanctioned or rewarded on the basis of its students' performance on standardized tests. Test-driven, standardized teaching is one product of this agenda, except in selective or high-scoring schools that negotiate or are exempted from it.[2] In practice, having served as a stalking horse for NCLB, Chicago is now ironically circumscribed by it even as some officials talk about new teaching initiatives. In a NCLB world of state regulation, deviation from this agenda has become even more difficult. In my last interview with Ms. Grimes, Westview's principal, she defined the power of the national policy context: "If they're not able to master what's on that Iowa, I don't care what other things you're taught. Looking at it from what Bush is looking for, you're not taught. You are a failing school" (January 2001). What we can learn from accountability, centralized regulation, standardization, and differentiated schools in Chicago has implications for what is meant to be the national norm.

Chicago has a specific history and the school district has its own particularities. And the four schools in this study have their own institutional characters, micropolitics, and histories. What happens behind their brick façades is only partially determined by dominant policies. Moreover, my research is just a brief look at each school. I do not suggest that Chicago and these four schools are representative of U.S. schools or urban school systems. Yet I have attempted, through an overview of CPS policies and an examination of how they play out in four different contexts, to tell stories not told about a hegemonic national education agenda. Thus I hope to say something of what might be expected in other contexts, particularly in relation to issues of educational and social equity, the agency of adults and children, the valuing of cultures and languages, and possibilities for making schools places where children develop tools to critique authorized knowledge and challenge social injustice. In this chapter I summarize some main insights from the school case studies and analysis of districtwide policies and their implications in relation to processes of globalization. I counterpose this emphasis with an outline for an alternative educational agenda and three powerful examples of doing education very differently. These examples challenge hegemonic discourses about education by showing that teachers, administrators, students, and families can create schools and school systems that prepare children to be empowered subjects and critical actors for social change. These examples also concretize the strategic role of education in reconstructing the state and challenging neoliberal hegemony. I conclude by commenting on what these policies mean in a post-9/11 world and possibilities for linking education change with emerging, critically conscious social movements.

Lessons from Chicago

I have argued that the regime of accountability supports processes of economic and social dualization linked to globalization. Education policies concretely and symbolically produce a highly segmented and economically polarized labor force and the reconstitution of urban space as the cultural and material province of real estate developers, corporate headquarters, and the new urban gentry. Accountability language, practices, social relations, and ways of valuing and thinking constitute a discourse of social discipline and subjugation that is highly racialized. They legitimate and produce the regulation and control of youth of color and support the eviction and criminalization of communities of color. In this section, I review these arguments and draw out their implications in the present political context.

Changing the Discourse of, and about, Education

Aligned with a broad social agenda that is retrenching on every social gain wrung from the state in the post-World War II era, neoliberal education discourses shift responsibility for inequality produced by the state onto parents, students, schools, communities, and teachers. Chicago's policies bring these discourses to life. *Equity* ("ending the injustice of social promotion," "holding all students to the same high standards," expanding "a variety of education opportunities") is tied to *individual responsibility* (students who progress are those who "work hard"; failure is publicly penalized through grade retention, assignment to remedial high schools, and school probation). *Technical rationality and efficiency* (educational processes are standardized, centrally prescribed and scripted, and subject to accounting measures) are substituted for the complex ethical and social processes and goals of education. This is lived through test-prep drills, educational triage, and semiscripted curricula. *Business metaphors* of quality control, accountability, and standards replace any notion of democratic participation in education as a public good in a democratic society. The purpose of education is redefined to develop the skills and dispositions necessary for the labor market of a post-Fordist, globalized capitalism.

The four case studies demonstrate the power of the dominant policy agenda to change educational discourse at the level of the classroom and school. In all four schools, to varying degrees, accountability redefined what it means to be a "good school" in technical and narrowly instrumental terms (Ball, 1997a). The practices induced by accountability and centralized regulation created and exacerbated contradictions between substantive long-term projects to change teaching and learning and short-term accountability-driven goals. This process was illustrated by dropping rich mathematics curricula at Grover and Brewer; undermining a budding process of collective, critical reflection at Brewer; channeling Westview teachers' commitment to their students into raising test scores; and chipping away at Farley teachers' sense of professional efficacy.

In this discourse, teachers who were "good" according to multidimensional and complicated criteria, including those constructed by families and communities, became less so. Teachers recognized for their commitment to children and the community, their determination to help students become people who could "read" and "write" the world (Freire & Macedo, 1987), and their defense of children's language and home culture were ultimately judged by a single, instrumental measure. Students, as well as teachers, with all their varied talents and challenges, were reduced to a test score. And schools, as well as their communities, in all their complexity— their failings, inadequacies, strong points, superb and weak teachers, ethical commitments to collective uplift, their energy, demoralization, courage, potential, and setbacks—were blended, homogenized, and reduced to a stanine score and a narrow business model of "success" or "failure." In the process, brilliant spots in the schools were rubbed out rather than cultivated and extended. A few uncommitted and unprepared teachers were driven out, and others were upgraded to standardized teaching. Instead of inducing schools to develop their curricular and pedagogical strengths, accountability policies promoted or reinforced a narrow focus on specific skills and on test-taking techniques. Instead of supporting and extending the strengths of culturally relevant, critical teachers at Grover and Brewer, the policies drove them out or forced them to accommodate. Even when accountability exposed weaknesses, such as racial disparities in achievement at Farley, the policies did little to help address them and may have reinforced conservatism, out of fear of not drawing attention to issues of race. Despite a vocabulary of excellence that clothes school accountability, this is a discourse that produces mediocrity, conservatism, and narrowly instrumental conceptions of people, learning, and the purposes of education. The policies are given life through social practices in specific contexts. The four schools provide a glimpse of how the "ethical retooling of the public sector to emphasize excellence, effectiveness and quality that can be measured" (Ball, 1990, p. 259) is actually *lived* inside the discourses of accountability in schools.

Reproducing and Extending Inequality

I have also demonstrated that Chicago's education policies reproduce existing educational and social inequalities and create new ones. In the name of "choice" of educational "opportunities," Chicago has superimposed new forms of educational tracking on an already tracked system. This differentiated system illustrates the strategic relationship between new forms of educational tracking and the production of a stratified labor force for the new economy. Carlson's (1997) outline of this trend is remarkably close to Chicago's policies: The academic track is becoming more differentiated from other tracks and more spatially separate through magnet and specialty schools and separate academic programs within schools, thus stripping academic track students from the general high school. These selective programs, employing more constructivist and "higher-order-thinking" curricula, as well as advanced course offerings, prepare students to be knowledge producers in the new economy. The new vocationalism of Education-to-Career Academies creates a closer link between applied vocationalism and academics. At the same time, general high schools provide the new basic literacies (i.e., better than eighth grade reading and math skills and compliant and amiable social dispositions) that correspond to the skills required for the large number of low-skill, low-wage service jobs. Because of the fairly low level of these skills and the emphasis on test-driven practices, the new functional literacies are not conducive to critical literacy. As a whole this system constructs new "selective mechanisms within a system that claims inclusivity" (Ozga, 2000, p. 104). As I have argued, this stratified education produces identities for a stratified labor force, stratified city, and stratified society. Gee, Hull, and Lankshear (1996) point to the social logic of these policies in the context of the capitalist informational economy:

> "Education reform" in terms of ensuring quality schools for everyone is deeply
> paradoxical, because if everyone were educated there would be no servants.
> The new capitalism is in danger of producing and reproducing an even steeper
> pyramid than the old capitalism did. And, just as in the old capitalism, it will
> need institutions—like schools, first and foremost—to reproduce that social
> structure. (p. 47)

At the school level, although accountability has pushed some schools, such as Grover, to focus more on curriculum coordination and planning of instruction, my data suggest that it reinforces, even extends inequalities. I observed Farley, a high-scoring multiracial, mixed-class school, to be much less oriented to test-prep than the other three schools that served low-income and working-class African American and Latino/a children. There is virtually no evidence in the data from Grover, Westview, and Brewer that accountability policies helped them develop rich literacies, rigorous curriculum, or challenging intellectual experiences for students. The new policies also created a schism between the professional culture of these three schools, which became more regulated, and that of Farley, whose teachers were able to maintain some independent professional judgment. Particularly at Grover, probation and the school's array of external supervisors promoted technical and routinized approaches to improving instruction, deskilling teachers rather than enriching their thinking and knowledge. Accountability undermined the collective self-study at Brewer and practices and orientations that promoted bilingualism and biculturalism. It worked against critical literacy practices and drove out some of the strongest teachers at Brewer and Grover.

In short, the technical and routinized practices promoted by accountability policies have not helped Grover, Brewer, and Westview acquire the strengths of Farley's rich culture of literacy. Nor have they helped teachers to develop the professional competencies and independent professional judgment of some Farley teachers. These strengths are important elements to ensure that all children have access to an intellectually rigorous and multifaceted literacy curriculum. If anything, accountability has made them more routinized and pushed out teachers who embodied this professional culture making these schools less like Farley. (See McNeil, 2000; Valenzuela, 1999, for similar findings.) However, the other important issue is that accountability-as-surveillance is likely to promote conservatism in high-scoring schools, reinforcing existing tendencies to avoid controversy and in-depth analysis of politically charged issues of race, culture, educational disparities, as well as critical pedagogies. Taking up these issues is a central challenge, but it is made even more difficult in a coercive climate in which public attention might produce closer monitoring and thus pressures to conform to the dominant agenda.

Education for Social Control

The Chicago example demonstrates how accountability and centralized regulation of schools constitute a regime of social control. This is a system that robs principals, teachers, students, and communities of agency. Through accountability the state shifts responsibility for "success" and "improvement" to the school but gives it less control over its evaluation and less room to maneuver. As a Grover teacher said, "You really don't have too much power or say-so in what goes on." The four schools illustrate concretely how regulation of teaching through direct external oversight, standards, and assessment by high stakes tests strips teachers of opportunities for professional and ethical judgment, further eroding whatever agency teachers, principals, and communities have in relation to their schools. As a result of mandated curricula, imposed standards, and the exigencies of preparing for standardized tests, teachers and communities are losing control of knowledge, to the extent they ever had any. This trend was reflected in the thirteen weeks of test preparation at Westview, the instructional routines dictated by Grover's probation partner, the pressure to teach children English at the expense of their Spanish at Brewer, and the curricular compromises pressed on Farley teachers.

This is a complex set of issues because some teachers need more content and pedagogical knowledge, and in its absence, routines and semiscripted curricula fill this gap, as they did for teaching interns at Grover. But no middle-class school would be likely to accept these technical fixes as a substitute for thoughtful pedagogical decisions. Nor is this an acceptable substitute for the pedagogical judgment, sociopolitical knowledge, and cultural sensitivity of teaching that is culturally and politically relevant to students and their communities. Moreover, imposed standardization negates the contested nature of what should constitute common knowledge (Apple, 1996, 2001; Bohn & Sleeter, 2000) and of what constitutes a good school and good teaching (e.g., Darder, 1995; Delpit, 1988; Ladson-Billings, 1994).

In the schools I studied, teachers faced a moral crisis as they were, to paraphrase one teacher, forced to compromise their beliefs. The public display of individual and school failure and the meting out of punishment by the state remind students, teachers, and communities that they have little power, that they are all "on probation" or in danger of being put there. Accountability becomes a totalizing system that infiltrates all aspects of school life and demands that each level of authority, each classroom, each school, and each grade level capitulate, more or less, even if a given class or school is not immediately threatened with sanctions. This process is undergirded by a logic of inevitability. "There will always be tests, each grade needs to prepare students to be tested at the next grade, and if we don't comply, we too may be under tighter surveillance"—so goes the refrain. However, this system is deployed differentially. In the four schools in this study there was a continuum of enforcement, from near-total supervision of Grover to relative flexibility at Farley. This mirrors citywide patterns of race and class differentiation as revealed by the pattern of schools on probation—all enrolling predominantly low-income African Americans or Latinos/as. Thus, although everyone is swallowed up in this system, the accrued race and class advantages of some schools versus others mean that there are different constraints and that policies are "read" and accommodated differently in different contexts with different consequences for human agency.

Accountability works as a panoptic system of surveillance that teaches people to comply and to press others into compliance. This works, in part, because "deficiency" is made visible, individual, easily measured, and highly stigmatized within a hierarchical system of authority and supervision. By holding individuals all along the line—students, teachers, parents—responsible for their own "failure," the system and culture of accountability encourage both self-blame (as with Brewer students who failed the eighth grade ITBS) and passing on of the blame to others in a pecking order that originates in the CPS central office and ends at the student's and teacher's desk and parent's living room. This individualization of blame reinforces race-, ethnicity-, and class-based ideologies of deficient "others."

The four case studies illustrate that accountability, centralized regulation, and differentiated schools are (collectively) a system of social discipline that works through everyday practices in schools to shape student and teacher identities. The policies create actual material conditions—military discipline, routines of Direct Instruction, classroom language of accountability, unending test preparation, privileging of English over students' home language, challenging intellectual discussions, International Baccalaureate programs of study—"that construct the truth of who we are" (Ferguson, 2000, p. 59). Within this continuum, routinized, basic skills and highly regulated and assimilationist practices—delivered without critique—produce docile subjectivities:

> These are forms of power that are realized and reproduced through social interaction within the everyday life of institutions. They play upon the insecurities of the discipline subject. . . . They do not so much bear down upon but take shape within the practices of the institution itself and construct individuals and their social relations through direct interaction. (Ball, 1997b, p. 261)

Education Policy as a Racialized System of Regulation

Although all Chicago public schools are subject to surveillance and control by the state, patterns of racial subjugation are clear. Schools in low-income neighborhoods of color are the least in charge of their own destiny. (This is clear from the demographics of schools on probation and is illustrated by the differential regulation of the four schools in this study.) These are schools where both students and teachers are disciplined by the routines and frameworks of standardized tests and external supervision. As Ms. Dupree, a Grover teacher, said: "I don't think their [CPS leaders] children are going through this. And they need to realize that these are human beings. And what kind of effects are you having on the students?" (March 2000). School accountability is not a policy of public engagement in the improvement of schooling. Without any real public discussion or participation of teachers, school administrators, students, and parents, powerful city and school officials have held up these schools in Black and Latino/a neighborhoods, and by implication, their communities, as examples of failure, dictated what will happen in their schools; and undermined Local School Councils. As these policies are "rolled out" nationally, through state accountability systems under *No Child Left Behind,* this trend has serious implications for African Americans and Latinos/as, who are most likely to attend schools with low test scores and thus are most likely to be subject to a model of education as social regulation.

This is a form of colonial education governed by powerful (primarily white) outsiders. It signals that the communities affected have neither the knowledge nor the right to debate and act together with educators to improve their children's education. At Grover and Brewer this process also drove out some of the most committed, critical, and culturally relevant teachers. The loss of these teachers and the consolidation of a technical, instrumental version of education disarm African American and Latino/a students, particularly in a context of growing economic polarization, racial repression, and marginalization. Ladson-Billings's argument (1994) is important here:

> Parents, teachers, and neighbors need to help arm African American children with the knowledge, skills, and attitude needed to struggle successfully against oppression. These, more than test scores, more than high grade point averages, are the critical features of education for African Americans. If students are to be equipped to struggle against racism, they need excellent skills from the basics of reading, writing, and math, to understanding history, thinking critically, solving problems, and making decisions; they must go beyond merely filling in test sheet bubbles with Number 2 pencils. (pp. 139–40)

Accountability is also a highly racialized discourse of deficits. The separation of "good" and "bad" schools, of "failing" and "successful" students, that is accomplished through the testing, sorting, and ordering processes of standardized tests, distribution of stanine scores, retention of students, and determination of probation lists constructs categories of functionality and dysfunctionality, normalcy and deviance. In this sense, the test is, in Foucault's language, "a ritual of power." It embodies the power of the state to sort and define students and schools, creating and reinforcing oppressive power relations (Carlson, 1997) of race and class. "Failing" schools and "failing" students (and by implication, "failing" communities), most African American and Latino/a, are measured against the "success" of schools that are generally more white, more middle-class. Low-income schools of color that are defined as relatively successful in this scheme (Brewer is an example) are marked as exceptions, models of functionality in a sea of dysfunctional "others," much as the military high schools demarcate disciplined youth from undisciplined "others." Policies that regulate and punish especially African American, and to some extent Latino/a, students and schools also contribute to the pathologizing of African American and Latino/a communities. In this way, education policy contributes to the construction of consciousness about race in the city and justifies the containment and eviction of African American and Latino/a communities.

Education Policy and Global Transformations

Education policy in Chicago is strategically linked to the restructured economy, urban development and gentrification, transnational migrations, and the politics of race, ethnicity, and racial exclusion in the city. The social, economic, spatial, and cultural changes in Chicago are both products of and responses to transformations in the global economy since the 1970s. The contradictions and tensions of globalization play out on the streets of the city. Here we see a new urban geography—sweeping contrasts of wealth and poverty, centrality and marginality, blatant corporate and financial power, and growing masses of people of color and immigrants whose labor is essential but whose presence (language, culture, place-making practices, and demands for justice) is unwelcome. These tensions and contradictions also play out in the city's public schools. The story of urban education policy today is embedded in this larger narrative of globalization with its social and economic polarization, urban displacement and exclusion, and the salience of race and ethnicity as well as class. The significance of Chicago's education policies lies in their intersection with these economic, political, and cultural processes.

When we say education policy is another front in the struggle over the direction of globalization (Lipman, 2002), this is not a rhetorical flourish but a statement about material and cultural survival and space for agency and transformation. The policy regime I have described is producing stratified knowledge, skills, dispositions, and identities for a deeply stratified society. Under the rubric of standards, the policies impose standardization and enforce language and cultural assimilation to mold the children of the increasingly linguistically and culturally diverse workforce into a more malleable and governable source of future labor. This is a system that treats people as a means to an end. The "economizing of education" and the discourse of accounting reduce people to potential sources of capital accumulation, manipulators of knowledge for global economic expansion, or providers of the services and accessories of leisure and pleasure for the rich. Students are reduced to test scores, future slots in the labor market, prison numbers, and possible cannon fodder in military conquests. Teachers are reduced to technicians and supervisors in the education assembly line—"objects" rather than "subjects" of history. This system is fundamentally about the negation of human agency, despite the good intentions of individuals at all levels.

The nature of this regime is to produce the docile subjectivities necessary for the maintenance of a world of nearly unfathomable contrasts of wealth and poverty. As Gee, Hull, and Lankshear point out, this is a world "in which a small number of countries and a small number of people within them will benefit substantively from the new capitalism, while a large number of others will be progressively worse off and exploited" (1996, p. 44). Such a polarized world requires the sort of domestication of critical thought and agency that is integral to the regime of accountability and discourses of high stakes testing and centralized regulation of schooling. It also requires intensified policing, nationally and locally, as well as internationally. The militarization of schooling and regimentation, policing, and criminalization of youth of color become increasingly useful as some African American and Latino/a communities, and especially the youth, are becoming a "fourth world" inside the United States. Again, Gee, Hull and Lanshear (1996): "[I]t has become possible for vast tracts of humanity to be dismissed now as simply having nothing of relevance to contribute to the new world economy" (p. 149). These are key targets of social control.

As global economic processes make gentrification "the cutting edge of urban change" (Smith, 1996, p. 8), education policies become a material force supporting the displacement of working-class and low-income communities, the transformation of others into urban ethnic theme parks, and the consolidation of the city as a space of corporate culture, middle class stability, and whiteness. This is what Neal Smith calls the "class conquest" of the city. New forms of selectivity within and among schools are an important quality of life factor in attracting the high-paid knowledge workers central to globalization and the global city.

At the other end of the spectrum, specialized schooling, such as military schools, that discipline and regulate African Americans and some other people of color also mark them as requiring special forms of social control. This is particularly significant in the context of the global city, with its simultaneous dependence on low-paid labor of people of color, exclusion of those superfluous to the labor force, and need to recruit high-paid, primarily white knowledge workers who want to appropriate the city—neatly boulevarded, gated, and skyscrapered—as their own. Although the racialized policing of youth is nothing new, this has become a vastly expanded social policy and practice as the economy excludes whole sectors and as transnational migrations create a more diverse population of youth. The criminalization of some is related to the assimilation of others as part of the process of differentiated racialization. Schools are central to this process. The ideological force of these policies is deeply implicated in struggles over representation and power in increasingly racially and ethnically diverse urban contexts.

Toward an Alternative Educational Agenda

There is good reason why people back tough measures to ensure that when their children are sent to school, they are taught. That these policies resonate with families and communities is a measure of the persistent and urgent need to act immediately and decisively to address the abysmal material and intellectual conditions in too many urban schools. Support for accountability also reflects the absence of a viable alternative that grasps this urgency *and* makes a liberatory agenda concrete. In schools, as well as in the broader public, there is an absence of counterhegemonic discourses that capture the gravity of the current situation in urban schools *and* press for rich intellectual experiences, cultural and social relevance, democratic participation, and critical thought. More equitable, humane, and liberatory schooling can only grow out of a rich dialogue that includes the multiple perspectives of committed educators and students, families, and communities about what is in the best interest of their children (Delpit, 1988). Specifically, this requires the broad participation and cultural resources of the diverse racially, ethnically, and economically marginalized communities most failed by public schools in the United States. A central problem in Chicago is that city and school officials have captured the common sense about school reform. There an absence of public debate and there is no public forum for fundamentally different perspectives. Moreover, some of the best, most committed teachers who might provide leadership in a more democratic process at the school level, whose practices might be the basis for a liberatory educational program, are being driven out by the current policies.

In part, neoliberal education programs and the drive to accountability and standardization have won out because they have captured the national, even international conversation about education as the only alternative for the "failure" of public schooling. Their hegemonic project has succeeded in redefining education as job preparation, learning as standardized skills and information, educational quality as measurable by test scores, and teaching as the technical delivery of that which is centrally mandated and tested. By defining the problem of education as standards and accountability they have made simply irrelevant any talk about humanity, difference, democracy, culture, thinking, personal meaning, ethical deliberation, intellectual rigor, social responsibility, and joy in education. Challenging the dominant discourse and posing alternative frameworks are strategic aspects of reversing the present direction. Parents, students, and committed teachers—especially those in the communities most affected—can provide a new language of critique and possibility that is grounded in their own knowledge, experiences, and commitments. Critics of current policies need to work together with them, and their perspectives need to be injected into discussions about education. The power of such a participatory process is illustrated by the development of Citizen Schools in Brazil, which I discuss in this chapter.

In the spirit of dialogue, I have suggested (Lipman, 2002) several premises of an alternative agenda. First, all students need an education that is intellectually rich and rigorous and that instills a sense of personal, cultural, and social agency. Students need both the knowledge and skills traditionally associated with academic excellence and a curriculum that is meaningfully related to their lives. They need an education that teaches them to think critically about knowledge and social institutions and locate their own history and cultural identity within broader contexts. Students need an education that instills a sense of hope and possibility that they can make a difference in their own family, school, and community and in the broader national and global community while it prepares them for multiple life choices.

Second, a commitment to educate all students requires the deployment of significant resources. This point almost seems a hollow joke at a moment when the U.S. government spends billions of tax dollars on global military domination and corporate enrichment while there are cutbacks in education funding. But what is needed is nothing short of a massive reconstruction and renewal project. Without new intellectual, cultural, material, and ideological resources, urban schools cannot overcome long-standing problems rooted in racism and a history of neglect. In most urban schools, if not most school systems, there is a compelling need to reduce class size substantially; to provide consistent high-quality professional development and time for teachers to plan and reflect in order to transform the nature of teaching, learning, and assessment; to recruit and retain expert committed teachers in schools in the poorest communities; to provide up-to-date science labs, current and well-stocked school libraries, arts and foreign language programs, state of the art and well-run computer labs. The failure to marshal these resources leads to blaming of communities and democratic policy itself for educational failure. This was the case in Chicago when business leaders and political officials declared that Local School Councils were not "working." Failure due to lack of resources provides a justification for the state to impose controls (Apple, 1991) to overcome the "failed policies of the past," as in Chicago, or to privatize public education, as in Philadelphia. In a period of retrenchment of social benefits at home and squandering of billions in military conquest abroad, the lack of political will for such an investment is self-evident. With huge local and state budget deficits, the necessity to reprioritize federal funding for education is obvious. Although reversing historical inequities requires reciprocal responsibility and participation of educators, students, parents, school leaders, and policy makers, political officials should be held accountable to ensure necessary resources. Obviously, this is a question of political priorities, and will require a social movement to enforce the reallocation of resources from militarism and support of corporate profit to these human needs.

Third, transforming urban schools entails a protracted cultural campaign directed against deficit notions about the potential of low-income children and children of color (Lipman, 1998). Changing entrenched discourses of "ability" and of children and communities as "problems" is obviously complex, long-term, and multifaceted. Clearly it requires the active involvement of parents and children as well as committed educators of children of color and others. The work of urban educators has provided a wealth of knowledge about rich, culturally relevant, critical pedagogies. The beginning process of collective reflection about some of these issues at Brewer hints at possibilities for examining assumptions and ideologies at the school level, as do more developed and systematic programs of preparing teachers to teach in diverse classrooms (e.g., Cochran-Smith, 1995; Ladson-Billings, 2001). There is also a substantial body of research that outlines pedagogical theories that build on the experience, language, and cultural identity of students as a basis for learning and that support the development of critical consciousness and the agency of students of color in particular (e.g., Cummins, 1996; Darder, 1995; Delpit, 1988; Ladson-Billings, 1994).

Finally, the state of urban education is deeply embedded in the state of cities and national and global economic and social priorities. Although much needs to be done in schools, putting the onus on them overlooks the impact of the social–economic context. Although much can be done by committed, culturally relevant, critical educators, the state of education at schools like Grover and Westview cannot be separated from the reality of life in deeply impoverished neighborhoods. Nor can it be addressed without addressing the documented history of inequality and racism that has permeated public schooling in the United States, and urban education in particular. Thus, any serious effort to transform public schools ultimately can only succeed as part of a larger local and global social struggle for material redistribution and cultural recognition (Fraser, 1997).

Policy Borrowing from Below—Three Strategic Models of Counter Hegemonic Education

One effect of globalization has been rapid international policy borrowing among states (Blackmore, 2000). As I noted earlier, this policy borrowing *from above* is reflected in the convergence of neoliberal education policies in Western Europe, the United States, New Zealand, and elsewhere, and in the role of the World Bank in setting educational standards to promote market-driven economies in "developing countries" (Jones, 2000). But as globalization strives to bend all nations, all peoples, all economic sectors and organizations of civil society to the discipline of international capital, the ensuing economic and cultural dislocations and generalized immiseration have given rise to new solidarities and links between disparate social movements across the globe. This is globalization from below. The dialogue among social movements, embodied in the World Social Forum, provides a model of policy borrrowing *from below* (Coates, 2002). Examples of counterhegemonic practices drawn from disparate social contexts can deepen our understanding of how to proceed in a period in which discourses of inevitability preach every day that there is no alternative to the existing social order. Here I want to discuss three quite different, but theoretically linked examples and what we might learn from them.

The first are the Citizen Schools being created by the Workers Party Municipal Government in Porto Alegre, Brazil. In a powerful chapter, Luís Armando Gandin and Michael Apple (2003) describe ways in which these schools concretely challenge neoliberal conceptions of education and their role in the struggle for radical democracy in Brazil. My summary is drawn from their discussion, Gandin's research (2002), and my own investigation in Porto Alegre. The Citizen Schools Project was initiated by the Workers Party not only to create better schools for those students who have been excluded from education in Brazil, particularly the children of the *favelas* (the most impoverished neighborhoods), but also to initiate a pedagogical project in radical democracy. Gandin and Apple outline three aspects of this unfolding project. One, the schools respond to the historical exclusion, failure, and dropping out of poor students by reogranizing the structure of schooling to eliminate the mechanisms that have contributed to the problem in the past. New "cycles of formation" challenge notions of "failure" by assigning students to classes with children of their own age while providing a challenging environment in which they can fill in gaps in their development. Two, the schools reconstitute official knowledge by centering the curriculum on interdisciplinary "thematic commmplexes" grounded in the central issues facing the favella community. The new epistemological perspective is meant to ensure that students learn Brazilian "high culture," *but through new perspectives* grounded in their sociopolitical reality. A stated goal of the new curriculum is to move the culture and history of Afro-Brazilians to the center to openly challenge racism, a central issue in Brazilian society and a principle form of oppression.[1] Three, Citizen Schools are run by councils of teachers, school staff, parents, students, and one member of the school administration. The responsibility of the council to define the aims and direction of the school, allocate economic resources, and ensure implementation makes them schools of democratic participation and collective governance in their own right. The community power and democracy of these councils are redefining neoliberal notions of accountability, reframing it as collective responsibility to ensure that the school serves the community. These three aspects of the project are captured in the idea of democratization of access, knowledge, and management (Gandin, 2002).

While the schools are attempting to productively address the very serious issues of educational exclusion, most important, their goal is to generate a new way of thinking about society as a whole and who should run it. Gandin and Apple report that the schools—their structure, curriculum, and governance—are part of the creation of a movement that "contains as a real social process, the origins of a new way of life" (p. 196). The Citizen Schools provide a powerful example that education projects can be part of a conscious strategy to challenge dominant discourses about schooling and citizenship. Gandin and Apple (2003) emphasize this point:

> . . . there is a constant struggle to legitimize the experience of the Citizen School, to make it socially visible, to pose the discussion over education in terms other than those of neoliberalism, to pull education from the technical economistic realm favored by neoliberal assumptions and to push it to a more politicized one that has as its basic concern the role of education in social emancipation. (p. 200)

The democratic participatory experiences of creating and running the schools redefine the relationship of communities to schools and of communities to the state. "They develop the collective capacities among people to enable them to continue to engage in the democratic administration and control of their lives" (p. 195). By reconstructing school knowledge to draw on the experiences of the community and developing the democratic leadership of the councils, Citizen Schools are also attempting to transform the "separation between the ones who 'know' and . . . ones who 'don't know'" (p. 211).

The Citizen School Project clarifies strategic relationships between educational change and the protracted process of concretely transforming society. This is an important theoretical foundation for conceptualizing education reform and its relationship to a larger liberatory social project. The schools embody reforms that build up democratic participation, reconceptualize school knowledge around the perspectives and experiences of the oppressed, and create conditions for poor and marginalized people to see themselves as people with the capacity to run society and experiences in doing so. Although the actual practice is fraught with challenges, this framework is a powerful lens through which to assess the liberatory potential of specific educational policy agendas. It provides an orientation for both the process and the content of policies that move in a liberatory direction. The Citizen Schools also challenge neoliberal educational frameworks by rearticulating elements of the dominant agenda to a liberatory educational framework. This insight helps us think about the ways in which neoliberalism articulates equity to accountability, for example, and how we might rearticulate it to a democratic agenda. In short, the Citizen Schools give us new tools to think and act in the field of education in more strategic ways in the context of neoliberalism.

The second example is the Rethinking Schools project anchored in the Milwaukee-based teacher journal *Rethinking Schools*. Since 1986 the editors of *Rethinking Schools*, most of them teachers, have provided a space for educators to read about social justice curriculum in action as well as educational issues from a critical, antiracist prespective. Articles about teaching, from kindergarten through high school, demonstrate that teachers can develop pedagogies that help children grapple with issues of racism, sexism, homophobia, social inequality, destruction of the environment, globalizaton, war, militarism, repressive discipline, community disinvestment, and more. The power of this journal is that it presents the writing of real teachers going against the grain in real schools, working under real ideological and material constraints. The classrooms they describe provide concrete examples of what critical, antiracist, participatory education looks like. They make possibility tangible, concretely challenging discourses of inevitability and disempowerment. Taken as a whole and over time, the journal constructs a counterhegemonic educational discourse grounded in critical social praxis. *Rethinking Schools* books on topics of curriculum and classroom practice (*Rethinking Our Classrooms*, 1994, 2001), *Rethinking Columbus* (Bigelow & Peterson, 1998), The Real

Ebonics Debate (Perry & Delpit, 1998), *Reading, Writing, and Rising Up* (Christensen, 2000), and *Rethinking Globalization* (Bigelow & Peterson, 2002, among others), provide a powerful knowledge base for teaching that is grounded in critical social theory, thus directly challenging neoliberal assumptions of teachers as technicians.

These publications and the Rethinking Schools critical listserv are nodes of a national network of critical educational praxis. They establish a community across distance, a center at a time when discourse of inevitability drives out all notions that there are others who also dare to think and act differently. A central insight from the Rethinking Schools project is the strategic importance of social justice teachers' creating public spaces for dialogue and presentation of theoretically grounded alternative practices. These concrete models of practice are an important aspect of building up schools and classrooms that instantiate a counternarrative about schooling, ideologically and practically.

The third example is the practice of culturally relevant, liberatory teachers of African American students. Since the late 1980s, an important body of literature by African American scholars (e.g., Delpit, 1988, 1992b; Foster, 1997; Irvine, 1991; King, 1991; Ladson-Billings, 1994, 2001) has made visible the practices of teachers who draw on the culture of African American students to promote their academic competence and sociopolitical awareness. From studies of the practices of these teachers and the history of Black education in the United States, these scholars have constructed an ensemble of theories of culturally relevant, culturally responsive, emancipatory education for African American students. Drawing on students' African American cultural frame of reference, teachers who are the subjects and collaborators in these studies link literacy with students' social identities. Academic success is connected with developing tools to resist racism and oppression and with social analysis of community issues such as homelessness and global issues such as the Gulf War. Students are encouraged to see themselves as African American intellectual leaders. These theories have made their way into some teacher education programs, into scholarly journals, and onto the programs of national education conferences and have become a fashionable part of conversations among educational researchers. Yet, teaching remains largely color-blind (i.e., white-centered) and disconnected from the sociopolitical realities and psychic experiences of children of color, and the practice of liberatory education for African American students is disconnected from the discourse about education as a whole, including some critical discourse. Yet, these practices and the historically grounded philosophy underpinning them constitute a powerful counterhegemonic discourse.

In an extended essay on African American education, Teresa Perry (2003) explains the philosophy of African American education as "freedom for literacy and literacy for freedom" (see also Murrell, 1997). Perry argues that this philosophy is grounded in African Americans' existential necessity to assert their humanness, their very existence as intellectual beings, in a white supremacist context that historically negated Black intellectual capacity as a central tenet. Literacy from this perspective is a means of personal and collective emancipation and is essential to develop leadership for liberation:

> Read and write yourself into freedom! Read and write to assert your identity as human! Read and write yourself into history! Read and write as an act of resistance, as a political act, for racial uplift, so you can lead your people well in the struggle for liberation! (p. 19)

Thus education is inherently an act of resistance, a political act, and a collective responsibility (see also Anderson, 1988).

I see this philosophy at work in the practices of eight culturally relevant teachers in Ladson-Billings's study (1994) who ground teaching in students' cultural identity, are connected with the students' community, and aim to foster their students' intellectual leadership and critical consciousness about their role in fighting injustice. Despite the restrictive public school settings in which they work, they deliberately go against the grain because they understand education as political. This philosophy is also at work in the narratives of Black teachers (Foster, 1997) who describe challenging racism as central to their work. An Oakland teacher, Carrie Secret (Miner, 1997), exemplifies pedagogy rooted in the centrality of culture and the intersection of culture and power. Secret's culturally responsive classroom foregrounds African American intellectual and creative production and the power of Ebonics as a literary language while developing students' linguistic and cultural competence in the dominant code.

As did Black schools during segregation as described by Perry (2003) and Delpit (1992a), these pedagogies create spaces of resistance, organized to counter the myth of Black inferiority. Perry describes segregated Black schools as " 'figured universes'—or more precisely counterhegemonic figured communities" (p. 91) where African Americans forged a collective identity as literate and achieving people. I would argue that the present-day examples of culturally relevant, liberatory pedagogy fit this description and stand as examples of a fundamentally subversive notion of education for African American students—one we can draw upon in general. Not just academic, education in these classrooms is described as social, cultural, and political—directly counter to the narrow test-driven, technical notions of neoliberal accountability oriented schooling. As a whole, this pedagogical discourse challenges the education-for-work agenda that dominates discussions of education and education reform, particularly for "low-achieving" students of color. This is a praxis that rearticulates equity (framed as test scores in the dominant accountability discourse) to its roots in liberation. Although localized and operating sometimes behind closed doors and in narrow spaces, it is like the Brazilian Citizen Schools that work to transform consciousness about one's subject position in society. In this sense, the practices of culturally relevant emancipatory teachers and the philosophy they embody are challenging the dominant discourse about education and are resources with which concretely to demonstrate a liberatory vision of education. Along with the other two, this is an example of an educational project that can concretize an alternative way of thinking about and doing education that embodies liberatory social processes and specifically challenges the dominant discourse.

Education Policy in a Post- 9/11, Preemptive-War Era

When we sort through all the nuances, differences, and complexities, the essence of educational accountability, centralized regulation, policing of youth of color, and standards is the imposition of the authority of the state on the work and consciousness of adults and children in schools. I have argued throughout this book that the new authoritarianism is both material and ideological, disciplining bodies and minds. In some respects it is hardly new at all. The neoliberal project of recent decades has been the steady erosion of the social welfare functions of the state and expansion of its policing functions. The responsibility of the state to educate children and provide educators and communities with the necessary resources to do so has fully morphed into the role of overseer, judge, and dispenser of rewards and punishments—as well as subcontractor to corporations and supplier for the armed services. But education policies that legislate the policing of schools and schooling take on new and ominous implications in a post–September 11 present of militarism and repression at home and war abroad. School policies that teach people to be docile subjects and that undermine critical thought, imposing a reign of surveillance, coercion, and intimidation, are magnified when we look at them through the lens of the U.S. Patriot Act, Total Information Awareness, legalized merger of the spying functions of the Central Intelligence Agency (CIA) with the domestic "investigation" functions of the Federal Bureau of Investigation (FBI), proposals to recruit ordinary people to spy on their neighbors, unlimited secret detention without civil liberties of several thousand people, racial profiling as national policy, and an orgy of jingoistic patriotism in what passes for the nightly newscast. This new political landscape justifies the criminalization and surveillance that have been a fact of life for some communities of color in the United States and extends it to everyone, targeting specific immigrant groups in particular.

The state's repressive response to September 11 and the Bush doctrine of preemptive war have ushered in, at mind boggling speed, the retrenchment of basic civil liberties. We are living in a dangerous historical moment when state repression is openly being bartered for supposed security from enemies within and without—in fact, the majority of the world's people. As I write this, the devastation wrought by the war against Iraq and threats of other U.S. military aggressions loom as a monstrous storm cloud on our global horizon, school districts all around announce they are forced to lay off teachers and eliminate programs, CPS has announced 15 percent budget cuts, and high school students have walked out of their classes in protest of these deeply interrelated disasters. A historical dialectic is beginning to unfold. A nascent social movement is building as the full ideological and material force of the state and the avaricious goals of transnational capital bear down on us.

Adjusting our lenses to align dual images of authoritarianism in the schools and in the streets puts in focus the political implications of education policies that impose a tight regulatory and surveillance regime. They have dangerous implications for the suppression of critical thought and agency just when we need them most. Despite the truism that there are multiple, potent pedagogical sites beyond schools, schools remain important ideological institutions and spaces for the construction of identities. What we need most right now are "problem posing pedagogies" (Freire, 1970/1994) that help students question and investigate questions such as, Why did September 11 happen? Why does so much of the world hate "us"? What is the history of the Middle East and U.S. involvement in it? How can the United States change its actions in the world to address the resentments so many peoples feel toward its policies? What is the relationship between U.S. militarism and racism in the U.S.?

Instead, accountabilty policies expand the state's function to police knowledge and educational practices and intensify the repression of critical thought and action. High stakes tests (with all their accoutrements) take on a whole new meaning as "rituals of power" in the present context when docile subjectivities serve not only new labor force demands and global city images but the politics of state repression. Education policies that sort students and schools into neat, simplified opposites of "failures" and "successes" also promote a kind of binary thinking that serves the new official discourse of "good" and "evil" countries, nationalities, and people. Policies that obscure the richly textured strengths and weaknesses of schools, teachers, students, and communities not only erase the possibility of addressing in complex ways the process of educational improvement and transformation. They impose definitions of winners and losers and teach us to identify quickly and absolutely those who are deviant and must be controlled.

The containment and policing of communities of color take on new dimensions in this political context. Black and Latino/a communities that have faced repression all along are now more vulnerable as national security legitimates police raids and singling out of individuals based solely on nationality. Just at the moment when racial profiling had begun to be subjected to national scrutiny and critique, the state's response to 9/11 made it official policy. At the same moment, in a sinister reversal, African Americans and Latinos/as are expected to join in the demonization of people of Arab descent and certain immigrant groups. And in a zero-tolerance world, zero-tolerance discipline policies in schools fit a new common sense of militarism and repression to crack down on dangerous "others." Intense surveillance in urban schools becomes one more part of a commonsense national agenda that allows the state to monitor every facet of private life in the name of national security. If the merger of the military and public schools might have been problematic for some before 9/11, it is now national policy writ large. A provision of No Child Left Behind gives military recruiters access to all high school juniors and seniors. We can be sure that those being recruited are not primarily at the select magnet schools. They are the graduates of general high schools in Chicago and elsewhere, mainly African American and Latino/a youth, eighteen-year-olds whose substandard education and subzero options make them prime candidates for what has been called an unofficial "poverty draft." Indeed the general high school may truly be a "military prep track" as U.S. plans for global military domination require expansion of the military ranks.

Education Change and Social Movements

What is to be done? One source of insight is the history of school reforms since the 1950s that pressed for equity and justice. Desegregation struggles, campaigns by African American communities and others for community control of schools, challenges to the Eurocentric and male-centric curriculum, and demands for bilingual education, equal education for children with disabilities, and equal funding for school programs for girls and women—all were born of, and sustained by, broad social justice movements. The educational demands they proposed were concrete expressions of these social movements and at the same time helped to build and extend them. At a moment when accountability has become a new regime of truth, the history of these movements provides an important counterdiscourse and an alternative perspective on the role of democratic participation and activism in shaping social policy. Although only partially successful in achieving their aims, these movements linked education reforms to wider social change and challenged existing power relations. This relationship was captured by African American parents in Chicago in their

1968 call for an education organizing conference titled "Judgment Day for Racism in West Side Schools" (Danns, 2002).

This is a language that names the political nature of education. Its challenges a system that treats people as a means to an end. There are kernels of organized resistance in Chicago Public Schools today. In fall 2002, twelve teachers at Curie High School refused to give the high stakes Chicago Academic Standards Exam; actions of "The Curie 12" and their support from others around the city led the district to drop the test. The Youth First *Youth Summit,* also in fall 2002, and subsequent public actions have injected the voice of several hundred high school youth into school policies affecting their lives. The high school student walk out against war on Iraq in March 2003 demonstrated heightened political consciousness. An alternative assessment proposal developed by a coalition of local school councils and school reform groups (LSC Summit, 2000) introduced an element of debate to the heretofore narrow discourse of high stakes tests in Chicago.

The three counter-hegemonic education projects that I describe above were born of social movements and the participation of educators in those movements. Educational projects grounded in critical social theories and democratic participation (especially by those who have been most marginalized) help make the emancipatory visions of social movements concrete. Culturally relevant, critical, democratic education can help develop "new people" and new social organization to challenge the exisitng social order. In the recent past, appeals (including my own, Lipman, 1998) to link education change with social and economic reconstruction have been largely rhetorical in the context of fragmented and largely quiescent social movements. But that may be changing. As globalization increasingly divides the world into a small number of superrich countries and people on one side and literally billions of increasingly impoverished and dislocated people on the other, it is sowing seeds of its own destruction. There are new solidarities manifested in a worldwide antiglobalization movement that is perhaps most sharply reflected in the diverse social movements that make up the Porto Alegre World Social Forum and its agenda of "globalization from the bottom": economic, social, and cultural justice and opposition to neoliberalism, war, and militarism (see Coates, 2002). The true face of the "neoliberal miracle" in economically developing countries is being exposed in the intensified exploitation of workers, displacement of peasants and small farmers, destruction of the environment, growing national debt, and regulation by transnational lending institutions. Voters in Latin America are rejecting these policies from Brazil to Bolivia to Venezuela, another sign of the times. This is coupled with a massive worldwide showing of opposition to the U.S.–U.K. war on Iraq. From a historical perspective, the world significance of these gathering social forces as a counter to the global hegemony of transnational capital and U.S. militarism should not be underestimated.

As the effects of globalization have also come home to roost in low-wage jobs, lack of health care and retirement security, a crisis in affordable housing, and homelessness they have begun to awaken the U.S. labor movement and infuse it with the energy of immigrant and women workers in new alliances with African American and white workers. The slogan *Si Se Puede* heard from Chicago's hotel workers signals the rumblings of a new labor militance fortified by new Asian, Latino/a, African, Arab, and Eastern European voices. As I write, the Bush doctrine of preemptive, unilateral military action has begun to give rise to an antiwar, antimilitarization movement with a scope not seen since the Vietnam era. Today's activists are beginning to make critical connections between militarism abroad and racism, economic crisis, labor explitation, and lack of high-quality education, housing, and health care at home.

These connections bear seeds of a significant new, socially conscious movement in education. It is also quite transparent that those who will fight on the front lines in the U.S. military are overwhelmingly African American and Latino/a, products of the general high schools and the military prep tracks. There is a new hopefulness in a socially conscious, hip hop generation represented by Chicago's Youth First Campaign (September 2002) that says: "We are the generation who asks the question: *Why?* Why do things have to be the way they are? We *challenge the system* by organizing *direct action* to gain respect and have our *opinions heard*, so that we can *make change!*"

Methodological Appendix

My interpretation of official CPS policy and policy discourses is based on review of CPS documents and press releases. To learn about new programs and schools, during the 1999–2000 school year and in the summer of 2001, my research assistants[1] and I conducted telephone interviews and face-to-face informal interviews with eight CPS directors of specific programs, visited one military high school, and attended CPS district-level meetings. I tracked Chicago economic and educational trends through a variety of archival sources, including newspapers, *Catalyst: Magazine of Chicago School Reform*, policy documents of the Commercial Club of Chicago (an elite organization of the city's top commercial, industrial, financial, real estate, philanthropic, and civic leaders), and business and real estate publications. For a quantitative picture of student outcomes and district trends, I used data and reports produced by CPS and the Consortium on Chicago School Research. I computed the percentage of Chicago public school students participating in new programs and schools and mapped the location of these programs and schools onto real estate patterns, workforce trends, and school and neighborhood demographics (Lipman, 2002).

To investigate the meanings of CPS policies for teachers, school administrators, and students in different contexts I conducted qualitative studies of four elementary schools (Grover, Westview, Farley, and Brewer) reflecting a variety of demographic and achievement characteristics as defined by CPS. The time I spent in each school, the depth of my immersion in the life of the school, my methods of data collection, and the degree of collaboration with school staff varied considerably. Although frankly not ideal, this was the result of practical constraints I was forced to work under in my professional situation.

I studied Westview and Grover from fall 1997 to winter 2001. The study was facilitated by my work with a larger research project. Although I did not design that project, I was somewhat guided by it in my choice of teachers, classrooms, and activities to observe. I was assisted by two research assistants. The assistance of these researchers must remain anonymous here to protect the anonymity of the schools. We conducted fifty-five audiotaped teacher interviews and thirty-two formal and informal administrator interviews with a total of thirty-three teachers and seven administrators.[2] Most interviews were about sixty minutes long, although some were longer, and about two-thirds were transcribed verbatim; the rest were summarized. We interviewed teachers across grade levels but focused on teachers of grades three, six, and eight, the grades most affected by accountability policies.[3] We interviewed fourteen parents and representatives of community and school reform groups who were chosen because they were active in the schools. Interviews were guided by a semistructured protocol designed by the larger study to examine school development. Beginning in 1998, I included my own open-ended questions, focusing on the influence of accountability policies on teaching and learning, teacher and student agency, the culture of the school, and critical literacy practices. Notes from informal conversations with teachers and administrators are also part of the data, as are transcribed interviews from a separate study of probation schools. We observed 118 classes (most of which were taught by teachers we interviewed) and numerous school meetings and professional development sessions, using a structured observation protocol[4] that focused on curriculum, instruction, classroom climate, and student engagement. I also maintained field notes of these observations and daily life in the schools. In addition, there were many informal conversations with teachers over the years. I informally shared observations and perceptions with teachers at both schools, and in 1998 I formally shared initial findings with Grover staff. Feedback from teachers and administrators helped shape my interpretations.

Eric Gutstein and I studied Brewer from 1995 to 1999. We were involved with the school in various capacities, including professional development, collaboration in teaching and school improvement, and research. We formally interviewed and intermittently talked with fifteen teachers (about a third of the faculty), the principal, and other administrators and talked informally with virtually all the school's teachers, teacher aides, and nonteaching staff. Gutstein and a research assistant interviewed twenty-two students.[5] From 1996 through 1998 we participated regularly in faculty meetings, worked with small groups of teachers, and observed or participated in classrooms at most grade levels. In 1999, I did in-depth interviews about CPS policies with the principal and four teachers, selected because they taught the benchmark grades and were teachers we had identified as oriented to culturally relevant teaching and social justice (Lipman & Gutstein, 2001). Gutstein has continued to work closely with the teachers and administrators up to the present moment, and I have continued to follow the school, maintaining contact with a few teachers and the principal since 1999. I studied Farley during the 2000–1 school year. I conducted open-ended interviews with seventeen teachers representing most grade levels (prekindergarten through eighth grade), though I focused on teachers of benchmark grades. I also interviewed the principal multiple times, the librarian, and other support staff. I was a participant observer in ten teachers' classes, most several times. I spent about five months studying the school.

At all four schools, I attended faculty meetings, committee meetings, and school events and spent time informally in teachers' lounges, lunch rooms, and the school office. I also collected school and school-district archival data. I shared emerging interpretations with teachers and administrators, and their ideas inform my final discussion. At Brewer we analyzed data collaboratively with some of the teachers.[6] Following standard qualitative research practices, I attempted to strengthen the credibility of data through multiple interviews and observations and multiple data sources. I probed for evidence that might disconfirm or complicate my interpretations, sought out multiple perspectives, and explored alternative explanations for my data (Hammersley & Atkinson, 1995). When I worked with research assistants and/or collaborators at the school level, I used interresearcher verification to explore contradictions and triangulate data and analysis. I read and reread interview, observational, and archival data, using standard qualitative methods of data coding (Emerson, Fretch, & Shaw, 1995). Beginning with a general theoretical framework, I constructed the analysis from descriptive and analytical patterns in the data.

My analysis is clearly partial. More in-depth, ethnographic data are needed to explore fully the meanings students and teachers make of programs and policies. Also, much relevant information about CPS programs is constantly changing and/or not readily available. I have had to construct this information from CPS documents and personal conversations with school officials. CPS policies are a moving target, constantly being revised, renamed, and tweaked. In the analysis I attempt to account for some of this change.

NOTES

Chapter 1

1. Part of the debate about globalization as a concept centers on whether the economic developments at its core signal a new world order or are an acceleration of the global reach of capital and movement of peoples that began with the rise of imperialism in the nineteenth century, or, as some argue, with the origins of capitalism itself and specifically sixteenth-century European mercantile capitalism. Although the global reach of capital has a long history in colonialism and imperialism, on this point I agree with Rizvi and Lingard (2000), who argue for the distinctive character of globalization in the present era. Another central issue is the role of the nation state in an era of dominance of transnational capital and supranational economic bodies like the World Trade Organization. For a discussion of these issues in relation to education see Burbules and Torres (2000), also Gill (2003).

2. Neoliberalism, the political program of globalization, inserts the primacy of the market into all spheres of society—from health care, to education, to retirement security. Neoliberal social policy has undermined the post–World War II social contract and replaced it with personal responsibility, privatization of social programs, deregulation of market forces, coupled with increased state regulation of the individual, particularly low-income people and people of color.

3. Ray and Mickelson (1993, p. 9) estimate 28 to 35 percent of all U.S. workers can be classified as contingent.

4. Sanjek (1998) sums up these trends succinctly: "[During the Reagan years] financial and business services accounted for 3.3 million new jobs, a quarter of the increase. Most of these jobs paid well, but that total also included low-paid data-entry, messenger, and office-cleaner positions. At the same time, low-paying retail and food service jobs grew by 4.5 million, clerical employment stagnated, and manufacturing jobs, paying twice the wages of service jobs, decreased" (pp. 124–25).

5. Castells (1996) projected the following model of the occupational structure in 2005: an increase in the upper-class (managers and professionals) share of employment from 23.7 percent in 1992 to 25.3 percent, a decline in the middle-class (technicians and craft workers) share from 14.7 to 14.3 percent; a decline in lower-middle-class occupations (sales, clerical, operators) from 42.7 to 40.0 percent, and an increase in lower-class occupations (service and agricultural workers) from 18.9 to 20 percent (p. 225).

6. Castells (1998) points out, however, that even within the highly educated, privileged minority, there is differentiation of a few "rewarded ones . . . who, for whatever reason, provide an edge to business in their specific field of activity: sometimes it has more to do with

image-making than with substance. This embodying of value-added induces an increasing disparity between a few, highly paid workers/collaborators/consultants, and a growing mass of individuals . . . who must usually accept the lowest common denominator of what the market offers them" (p. 135).

7. See Abu-Lughod, 1999; Betancur and Gills, 2000a; Clavel and Kleniewski, 1990; Ferman, 1996; Giloth and Weiwel, 1996; Squires, Bennet, McCourt, and Nyden, 1987; Weiwel and Nyden, 1991.

8. Lack of specificity about schools and individuals is necessary to protect anonymity.

Chapter 2

1. For example, Daley sponsored a city ordinance giving 25 percent of city contracts to minority contractors; several key Black business leaders are part of his inner circle; he has launched a few high-profile development projects in African American neighborhoods and supported a neighborhood industrial corridor redevelopment project.

2. Sanjek (1998, pp. 141–45) argues that in New York, global city discourse, rather than the reality of economic concentration, was used by financial and city-planning elites to promote development policies that favored the financial center and ignored neighborhoods.

3. The income gap between high- and low-income households in the Chicago region increased by 11 percent between 1999 and 2000, and there was an increase in child poverty during the same period (Metropolis Index, 2002). See Longworth (2002) on the growing gap between rich and poor in the city in the 2000 census.

4. In information processing sectors and some high-tech manufacturing, there is a simultaneous up-skilling and downgrading of labor. For example, although some clerical work requires greater information processing skills, it is often part-time and temporary. The same is true for robotized and high-tech manufacture, which requires many fewer workers than in the industrial era but workers with the education to program computers, troubleshoot, and solve problems in digitalized production processes. Despite increased demand for skills, many of these jobs do not offer the benefits and security of previously unionized industrial jobs.

5. See Wacquant and Wilson (1989) for an analysis of African American joblessness and economic exclusion in Chicago due to the process of spatial and economic restructuring of capitalism.

6. Rast (1999, p. 24) reports that medium and small manufacturers in and around the Loop (downtown) provided 115,000 jobs for Chicago residents in 1970, 23 percent of the city's total manufacturing jobs at the time.

7. According to Morenoff and Tienda (1997), in 1970, "transitional working class neighborhoods" were the most dominant neighborhood type in Chicago with 45 percent of census tracts, but by 1990 they comprised only 14 percent of all neighborhoods. The "yuppies" category doubled in the decade of the 1980s while "ghetto underclass" neighborhoods increased most from 3 percent of census tracts to 23 percent during the decade of the 1970s. These data do not reflect the displacement of low-income communities in the 1990s, but they demonstrate increased polarization.

8. Between 1990 and 1997, attendance at conventions and trade shows rose 61 percent (Podmolik, 1998).

9. In 1996, Congress mandated public housing authorities across the United States to conduct viability studies to determine whether existing units should be renovated or demolished. The Chicago Housing Authority (CHA), which had been on the U.S. Department of Housing and Urban Development (HUD) "troubled" list since 1979 and was taken over by HUD from 1995 to 1999, was found to have nineteen thousand nonviable units (Metropolitan Planning Council, 2002).

10. These included Designs for Change and Chicago Panel on Public School Policy and Finance.

11. These included People's Coalition for Educational Reform, United Neighborhood Organization (UNO), Hispanic Dropout Taskforce, Aspira, and other Latino/a grassroots groups.

12. This included Leadership for Quality Education and Chicago United, which grew out of the Commercial Club of Chicago.

13. Shipps, Kahne, and Smiley (1999) argue that both reforms were promoted by the city's business interests to stabilize and legitimize a failing, mismanaged school system; promote

economic growth; and improve school performance and achievement. They argue that business interests pushed the 1995 law to intensify the pace of reform.

14. Both laws reflect a transnational policy trend to devolve governance to the local school while further centralizing and regulating curriculum, instruction, and assessment (Apple, 2001; Ball, 1994; Coffey, 2001; Gillborn & Youdell, 2000; Whitty et al., 1998).

15. Some parent organization leaders believe that Leadership for Quality Education a business group, promotes special programs, such as the International Baccalaureate Program, and small schools and charter schools to undermines LSCs. (Parent organizer, personal communication, June 2002).

16. For example, a coalition of parents and school reformers has developed a proposal for multiple assessments of student progress, elimination of retention based on test scores, and community participation in school reform.

Chapter 3

1. Newman, Bryk, and Nagaoka define authentic intellectual work as assignments that demand higher-order thinking, in-depth understanding, elaborated communication, and connections with students' lives beyond school and that require students to apply, integrate, interpret, and analyze knowledge. They characterize basic skills instruction as memorization, drills, exercises, and tests that ask students to reproduce knowledge in the same form in which it was learned.

2. In 2002 there were eighty-one schools on probation (fifty-two elementary and twenty-nine high schools). Of these eighty-one schools, sixty-one had a student population that is at least 98 percent Black. Five schools had at least 84 percent "Hispanic" students, and most of the other students were identified as Black. The remaining fifteen schools were mixed Black and Hispanic. Seven of these fifteen schools with mixed populations had a student body that was at least 75 percent Black (CPS Office of Accountability, 2002).

3. The curriculum employs a strict hierarchy of skills and concepts (levels of lessons) and scripted questions and student responses that "leave(s) nothing to chance" (Kozloff, La-Nunziata, & Cowardin, 1999). Lessons are "quick paced" (Kozloff, et al.) with a single right answer that the whole group must master before the group can move on. The curriculum is based on a behaviorist model of learning. There does not appear to be room for student interpretation of text, culturally specific content, or connections with students' experiences.

4. A racial and economic breakdown by school is available on the Illinois Board of Education website at http://206.166.105.128/ReportCard/asps/

5. Teachers for Social Justice is a Chicago-area organization of primarily kindergarten to twelfth grade teachers committed to teaching that is antiracist, multicultural, projustice, participatory, and critical.

6. Haney found that during the 1990s when Texas implemented its high stakes Texas Assessment of Academic Skills, slightly less than 70 percent of students graduated from high school (one in three dropped out), and the racial gap in progression from ninth grade to graduation increased. By the time the ninth grade cohort entered twelfth grade, only about 50 percent of African American and Hispanic students graduated. There was also an increasing number of General Education Degree (GED) test takers below age twenty. (They are not counted as dropouts in Texas.)

7. Smith, Lee, and Neumann (2001) found that Chicago teachers most often used didactic instruction in low-achieving classes.

8. The CAS elaborates state standards; the CFS, more specific knowledge and skills. For example, CAS "E" for fifth grade science is "Analyze natural cycles, interactions, and patterns in the earth's land, water, and atmospheric systems." The first CFS under this standard is "Distinguish among evaporation, condensation, and precipitation phases of the water cycle" (Board of Education, 1997, pp. 4–6.)

9. CPS Office of Accountability lists forty-five direct instruction schools. This list varied slightly from 2000 to 2001. Implementation also varies among schools (Telephone and written communication and interviews, CPS officials, April 2000, January 2001, September 2001).

10. Uncategorized programs/schools include Elementary Magnet Clusters, Middle Years Prospective IB programs, Education to Career Clusters, International Language Academics, and Career Academies—all post-1995.

11. Map 2 shows two schools that are plus/minus; both have an ETC and an IB program.
12. Data on racial distribution by neighborhood are available from Northeastern Illinois Planning Commission at http://www.nipc.cog.il.us/. Housing prices and rental costs by neighborhood are available from City of Chicago, Department of Planning and Development at http://www.ci.chi.il.us/PlanAndDevelop/ChgoFacts
13. I use Allensworth and Rosenkranz's (2000) data and income classifications. They define median family income distribution as $0–$16,000, very-low-income; $16,000–$29,000 low-income; $29,000–$55,000 middle-income; $55,000–$151,000 upper-income. See Allensworth and Rosenkranz, pp. 26–27 for maps of median family income and race by region.
14. These calculations are based on data supplied by a CPS official (personal communication, February 2003).
15. These include International Baccalaureate, advanced placement, and honors courses.
16. The exact number of DI schools that employ DI schoolwide is not available, but schoolwide programs are the central office goal (Personal communication, CPS administrator, September 2001).
17. There are various explanations. Some sources in CPS claim the MSTAs were the brainchild of a few top administrators, and they were dropped when the administrators left their positions.
18. After three years of litigation, the Supreme Court declared the law unconstitutional in 1999. In 2000 the city government passed a new version limiting police actions to designated "hot spots." This designation allows police to continue legalized harassment and street sweeps of youth in specific neighborhoods.
19. A survey of sixty-eight top Chicago business leaders in 1988 also pointed to a poorly educated workforce as a prime reason for business loss (Mirel, 1993).

Chapter 4

1. Hamilton, quoted in Haymes (1995, p. 18).
2. Citywide, nineteen thousand CHA units are in the process of demolition.
3. I do not cite sources here because to do so would jeopardize the anonymity of the schools and their location.
4. HUD vouchers are used to obtain subsidized rent in privately owned apartments.
5. The state standardized test when I began my research in 1997 was the Illinois Goals Achievement Program (IGAP). In 1999, the state shifted to the Illinois State Achievement Test (ISAT).
6. Students who failed to meet the district's cut off score on the ITBS at benchmark grades (3, 6, 8) were required to attend summer school and could be retained in their grade.
7. See Coffey (2001) for a summary of similar inspections of failing schools in Britain.
8. The "scribble" was part of a reading lesson integrating graphic arts that was an ongoing project in this classroom in collaboration with a local artist.
9. Mumia Abu Jamal is an African American political activist and journalist on death row in Pennsylvania, convicted of killing a police officer. His case has become an international rallying point against the death penalty and unjust incarceration of African Americans. As part of a class project, the students had read about the case in the *Chicago Defender*, a venerable African American newspaper,
10. The proposal, the New ERA plan, calls for multiple assessments of student progress, elimination of retention based on test scores, and community participation in school reform.

Chapter 5

1. We use the term *Mexican* (instead of Mexican-American) because that is the way people generally refer to themselves in the community.
2. A pseudonym.
3. The 2002–3 CPS promotion policy stipulates that eighth-grade students must score at the 35th percentile on both mathematics and reading on the ITBS in order to graduate. Those students scoring between the 24th and 34th percentiles are evaluated by grades, attendance, homework completion, and behavior and may have to attend mandatory summer school; however, they can participate in spring graduation ceremonies. Students scoring below the 24th percentile cannot participate in spring graduation. For this latter group, there is an

August graduation ceremony by region for those who pass the ITBS at the end of summer school and who also pass and regularly attend the summer school program.

4. In Chicago, many teachers who have proficiency in a second language but no teaching qualifications are teaching bilingual classes under emergency certification.

5. The 1989 Standards focused on four core processes of mathematics: solving realistic and real-world, meaningful problems; using reasoning, proof, and justifications; communicating mathematical ideas to others via multiple representations including drawings and written and spoken language; and making connections between different mathematical domains, between mathematics and other school subjects, and to real-world contexts. The NCTM published the *Principles and Standards for School Mathematics* (National Council, 2000) as an update and synthesis of the previous volumes.

6. A major finding of the *Third International Mathematics and Science Study* (Schmidt, McKnight, & Raizen, 1997) is that traditional middle-school mathematics curricula in the United States are "a mile wide and an inch deep." Curricula like Meaningful Mathematics, based on the NCTM Standards (1989), do not necessarily cover the same material as the ITBS, but they go into much greater depth.

7. For example, MM starts algebra in the fifth grade (and at Brewer, teachers used it in the fourth), whereas the new curriculum does not start algebra until the seventh and also includes more practice in computation problems.

8. Principals may, at their discretion, grant individual students extensions of up to two years. However, CPS's public presentation of the policy is "three years and out" (personal communication, Brewer bilingual coordinator, November 2002).

9. Ironically, the CPS bilingual education policy also supports "dual language" by requiring two years of world language for all high school students while negating the language resources of thousands of students whose first language is not English.

10. For example, at Grover I was asked to pose for a photo after a meeting so the school could include it in its "documentation" of involvement with external agencies. At that school, the quality review consisted of administrators' putting together a portfolio of documents.

11. For example, the data indicated strong parental support for their children's education through nearly 100 percent compliance with the school's uniform policy, extraordinarily high attendance rates, and 98 percent family participation in the school's report card pickup. These data led to an examination of the assumption that parents "didn't care about their children's education." It also gave voice to previously silenced perspectives of Mexican teachers on this issue.

Chapter 6

1. Students get points for each DIR book they complete, and these points accumulate toward their language arts grade. Some teachers complained that DIR prompts students to read just for the extrinsic reward. They also pointed out that DIR is good for reluctant readers, but for students really engaged in reading, it is largely irrelevant.

2. I deliberately leave grade levels vague to protect anonymity.

3. Mastery Learning breaks up subject matter into small learning units. Students must master each unit, as indicated by a unit test, before proceeding to the next unit.

4. Northside College Prep High School, for example, uses a conceptually based mathematics curriculum exclusively; Whitney Young Magnet High School has won waivers from the board exempting it from the requirement that the standard standardized CASE exam constitute one-quarter of a student's final grade. The International Baccalaureate programs have their own curriculum.

5. Teachers attributed this to the changed format of the ITBS in third grade and the fact that third grade is the first year that the test is high stakes for students, for example, that they are required to attend summer school and potentially are retained if they fail it. Third grade is also the first time students have to read the test questions themselves; teachers read the test questions to first and second graders.

6. This is not unwarranted paranoia. In several schools, public LSC disputes have been the grounds for central administrators to declare the LSC dysfunctional and to dissolve or reconstitute it.

7. The research on effects of class size on student achievement is quite definitive. See, for example, Nye, Hedges, and Konstantopoulos (2000).

Chapter 7

1. This agenda has a long history, going back to the free market proposals of Milton Friedman (1962), Chubb and Moe's (1990) argument for the introduction of market forces and school choice, *A Nation at Risk* (National Commission, 1983), and the business-centered reforms advocated under President Reagan.
2. New York's Board of Education mandated a standard curriculum for all its 1,291 schools but then exempted 208, five-sixths of which are in middle- or upper-income neighborhoods (Hoff, 2003).
3. Racism is deeply entrenched in Brazilian society and in schooling, but one hopeful development is the initiative of the municipal education department (SMED) racial justice working group to make racism visible through the Citizen Schools (personal communication, SMED official, July 2003).

Methodological Appendix

1. I was assisted by Lori Huebner.
2. We conducted a total of thirteen teacher interviews in 1997–98, twenty in 1998–99, eight in 1999–2000, fourteen in 2000–1. Some were repeat interviews of the same teachers, others of new teachers. These were in addition to informal conversations with teachers across the schools.
3. Students in these grades who score below a certain "cut score" on the Iowa Test of Basic Skills must attend summer school. If they fail the test in summer school they must repeat the grade.
4. I made these observations in conjunction with the larger study, which utilized a structured protocol. My own notes utilized more ethnographic methods.
5. Our research assistant must remain anonymous to protect the anonymity of the school.
6. Variation in research plans and degree of teacher collaboration reflects the different conditions under which I studied each of the schools. Grover and Westview studies were partly shaped by my participation in a large research project. Variations also reflect specific issues posed by the schools; e.g., issues of culture and language were very prominent at Brewer and shaped that study.

REFERENCES

Abu-Lughod, J. L. (1999). *New York, Chicago, Los Angeles: America's global cities*. Minneapolis: University of Minnesota Press.

Allen, L. J., & Richards, C. (1999, February 9). Boomtown. *Chicago Tribune*, Sec. 1, pp. 1, 8.

Allensworth, E. M., & Easton, J. Q. (2001). Calculating a cohort dropout rate for the Chicago public schools: A technical report. Chicago: Consortium on Chicago School Research

Allensworth, E. M., & Rosenkranz, T. (2000). *Access to magnet schools in Chicago*. Chicago: Consortium on Chicago School Research and Mexican American Legal Defense and Education Fund.

Anderson, J. D. (1988). *The education of blacks in the South, 1860–1935*. Chapel Hill: University of North Carolina Press.

Anyon, J. (1997). *Ghetto schooling*. New York: Teachers College Press.

Apple, M. W. (1988). *Teachers and texts: A political economy of class and gender relations in education*. New York: Routledge.

Apple, M. W. (1991). Conservative agendas and progressive possibilities: Understanding the wider politics of curriculum and teaching. *Education and Urban Society, 23*(3), 279–291.

Apple, M. W. (1996). *Cultural politics and education*. New York: Teachers College Press.

Apple, M. W. (2001). *Educating the "right way."* New York: Routledge.

Apple, M. W., & Beane, J. A. (Eds.). (1995). *Democratic schools*. Alexandria, VA: Association for Supervision and Curriculum Development.

Apple, M. W. et al. (2003). *The state and the politics of knowledge*. New York: Routledge.

Ball, S. J. (1990). *Politics and policy making in education*. London: Routledge.

Ball, S. J. (1994). *Education reform: A critical and post-structural approach*. Buckingham, England: Open University Press.

Ball, S. J. (1997a). Good school/bad school: Paradox and fabrication. *British Journal of Sociology of Education, 18*(3): 317–336.

Ball, S. J. (1997b). Policy sociology and critical social research: A personal review of recent education policy and policy research. *British Educational Research Journal, 23*, 257–274.

Bartlett, L., & Lutz, C. (1998). Disciplining social difference: Some cultural politics of military training in public high schools. *The Urban Review, 30*, 119–136.

Bartolome, L. I. (1994). Beyond the methods fetish: Toward a humanizing pedagogy. *Harvard Educational Review, 64*, 173–194

Becker, W. (1977/2001). Teaching reading and language to the disadvantaged. Reprinted in *Journal of Direct Instruction, 1*(1), 31–52.

Betancur, J. J., Cordova, T., & de los Angeles Torres, M. (1993). In R. Morales & F. Bonilla (Eds.), *Latinos in a changing U.S. economy* (pp. 109–132). Newbury Park, CA: Sage.

Betancur, J. J., & Gills, D. C. (2000a). The restructuring of urban relations. In J. J. Betancur & D. C. Gills (Eds.), *The collaborative city: Opportunities and struggles for Blacks and Latinos in U.S. cities* (pp. 17–40). New York: Garland.

Betancur, J. J., & Gills, D. C. (2000b). The African American and Latino coalition experience in Chicago under Mayor Harold Washington. In J. J. Betancur & D. C. Gills (Eds.), *The collaborative city: Opportunities and struggles for Blacks and Latinos in U.S. cities* (pp. 59–87). New York: Garland.

Bettis, P. J. (1994). Deindustrialization and urban schools: Some theoretical considerations. *Urban Review, 26*, 75–94.

Bigelow, B., & Peterson, B. (Eds.). (1998). *Rethinking Columbus: The next 500 years.* Milwaukee: Rethinking Schools.

Bigelow, B., & Peterson, B. (Eds.). (2002). *Rethinking globalization: Teaching for justice in an unjust world.* Milwaukee: Rethinking Schools.

Blackmore, J. (2000). Warning signals or dangerous opportunities? Globalization, gender, and educational policy shifts. *Education Theory, 50*(4), 467–486.

Board of Education of the City of Chicago. (1997). *Expecting more: Chicago academic standards and frameworks.* Chicago: Author.

Board of Education of the City of Chicago. (n.d.). *Education Opportunities in Chicago Public Schools 2000.* Chicago: Author.

Bohn, A. P., & Sleeter, C. E. (2000). Multicultural education and the standards movement. *Phi Delta Kappan, 82*(2), 156–159.

Bonilla, F. & Morales, R. (1993). Critical theory and policy in an era of ethnic diversity: Economic interdependence and growing inequality. In Morales, R. & Bonilla, F. (Eds.), *Latinos in a changing U.S. economy* (pp. 226–240). Newbury Park, CA: Sage Publications.

Bryk, A. S., Sebring, P. B., Kerbow, D., Rollow, S., & Easton, J. Q. (1998). *Charting Chicago school reform: Democratic localism as a lever for change.* Boulder, CO: Westview Press.

Bryk, A. S., Thum, Y. M., Easton, J. Q., & Luppescu, S. (1998). *Academic productivity of Chicago public elementary schools.* Chicago: Consortium on Chicago School Research.

Burbules, N. C., & Torres, C. A. (2000). Globalization and education: An introduction. In N. C. Burbules & C. A. Torres (Eds.), *Globalization and education: Critical perspectives* (pp. 1–26). New York: Routledge.

Carlson, D. (1996). Education as a political issue: What's missing in the public conversation about education? In J. L. Kincheloe & S. R. Steinberg (Eds.), *Thirteen questions: Reframing education's conversatio*, (2nd ed., pp. 281–91) New York: Peter Lang.

Carlson, D. (1997). *Making progress: Education and culture in new times.* New York: Teachers College Press.

Castells, M. (1989). *The informational city.* London: Blackwell.

Castells, M. (1996). *The rise of the network society.* London: Blackwell.

Castells, M. (1998). *End of the millennium.* London: Blackwell.

Catalyst: Voices of Chicago school reform. (1990, February), *1* (1). Chicago: Community Renewal Society.

Catalyst: Voices of Chicago school reform. (1991, June), *2* (9). Chicago: Community Renewal Society.

Catalyst: Voices of Chicago school reform. (2000, December), *12*(4). Chicago: Community Renewal Society.

Catholic Charities of the Archdiocese of Chicago. (1999). *The housing crisis in our neighborhoods.* Chicago: Author.

Census 2000: General profiles for the 77 Chicago community areas. (2002). Northeastern Illinois Planning Commission. Retrieved August 15, 2002 from http://www.nipc.cog.il.us/

Central Area Plan to help guide downtown growth. (2002, July 2). City of Chicago, Department of Planning and Development. Retrieved September 5, 2002 from http://www.ci.chi.il.us/PlanAndDev . . . PressReleases/centralareaplan.html

Chicago Public Schools Announce Major Initiative to Close Low-Performing Schools (2002, April 10). [Press Release] Retrieved November 29, 2002 from http//www.cps.k12.il.us/AboutCPS/PressReleases/April_2002

Chomsky, N. (1999). *Profit over people: Neoliberalism and global order.* New York: Seven Stories Press.

Christensen, L. (2000). *Reading, writing, and rising up: Teaching about social justice and the power of the written word.* Milwaukee: Rethinking Schools.

Chubb, J. M. & Moe, T. E. (1990). *Politics, markets, and America's schools.* Washington, D.C.: Brookings Institution.

City of Chicago, Department of Planning and Development (2002). *Chicago fact book: Housing.* Retrieved February 6, 2002 from http://www.ci.chi.il.us/PlanAndDevelop/ChgoFacts

Clavel, P. , & Kleniewski, N. (1990). Space for progressive local policy: Examples from the United States and the United Kingdom. In J. R. Logan & T. Swanstrom (Eds.), *Beyond the city limits: Urban policy and economic restructuring in comparative perspective* (pp. 199–234). Philadelphia: Temple University Press.

Coates, K. (Ed.). (2002). A better world is possible. *The Spokesman, 74.*

Cochran-Smith, M. (1995). Uncertain allies: Understanding the boundaries of race and teaching. *Harvard Educational Review, 65* (4), 541–570.

Coffey, A. (2001). *Education and social change.* Buckingham, England: Open University Press.

Commercial Club of Chicago. (1973). *Chicago 21: A plan for the central area communities.* Chicago: Author.

Commercial Club of Chicago. (1984). *Make no little plans: Jobs for metropolitan Chicago.* Chicago: Author.

Commercial Club of Chicago. (1990, August). *Jobs for metropolitan Chicago—an update.* Chicago: Author.

Community Renewal Society. (2002). Conference. Injustice in Brick and Mortar: A Crisis in Affordable and Public Housing. Chicago, November 9.

CPS Office of Accountability. (2002). Schools on academic probation fiscal year 2001–2002. Retrieved October 1, 2002, from http://acct.multi1.cps.k12.il.us/probationfy02.html

CPS promotes retained students. (1999, January 22). [Press release]. Chicago Public Schools.

Cummins, J. (1986). Empowering minority students: A framework for intervention. *Harvard Educational Review, 56*(1), 18–36.

Cummins, J. (1996). *Negotiating identities: Education for empowerment in a diverse society.* Ontario, CA: California Association for Bilingual Education.

Cummins, J. (2000). *Language, power and pedagogy.* Clevedon, England: Multilingual Matters.

Danns, D. (2002). Black student empowerment in Chicago: School reform efforts in 1968. *Urban Education, 37*(5), 631–655.

Darder, A. (1995). Buscando America: The contribution of critical Latino educators to the academic development and empowerment of Latino students in the U.S. In C. E. Sleeter & P. L. McLaren (Eds.), *Multicultural education, critical pedagogy, and the politics of difference* (pp. 319–348). Albany, NY: SUNY Press.

Davis, M. (2001). *Magical urbanism: Latinos reinvent the U.S. city.* London: Verso.

Deerin, M. M. (2001). Schools put individual stamp on dual language. *Catalyst, 12*(3), 10–11.

Delgado, R., & Stefancic, J. (2001). *Critical race theory.* New York: New York University Press.

Delpit, L. (1988). The silenced dialogue: Power and pedagogy in educating other people's children. *Harvard Educational Review, 58,* 280–298.

Delpit, L. D. (1992a). Acquisition of literate discourse: Bowing before the master? *Theory into Practice, 31,* 296–302.

Delpit, L. D. (1992b). Education in a multicultural society: Our future's greatest challenge. *Journal of Negro Education, 61,* 237–249.

Designs for Change. (1999, December). *Comment on ending social promotion: The first two years.* Chicago: Author.

Duffrin, E. (1999a). Classes revolve around test prep. *Catalyst, 10*(6), 9–11.

Duffrin, E. (1999b). Transition centers: Services praised, instruction questioned, results withheld. *Catalyst, 10*(6)(1), 4–8.

Easton, J. Q. Rosenkranz, T., Bryk, A. S., Jacob, B. A., Luppescu, S., & Roderick, M. (2000). *Annual CPS test trend review, 1999.* Research Data Brief. Chicago: Consortium on Chicago School Research.

Emerson, R., Fretz, R., & Shaw, L. (1995). *Writing ethnographic fieldnotes.* Chicago: University of Chicago Press.

English as a Second Language Goals and Standards (1998). Chicago: Chicago Board of Education.

Every child, every school: An education plan for the Chicago public schools. (2002, September). Chicago: Chicago Public Schools.

Fair Test Examiner. Cambridge, MA: National Center for Fair and Open Testing.

Feagin, J. R. (1998). *The New urban paradigm: Critical perspectives on the city.* Lanham, MD: Roman & Littlefield.

Feagin, J. R., & Smith, M. P. (1987). Cities and the new international division of labor: An overview. In M. R. Smith & J. R. Feagin (Eds.), *The capitalist city: Global restructuring and community politics* (pp. 3–34). Oxford, England: Basil Blackwell.

Ferguson, A. A. (2000). *Bad boys: Public schools in the making of Black masculinity.* Ann Arbor: University of Michigan Press.

Ferman, B. (1996). *Challenging the growth machine.* Lawrence: University of Kansas Press.

Fine, M. (1993). [Ap]parent involvement: Reflections on parents, power, and urban public schools. *Teachers College Record, 94*(4), 682–710.

Flecha, R. (1999). New educational inequalities. In M. Castells et al. (Eds.), *Critical Education in the New Information Age* (pp. 65–82). Lanham, MD: Rowman & Littlefield.

Foster, M. (1997). *Black teachers on teaching.* New York: New Press.

Foucault, M. (1995/1977). *Discipline and punish: The birth of the prison* (Trans. Alan Sheridan). New York: Vintage Books.

Franke, M., Fennema, E., & Carpenter, T. P. (1997). Changing teachers: Interactions between beliefs and classroom practices. In E. Fennema & B. Scott Nelson (Eds.), *Mathematics teachers in transition* (pp. 255–282). Mahway, NJ: Erlbaum Press.

Fraser, N, (1997). *Justice interruptus: Critical reflections on the "postsocialist" condition.* New York: Routledge.

Freire, P. (1970/94). *Pedagogy of the oppressed* (Trans. M. B. Ramos). New York: Continuum.

Freire, P., & Faundez, A. (1989). *Learning to question: A pedagogy of liberation.* New York: Continuum.

Freire, P., & Macedo, D. (1987). *Literacy: Reading the word and the world.* Westport, CT: Bergin & Garvey.

Friedman, M. (1962). *Capitalism and Freedom.* Chicago: University of Chicago Press.

Gabbard, D. A. (Ed.). (2000). *Knowledge and power in the global economy: Politics and rhetoric of school reform.* Mahwah, NJ: Lawrence Erlbaum.

Gandin, L. A. (2002). *Democratizing access, governance, and knowledge: The struggle for educational alternatives in Porto Alegre, Brazil.* Unpublished doctoral dissertation, University of Wisconsin, Madison.

Gandin, L. A., & Apple, M. W. (2003). Educating the state, democratizing knowledge: The Citizen School Project in Porto Alegre, Brazil. In M. W. Apple, *The state and the politics of knowledge* (pp. 193–219). New York: Routledge.

Garcia, E. E. (1995). Educating Mexican American students: Past treatments and recent developments in theory, research, policy, and practice. In J. A. Banks & C. A. M. Banks (Eds.), *Handbook of research on multicultural education* (pp. 372–388). New York: Macmillan.

Gee, J. P., Hull, G., & Lankshear, C. (1996). *The new work order: Behind the language of the new capitalism.* Boulder, CO: Westview Press.

Generation Y. (2001). Right to learn campaign. Retrieved December 5, 2001 from http://www.pureparents.org/pencil.html

Generation Y. (2002). *Higher learning: A report on educational inequities and opportunities facing public high school students in Chicago.* Chicago: Generation Y.

Gewertz, C. (2002, October 9). More Chicago pupils flunk grade. *Education Week, XXII*(6), 1, 13.

Gill, S. (2003). *Power and resistance in the new world order.* New York: Palgrave Macmillan.

Gillborn, D., & Youdell, D. (2000). *Rationing education: Policy, practice, reform, and equity.* Buckingham, England: Open University Press.

Gilmore, P. (1985). "Gimme room": School resistance, attitude, and access to literacy. *Journal of Education, 167*(1), 111–128.

Giloth, W., & Mier, R. (1989). Spatial change and social justice: Alternative economic development in Chicago. In R. A. Beauregard (Ed.), *Economic restructuring and political response.* Urban Affairs Annual Reviews (Vol. 34, pp. 181–208). Newberry Park, CA: Sage.

Giloth, W., & Weiwel, W. (1996). Equity development in Chicago: Robert Mier's ideas and practice. *Economic Development Quarterly, 10,* 204–206.

Giroux, H. A. (1983). *Theory and resistance in education.* New York: Bergin & Garvey.

Giroux, H. A. (1988). *Schooling and the struggle for public life.* Minneapolis, MN: University of Minnesota Press.

Giroux, H. (2002). Democracy, freedom, and justice after September 11th: Rethinking the role of education and the politics of schooling. *Teachers College Record.* Retrieved March 2, 2003, from http://www.tcrecord.org/Content.asp?ContentID=10871

Goldberg, D. T. (1993). "Polluting the body politic": Racist discourse and urban location. In M. Cross & M. Keith (Eds.), *Racism, the city and the state* (pp. 45–60). London: Routledge.

Grace, G. (1984). Urban education: Policy science or critical scholarship. In G. Grace (Ed.), *Education and the city: Theory, history and contemporary practice* (pp. 3–59). London: Routledge & Kegan Paul.

Grace, G. (1994). Urban education and the culture of contentment: The politics, culture, and economics of inner-city schooling. In N. P. Stromquist (Ed.), *Education in urban areas: Cross-national dimensions.* Westport, CT: Praeger.

Gramsci, A. (1971). *Selections from the prison notebooks.* New York: International Publishers.

Gusfield, J. R. (1986). *The symbolic crusade* (2nd ed). Urbana: University of Illinois Press.

Gutstein, E. (1999). Untitled. Unpublished manuscript.

Gutstein, E. (2001). *Consequences of Chicago school policy for Latino students and their teachers: One school's story.* Presentation at the Annual Meeting of the American Educational Research Association, Seattle, WA.

Gutstein, E. (2003). Teaching and learning mathematics for social justice in an urban, Latino school. *Journal for Research in Mathematics Education, 34*(1), 37–73.

Hammersley, M., & Atkinson, P. (1995). *Ethnography* (2nd ed.). New York: Routledge.

Haney, W. (2000). The myth of the Texas miracle in education. *Education Policy Analysis Archives, 8* (41). Retrieved January 26, 2001 from http://epaa.asu.edu/epaa/v8n41/

Haney, S., & Shiller, B. (1997, May 16–31). Cabrini redevelopment: It's here! *Streetwise,* pp. 3, 8.

Harvey, D. (1973). *Social justice and the city.* Baltimore: Johns Hopkins University Press.

Hauser, R. (1999). On "ending social promotion" in Chicago. In D. Moore, Comment on Ending social promotion: The first two years, Attachment B. Chicago: Designs for Change.

Haymes, S. N. (1995). *Race, culture and the city.* Albany: State University of New York Press.

Haymes, S. N. (1996). Educational reform: What have been the effects of attempts to improve education over the last decade? In J. L. Kincheloe & S. R. Steinberg, (Eds.). *Thirteen questions: Reframing education's conversation* (2nd ed., pp. 239–250). New York: Peter Lang.

Hess, G. A. (1991). *School restructuring Chicago style.* Newbury Park, CA: Corwin Press.

Heubert, J. P., & Hauser, R. M. (Eds.) (1999). *High stakes: Testing for tracking, promotion, and graduation.* Washington, DC: National Research Council, National Academy Press.

Hiebert, J., & Carpenter, T. P. (1992). Learning and teaching with understanding. In D. A. Grouws (Ed.), *Handbook of research on mathematics teaching and learning* (pp. 65–97). New York: Macmillan.

High court is the final chapter in gang ordinance controversy. (1998, September). *Chicago Reporter.* Retrieved August 21, 2001 from http://.www.chicagoreporter.com/1998/09/0998court.htm

Higher learning. (2002, October). Generation Y: Youth Activist Organization. Chicago, IL.

Hoff, D. J. (2003, March 9). Complaints pour in over NYC curriculum exemptions. *Education Week.* Retrieved March 14, 2003, from http://www.edweek.org

Homel, M. W. (1984). *Down from equality: Black Chicagoans and the public schools, 1920–41.* Urbana: University of Illinois Press.

Hursh, David. 2001. Neoliberalism and the Control of Teachers, Students, and Learning. *Cultural Logic, 4*(1). Retrieved November 16, 2001 from http://eserver.org/clogic/4-1/4-1.html

Illinois state school report cards (2002). Retrieved December 10, 2002 from http://statereportcards.cps.k12.il.us/

Irvine, J. J. (1991). *Black students and school failure: Policies, practices, and prescriptions.* New York: Praeger.

Johnson, D. (2002, January 21). High school at attention. *Newsweek.* Retrieved January 25, 2002 from http://www.msnbc.com/news/686928.asp?cp1=1

Johnson, E. (1998, November). *Chicago metropolis 2020: Preparing metropolitan Chicago for the 21st century: Executive summary.* Chicago: Commercial Club of Chicago.

Jones, P. W. (2000). Globalization and internationalism: Democratic prospects for world education. In N. P. Stromquist & K. Monkman, (Eds.), *Globalization and education.* Lanham, MD: Rowman & Littlefield.

Joseph, L. B. (1990). *Creating jobs, creating workers: Economic development and employment in metropolitan Chicago.* Champaign: University of Illinois Press.

Kantor, M. B., & Brenzel, B. (1993). Urban education and the "truly disadvantaged": The historical roots of the contemporary crisis, 1945–1990. In M. B. Katz (Ed.), *The underclass debate: Views from history* (pp. 366–402). Princeton, NJ: Princeton University Press.

Katz, B., & Nguyen, D. (1998). A rise in downtown living. Washington, DC: The Brookings Institution. Retrieved March 4, 2000 from http://www.brook.edu/ES/urban/publications.htm.

Katz, M. B. (1992). Chicago school reform as history. *Teachers College Record, 94*(1), 56–72.

Katz, M. B. (2001). *The Price of Citizenship.* New York: Metropolitan Books.

Katz, M. B. Fine, M., & Simon, E. (1997). Poking around: Outsiders view Chicago school reform. *Teachers College Record, 99*(1), 117–157.

Keith, M. (1993). From punishment to discipline? Racism, racialization, and the policing of social control. In M. Cross & M. Keith (Eds.), *Racism, the city and the state* (pp. 193–209). London: Routledge.

King, J. E. (1991). Unfinished business: Black student alienation and Black teachers' emancipatory pedagogy. In M. Foster (Ed.), *Readings in equal education: Qualitative investigations into schools and schooling* (Vol. 11, pp. 245–271). New York: AMS Press.

King, J. E. (1992). Dysconscious racism: Ideology, identity, and the miseducation of teachers. *Journal of Negro Education, 60*, 133–146.

Korten, D. C. (1995). *When corporations rule the world.* West Hanford, CT: Kumarian Press.

Kozloff, M. A., LaNunziata, L., Cowardin, J. (1999). Direct instruction in education. Retrieved October 18, 2001 from http://www.uncwil.edu/people/kozloffm/diarticle.html

Kozol, J. (1992). *Savage inequalities.* New York: Perennial.

Krashen, S. (1996). *Under attack: The case against bilingual education.* Culver City, CA: Language Education Associates.

Kyle, C. L., & Kantowicz, E. R. (1992). *Kids first—primero los niños: Chicago school reform in the 1980s.* Springfield, IL: Sangamon State University.

Ladson-Billings, G. (1994). *Dreamkeepers: Successful teachers of African American students.* San Francisco: Jossey Bass.

Ladson-Billings, G. (1997). I know why this doesn't feel empowering: A critical race analysis of critical pedagogy. In P. Freire (Ed.), *Mentoring the mentor: A critical dialogue with Paulo Freire* (pp. 127–141). New York: Peter Lang.

Ladson, Billings, G. (1999). Just what is critical race theory and what's it doing in a *nice* field like education? In L. Parker, D. Deyhle, & S. Villenas (Eds.), *Race is, race isn't: Critical race theory and qualitative studies in Education* (pp. 7–30). Boulder, CO: Westveiw Press.

Ladson-Billings, G. (2000). Racialized discourses and ethnic epistemologies. In N. Denzin & Y. K. Lincoln (Eds.), *Handbook of qualitative research* (pp. 257–277). Thousand Oaks, CA: Sage.

Ladson-Billings, G. (2001). *Crossing over to Canaan: The journey of new teachers in diverse classrooms.* San Francisco: Jossey Bass.

Language and cultural education initiatives. (1998). Chicago Public Schools, Department of Language and Cultural Education. Retrieved December 18, 2002, from http://www.cps.k12.il.us/AboutCPS/Departments/LanguageCulture

Lewis, D. A., & Nakagawa, K. (1995). *Race and educational reform in the American metropolis: A study of decentralization.* Albany: State University of New York Press.

Lewis, L. (1997, September). Law, policy changes dilute LSC power. *Catalyst, 9* (1). Community Renewal Society. Retrieved September 3, 2001 from http://www.catalyst-chicago.org/09–97/097law.htm

Lingard, B., & Rizvi, F. (Eds.) (2000). A symposium on globalization and education: Complexities and contingencies. *Education Theory, 50,* 4.

Lipman, P. (1998). *Race, class, and power in school restructuring.* Albany: State University of New York Press.

Lipman, P. (2000, November). *Chicago school policy at ground level: Implications for equity and agency in the new urban economy.* Paper presented at the annual meeting of the American Anthropology Association, San Francisco, CA.

Lipman, P. (2001a). Bush's education plan, globalization, and the politics of race. *Cultural Logic, 4,* 1. Retrieved November 16, 2001 from http://eserver.org/clogic/41/4–1.html

Lipman, P. (2001, April). *The politics of Chicago school policy and emerging resistance.* Paper presented at the Annual meeting of the American Education Research Association, Seattle, WA.

Lipman, P. (2002). Making the global city, making inequality. Political economy and cultural politics of Chicago school policy. *American Educational Research Journal, 39*(2), 379–419.

Lipman, P. (2003). Cracking down: Chicago school policy and the regulation of black and Latino/a youth. In D. Gabbard & K. L. Saltman (Eds.), *Education as enforcement* (pp. 81–101). New York: Routledge.

Lipman, P., & Gutstein, E. (2001). Undermining the struggle for equity: A case study of Chicago school policy in a Latino/a school. *Race, Gender, and Class, 8*(1), 57–80.

Logan, J. R., & Molotch, H. L. (1987). *Urban fortunes: The political economy of place.* Berkeley: University of California Press.

Logan, J. R., & Swanstrom, T. (Eds.). (1990). *Beyond the city limits.* Philadelphia: Temple University Press.

Longworth, R. C. (2002, August 25). Chicago has entered the global era. *Chicago Tribune,* Sec. 2, pp. 1,8.

Longworth, R. C., & Burns, G. (1999, February 7). Progress, trouble on economic front. *Chicago Tribune,* pp. A1, 14–15.

LSC Summit. (2000). *The new ERA plan.* Chicago: Author. Contact: Parents United for Responsible Education. Retrieved October 21, 2000 from http://www.pureparents.org

Macedo, D. (1994). *Literacies of power: What Americans are not allowed to know.* Boulder, CO: Westview Press.

Mander, J., & Goldsmith, E. (Eds.). (1996). *The case against the global economy.* San Francisco: Sierra Club Books.

Martinez, M. (1999, March 19). New magnet school race goals face US query. *Chicago Tribune,* Sec. 2, pp. 1–2.

McLaren, P. (1999). Traumatizing capital: Oppositional pedagogies in the age of consent. In M. Castells et al. (Eds.), *Critical education in the new information age* (pp. 1–36). Lanham, MD: Rowman & Littlefield.

McNeil, L. M. (2000). *Contradictions of school reform: Educational costs of standardized testing.* New York: Routledge.

McNeil, L. M. (2002). Private asset or public good: Education and democracy at the crossroads (Editor's introduction). *American Educational Research Journal 39*(2), 243–248.

Mendell, D., & Little, D. (2002, August 20). Rich 90's failed to lift all: Income disparity between races widened greatly, census analysis shows. *Chicago Tribune.* Retrieved January 18, 2003, from http://www.chicagotribune.com/news/showcase/chi-0208200185aug20,1,3880199. story

Metropolis Index. (2002). Chicago: Chicago Metropolis 2020.

Metropolitan Planning Council. (2002, February). *Public housing in the public interest,* MPC Fact Sheet #3. Retrieved October 20, 2002, from http://www.metroplanning.org

Mickelson, R. A. (Ed.). (2000). Children on the streets of the Americas: Globalization, homelessness and education in the United States, Brazil and Cuba. London: Routledge.

Mickelson, R. A., Ray, C., & Smith, S. (1994). The growth machine and the politics of urban educational reform: The case of Charlotte, North Carolina. In N. P. Stromquist (Ed.), *Education in urban areas: Cross-national dimensions.* Westport, CT: Praeger.

Mills, C. W. (1997). *The racial contract.* Ithaca, NY: Cornell University Press.

Miner, B. (1997, Fall). Embracing Ebonics and teaching standard English: An interview with Oakland teacher Carrie Secret. *Rethinking Schools, 12*(1), 18–19, 34.

Mirel, J. (1993). School reform Chicago style: educational innovation in a changing urban context, 1976–1991. *Urban Education, 28,* 116–149.

Moberg, D. (1997). Chicago: To be or not to be a global city. *World Policy Journal, 14,* 71–86.

Moll, L. C., Amanti, C., Neff, D., & Gonzalez, N. (1992). Funds of knowledge for teaching: Using a qualitative approach to connect homes and classrooms. *Theory into Practice, 31*(2), 132–141.

Morales, F., & Bonilla, R. (1993). Critical theory and policy in an era of ethnic diversity: Economic interdependence and growing inequality. In R. Morales and F. Bonilla (Eds.), *Latinos in a changing U.S. economy* (pp. 226–240). Newbury Park: Sage.

Morenoff, J. D., & Tienda, M. (1997). Underclass neighborhoods in temporal and ecological perspective. *Annals, AAPSS, 551,* 59–136.

Morrow, R. A., & Torres, C. A. (2000). The state, globalization, and educational policy. In N. C. Burbules & C. A. Torres (Eds.). *Globalization and education: Critical perspectives* (pp. 27–56). New York: Routledge.

Murnane, R. J., & Levy, F. (1996). *Teaching the new basic skills.* New York: The Free Press.

Murrell, P. C., Jr. (1997). Digging again the family wells: A Freirian literacy framework for emancipatory pedagogy for African American children. In P. Freire (Ed.), *Mentoring the mentor: A critical dialogue with Paulo Freire* (pp. 19–58). New York: Peter Lang.

National Center on Education and the Economy. (1990). *America's choice: High skills or low wages.* Rochester, NY: Author.

National Center for Research in Mathematical Sciences Education and Freudenthal Institute. (1997–1998). *Mathematics in context: A connected curriculum for grades 5–8.* Chicago: Encyclopedia Britannica Educational Corporation.

National Commission on Excellence in Education. (1983). *A nation at risk: The imperative for educational reform.* Washington, DC: Government Printing Office.

National Council of La Raza. (1990). *Hispanic education: A statistical portrait, 1990.* [Prepared by Denise de la Rosa and Carlyle E. Maw.] Washington, DC: Author.

National Council of Teachers of Mathematics. (1989). *Curriculum and evaluation standards for school mathematics.* Reston, VA: Author.

National Council of Teachers of Mathematics. (1991). *Professional standards for teaching mathematics.* Reston, VA: Author.

National Council of Teachers of Mathematics. (1995). *Assessment standards for school mathematics.* Reston, VA: Author.

National Council of Teachers of Mathematics. (2000). *Principles and standards for school mathematics.* Reston, VA: Author.

National Priorities Project. (1998). *Working hard, earning less: The story of job growth In Illinois.* Grassroots Factbook (Vol. I, Series 2). Northhampton, MA: Author.

Newman, K. S. (1988). *Falling from grace: Downward mobility in the age of affluence.* Berkeley: University of California Press.

No Child Left Behind Act of 2001. US Public Law 107–110. 107th Congr., 1st sess., 8 January 2002.

Newmann, F. M., Bryk, A. S., & Nagaoka, J. K., (2001, January). *Authentic intellectual work and standardized tests: Conflict or coexistence?* A report of the Chicago Annenberg Research Project. Chicago: Consortium on Chicago School Research.

Nye, B., Hedges, L. V., & Konstantopoulos, S. (2000). The effects of small classes on academic achievement: The results of the Tennessee class size experiment. *American Educational Research Journal, 37*(1), 123–151.

Oakes, J. (1985). *Keeping track: How schools structure inequality.* New Haven, CT: Yale University Press.

Oakes, J. (1990). *Multiplying inequalities: The effect of race, social class, and tracking on opportunities to learn mathematics and science.* Santa Monica, CA: RAND.

Oakes, J., Wells, A. S., Jones, M., & Datnow, A. (1997). Detracking: The social construction of ability, cultural politics, and resistance to reform. *Teachers College Record, 98*(3), 482–510.

Olson, L. (1997). *The school to work revolution,* Reading, MA: Perseus Books.

Olzewski, L., & Little, D. (2002, June 5). Even troubled schools see scores pick up. *Chicago Tribune,* Sec. 1, pp. 1, 16.

Orfield, G. (1990). Wasted talent, threatened future: Metropolitan Chicago's human capital and Illinois public policy. In L. B. Joseph (Ed.), *Creating jobs, creating workers: Economic development and employment in metropolitan Chicago* (pp. 129–160). Chicago: University of Chicago Center for Urban Research and Policy Studies.

Ozga, J. (2000). *Policy research in educational settings.* Buckingham, England: Open University Press.

Parenti, C. (1999). *Lockdown America: Police and prisons in the age of crisis.* London: Verso.

Parker, L., Deyhle, D., & Villenas, S. A. (Eds.). (1999). *Race is . . . Race isn't: Critical race theory and qualitative studies in education.* Boulder: Westview.

Perry, T. (2003). Up from the parched earth: Toward a theory of African American achievement. In T. Perry, C. Steele, & A. Hilliard III (Eds.), *Young gifted and Black: Promoting high achievement among African-American students* (pp. 1–108). Boston: Beacon Press..

Perry, T., & Delpit, L. (Eds.). (1998). *The real Ebonics debate: Power, language and the education of African-American children.* Boston: Beacon Press.

Peterson, P. E. (1976). *School politics Chicago style.* Chicago: University of Chicago Press.

Phillips-Fein, K. (1998, September–October). The still-industrial city: Why cities shouldn't just let manufacturing go. *The American Prospect, 9*(40), 28–37.

Phuong Le & Malone, H. (1998, June 1). Parents see politics in conversion of school. *Chicago Tribune*, Sect. 2, p. 2.

Pitt, L. (1998, August 31). Hot houses. *Chicago Sun Times*, p. N8.

Pitt, L. (1998, September 1). Hot houses. *Chicago Sun Times*, p. N12.

Podmolik, M. E. (1998). Downtown spreading out as residents pour in. *Chicago Sun Times*, pp. A20–A21.

Popkewitz, T. S. (2000). The denial of change in educational change: Systems of ideas in the construction of national policy and evaluation. *Educational Researcher, 29* (1), 17–29.

President Lynch responds to charges of test cheating. (2002, October). *Chicago Union Teacher,* 66(2), 6.

Preteceille, E. (1990). Political paradoxes of urban restructuring: Globalization of the economy and localization of politics. In J. R. Logan & T. Swanstrom (Eds.), *Beyond the city limits* (pp. 27–59). Philadelphia: Temple University Press.

Public schools receive $25 million grant for after-school programs. (1998, November 12). [Press release]. Chicago: Chicago Public Schools. Retrieved September 1, 2000 from http://www.cps.k12.il.us/About CPS/PressRelease/Arch

PURE—Office of Civil Rights Letter. (1999, October 21). Retrieved February 20, 2000 from http//:pureparents@pureparents.org/OCRletterPURE.htmt

Quintanilla, R. (1999, August 12). It's not just school, it's an adventure. *Chicago Tribune*, Sec. 1, pp. 1, 26.

Quintanilla, R. (2001, March 13). It's more than a school, it's the drill. *Chicago Tribune*, Sec. 1, pp. 1, 10.

Rast, J. (1999). *Remaking Chicago: The political origins of urban industrial change.* Dekalb: Northern Illinois University Press..

Ray, C. A., & Mickelson, R. A. (1993). Restructuring students for restructured work: The economy, school reform, and non-college-bound youths. *Sociology of Education, 66,* 1–20.

Regional realities. (2001). Chicago: Chicago Metropolis 2020.

Reich, R. B. (1991). *The work of nations.* New York: Vintage.

Rethinking Columbus. (2001). Milwaukee: Rethinking Schools..

Rethinking our classrooms (Vol. 1). (1994). Milwaukee: Rethinking Schools.

Rethinking our classrooms (Vol. 2). (2001). Milwaukee: Rethinking Schools.

Rivlin, G. (1992). *Fire on the prairie: Chicago's Harold Washington and the politics of race.* New York: Henry Holt.

Rizvi, F., & Lingard, B. (2000). Globalization and education: Complexities and contingencies. *Education Theory, 50*(4), 419–426.

Roderick, M., Bryk, A. S., Jacob, B. A., Easton, J. Q., & Allensworth, E. (1999). *Ending social promotion: Results from the first two years.* Chicago: Consortium on Chicago School Research.

Roderick, M., Nagaoka, J., Bacon, J., & Easton, J. Q. (2000). *Update: Ending social promotion.* Chicago: Consortium on Chicago School Research.

Rodriguez, R. (1982). *Hunger of memory: The education of Richard Rodriguez.* Toronto: Bantam.

Rogal, B. J. (2001). Alternative education: Segregation or solution? *Chicago Reporter, 30*(4), 6–8, 10.

Rosenbaum, J. E., & Binder, A. (1997). Do employers really need more educated youth? *Sociology of Education, 70,* 68–75.

Rossi, R. (2001, April 2). City's toughest prep schools: Only 5 percent of applicants to top-ranked Northside get in. *Chicago Sun Times*, pp. A1–2.

Ruiz, R. (1997). The empowerment of language-minority students. In A. Darder, R. D. Torres, & H. Gutíerrez (Eds.), *Latinos and education: A critical reader* (pp. 319–328). New York: Routledge.

Rury, J. R., & Mirel, J. E. (1997). "The Political Economy of Urban Education," In M. W. Apple (Ed.), *Review of Research In Education* (Vol. 22, pp. 49–110). Washington, D.C.: American Educational Research Association.

Saltman, K. J. (2000). *Collateral damage: Corporatizing public schools—a threat to democracy.* Lanham, MD: Rowman & Littlefield.

Sanjek, R. (1998). *The future of us all: Race and neighborhood politics in New York City.* Ithaca, NY: Cornell University Press.

Sassen, S. (1994). *Cities in a world economy.* Thousand Oaks, CA: Pine Forge Press.

Sassen, S. (1998). *Globalization and its discontents.* New York: The New Press.

Schaeffer, B. (2000). Some see elite schools as drain on system. *Catalyst, 12*(4), 12–13.

Schmid, J. (1998, September 4). City's loft, condo prices soaring. *Chicago Sun Times*, pp. N8–N9.

Schmidt, W. H. , McKnight, C. C., & Raizen, S. A. (1997). *A splintered vision: An investigation of U.S. science and mathematics education.* Dordrecht, The Netherlands. Kluwer Academic.

Secada, W. G. (1992). Race, ethnicity, social class, language, and achievement in mathematics. In D. A. Grouws (Ed.), *Handbook of research on mathematics teaching and learning* (pp. 623–660). New York: Macmillan.

Sheldon, K. M., & Riddle, B. J. (1998). Standards, accountability, and school reform: Perils and pitfalls. *Teachers College Record, 100,* 164–180.

Shipps, D. (1997). Invisible hand: Big business and Chicago school reform. *Teachers College Record, 99,* 73–116.

Shipps, D., Kahne, J., & Smiley, M. A. (1999). The politics of urban school reform: Legitimacy, city growth, and school improvement in Chicago. *Educational Policy, 13*(4), 518–545.

Sirotnik, K. A. (1987). *The school as the center of change* (Occasional Paper No. 5). Seattle: University of Washington. Center for Educational Renewal.

Skertic, M., Guerrero, L., & Herguth, R. C. (2002, August 27). Same neighborhood, different worlds. *Chicago Sun Times,* Sec. 1, p. 5.

Sleeter, C., & McLaren, P. (Eds.). (1995). *Multicultural education, critical pedagogy, and the politics of difference.* Albany, NY: State University of New York Press.

Smith, J. B., Lee, V. E., & Newmann, F. M. (2001). *Instruction and achievement in Chicago elementary schools.* Chicago: Consortium on Chicago School Research.

Smith, M. L. (in press). *Political spectacle and the fate of American schools.* New York: Routledge.

Smith, M. L., Heinecke, W., & Noble, A. J. (2000). Assessment policy and political spectacle. *Teachers College Record, 101,* 157–191.

Smith, M. P., & Tarallo, B. (1993). The post-modern city and the social construction of ethnicity in California. In M. Cross & M. Keith (Eds.), *Racism, the city and the state* (pp. 61–76). London: Routledge.

Smith, N. (1996). *The new urban frontier: Gentrification and the revanchist city.* New York: Routledge.

Solarzano, D., & Delgado Bernal, D. (2001). Examining transformational resistance through a critical race and LatCrit theory framework: Chicana and Chicano students in an urban context. *Urban Education, 36,* 308–342.

Squires, G. D., Bennett, L., McCourt, K., & Nyden, P. (1987). *Chicago: Race, class, and the response to urban decline,* Philadelphia: Temple University Press.

Stromquist, N. P., & Monkman, K. (Eds.). (2000). *Globalization and education.* Lanham. MD: Rowman & Littlefield.

Sutton, M., & Levinson, B. A. U. (2001). *Policy as practice: Toward a comparative sociocultural analysis of educational policy.* Westport, CT: Ablex.

Tate, W. F. (1997). Critical race theory and education: History, theory, and implications. In M. W. Apple (Ed.), *Review of research in education,* (Vol 22, pp. 195–247). Washington DC: American Educational Research Association.

Taylor, M. D. (1991). *Roll of thunder, hear my cry.* New York: Puffin Books.

Taylor, S., & Henry, M. (2000). Globalization and educational policy making: A case study. *Education Theory, 50*(4), 487–503.

Teachers for social justice: Policy forum on high stakes testing. (2000, November 11). Retrieved from http://www.teachersforjustice.org

Three More Schools approved for the International Baccalaureate program (1999, January 28). [Press release]. Retrieved February 12, 1999 from http://www.cps.k12.il.us/AboutCPS/Press Releases/January_28

Trending up: Four-year education progress report: July 1995–August 1999 (n.d.). Chicago: Chicago Public Schools.

Urow, C., & Sontag, J. (2001). Creating community—un mundo entero: The Inter-American experience. In E. Christian & F. Genesee, F. (Eds.), *Bilingual education* (pp. 11–26). Case Studies in TESOL Practice Series. Alexandria, VA: Teachers of English to Speakers of Other Languages.

U.S. Legislators to Tour Chicago Military Academy: First Visit for Durbin and Rush. (1999, October 18). [Press Release]. Retrieved January 8, 2000 from http://www.cps.k12.il.us/AboutCPS/Press Releases/October_18

Valenzuela, A. (1999). *Subtractive schooling: U.S. Mexican youth and the politics of caring.* Albany: State University of New York Press.

Vallas, P. (2000, January). Ending the injustice of social promotion. *The Chicago Educator, 5*(6), 5–6.

Vinson, K. D., & Ross, E. W. (2001). Education and the new disciplinarity: Surveillance, spectacle, and the case of SBER. *Cultural Logic, 41.* Retrieved November 16, 2001 from http://eserver.org/clogic/4-1/4-1.html

Wacquant, L. J. D., & Wilson, W. J. (1989). The costs of racial and class exclusion in the inner city. *Annals of the American Academy of Political and Social Science, 501,* 8–25.

Walters, S. (Ed,). (1997). *Globalization, adult education and training.* London: Zed Books.

Washburn, G. (2002, July 3). City maps downtown future. *Chicago Tribune,* Sec. 2, pp. 1, 6.

Weinstein, R. S. (1996). High standards In a tracked system of schooling: For which students and with what educational supports? *Educational Researcher 25*(8), 16–19.

Weissmann, D. (2002). High-income housing, low-income schools. *Catalyst 14*(3), 17–21.

Wells, A. S., Slayton, J., & Scott, J. (2002). Defining democracy in the neoliberal age: Charter school reform and educational consumption. *American Educational Research Journal, 39*(2), 337–361.

Whitty, G. Power, S., & Halpin, D. (1998). *Devolution and choice in education: The school, the state and the market.* Buckingham, England: Open University Press.

Wiewel, W., & Nyden, P. W. (1991). Introduction. In P. W. Nyden & W. Wiewel (Eds.), *Challenging uneven development: An urban agenda for the 1990s* (pp. 1–16). New Brunswick, NJ: Rutgers University Press.

Williams, D. (2000). Board gives north side preps lavish facilities, ample planning time. *Catalyst, 12*(4), 4–9.

Williams, D. (2000). Highlights of a decade: 1999. *Catalyst, 11*(5), 1.

Wintermute, W., & Hicklin, C. (1991). The employment potential of Chicago's service industries. In P. W. Nyden & W. Wiewel (Eds.), *Challenging uneven development: An urban agenda for the 1990s* (pp. 144–165). New Brunswick, NJ: Rutgers University Press.

Wolf, E. N. (1995). *Top heavy: A study of the increasing inequality of wealth in America,* New York: Twentieth Century Fund Press.

Wrigley, J. (1982). *Class politics and public schools: Chicago, 1900 to 1950.* New Brunswick, NJ: Rutgers University Press.

Youth First Campaign. (2002). Youth Summit on Education Issues. Conference October 9, 2002 at Daley College, Chicago, IL.

INDEX

Abu-Lughod, J. L., 25–26
Academic Preparatory Centers (APCs)
  demographics of, 43–44
  for ITBS failure, 47
accountability. *See also* No Child Left
    Behind Act
  bilingual education and, 120–124
  blame cultivated by, 46–47, 176
  at Brewer Elementary, 127–131
  Bush's agenda for, 2, 4, 9, 170
  categorization of, 177–178
  in CPS, 39–40, 68
  "democratic localism" and, 2, 38–39
  at Farley Elementary, 139–140
  funding rewarded for, 68
  hegemony of, 99
  measuring, 9
  for remediation, 47
  resistance and, 92–95
  social classes and, 45–47
  for social discipline, 46
  by surveillance, 96–98
  of teachers, 82–84, 92–95, 128,
    150–154
  for test preparation, 42–45, 112,
    129–131, 150–152
African American(s). *See also* Grover
    Elementary School; Westview
    Elementary School
  Chicago mayor, first, 32
  college prep percentage of, 53

  commuting to Farley Elementary,
    142–143
  criminalization of, 73
  in differentiated schools, 50–53, 64
  disciplining, 64, 74, 159–161
  displacement of, 24, 28, 30, 31, 72–74,
    198n1
  educational liberation of, 186–187
  expulsion rates of, 59
  graduation rate of, in Texas, 199n6
  marketing culture of, 134–135
  in military schools, 58
  in MSTAs, 54
  neighborhoods, 24, 28, 30, 31, 72–74,
    198n1
  political activists, 98, 200n9
  as principals, 74, 75, 76
  in probation schools, 43–44, 199n2
  protests held by, 32–34
  racial exclusion of, 1, 4, 17–18, 33, 177,
    187–188
  regulating schools for, 71–104
  schools closed to, 67
  social classes, 158–159
  social movements by, 32–34, 190–191
  strikes led by, 137
  as "surplus people," 60
  suspension rates of, 59
  teachers, 100–101, 140, 151, 186
  tests failed by, 45, 178
  wages for, 27, 198n5

after-school programs. *See* remediation
AIOs. *See* Area Instructional Officers
Allensworth, E. M., 200n13
"American" behaviors, 121
APCs. *See* Academic Preparatory Centers
Apple, Michael W., ix–x, 13–14, 183–185
Area Instructional Officers (AIOs), 66, 68
ARTS program, 89, 91
authoritarianism, 188–190

Ball, S. I.
   centralization noted by, 96
   critical policy noted by, 12–13
   social policy defined by, 14–15, 17
   state's roles noted by, 88
BCS. *See* Better City Schools
Bennett, William, 2
Better City Schools (BCS)
   addition to, 96
   CAS strategies of, 86, 90
   Grover Elementary monitored by, 75,
      83, 96, 97
   workshops, 89–91
bilingual education
   accountability of, 120–124
   at Brewer Elementary, 105–106,
      113–114, 119–124
   CPS policies on, 105–106, 113–114,
      119–124
   cultural assimilation by, 105–106,
      118–124
   limitations on, 36, 46, 119, 201n8
   "non-importance" of, 119–123
   teacher qualification for, 201n4
   test taking and, 113–114, 119, 124
Binder, A., 61–62
Black Power movement, 33–34
blame
   accountability cultivating, 46–47, 176
   failing students cultivating, 113–114
   test pressure cultivating, 95–96
boycotts
   CASE, 99–100
   Iraq war, 191
   ITBS, 99–100, 153–154
   low wage, 137
   school facility conditions, 33–34
   segregation, 33–34
Brazil
   Citizen Schools in, 183–185
   racism in, 184, 202n3
Brewer Elementary School

accountability at, 127–131
administration of, 125
bilingual education at, 105–106,
   113–114, 119–124
critical literacy development at, 109–114
dance music at, 123
demographics of, 108
educational change at, 124–131
evaluation of, self-, 125–127
facilities of, 108, 141
inquiry-based curriculum at, 109, 125
math curricula at, 114–118
neighborhoods of, 106–108
teaching approach at, 109–134
testing approach at, 110–112, 116–117,
   127–129
Bridge curriculum, 47
Brookings Institute, 28–29
Burbules, N. C., 197n1
Bureau of Labor Statistics, 61
Bush, George W.
   accountability agenda of, 2, 4, 9, 170
   preemptive war doctrine of, 189–190
Byrk, A. S., 43, 199n1

Cabrini Green public housing complex,
   30
capitalism
   contesting, 12
   differentiated schooling and, 63–64
   globalization originating from, 197n1
   reform for, 174
   restructuring, 7
Carlson, D., 57, 62, 173
Carver Military High School, 58
CAS. *See* Chicago Academic Standards
CASE (Chicago Academic Standards
   Exam)
   boycott against, 99–100
   waiver for, 201n4
Castells, M., 23, 197nn5–6
Catalyst, 38–39, 55, 67, 193
CCC. *See* Commercial Club of Chicago
CEOs (chief executive officers), 11, 36
CFS. *See* Curriculum Framework
   Statements
CHA. *See* Chicago Housing Authority
cheating, on tests, 44–45, 148
Chicago
   abandoned housing in, 30
   "buffer zone" of, 31
   Central Area Plan for, 24–25

corporate power of, 24–25, 27–28
development by Daley, Richard J., 27–28
development by Daley, Richard M., 2,
  24–25, 28–29, 198n1
as "dual city," 23–32, 198n7
economy of, 24–25, 26–27
gentrification strategy for, 27–30,
  179–180
as "global city," 24–26
graduation rate in, 62
Latino/a population of, 136
manufacturing decrease in, 26–27
Marion Park, 106–108, 132–135
Mercantile Exchange, 24, 25
North River, 142–143
real estate power in, 29–30, 55
taxation in, 29–30
tourism in, 134–135
unemployment rates in, 72
wages in, 26–27, 198n5
Chicago 21 Plan (CCC), 28
Chicago Academic Standards (CAS)
  BCS strategy for, 86, 90
  as checklist, 86
  developing, 48
  Grover Elementary's use of, 85–88
  purpose of, 85, 199n8
  racial exclusion masked by, 87
  teacher's use of, 85–88
  Westview Elementary's use of, 85–86
Chicago Academic Standards Exam. *See*
  CASE
Chicago Defender, 200n9
Chicago Housing Authority (CHA)
  dilapidation allowed by, 72–73
  school surveillance reported to, 98
Chicago Metropolis 2020 (CCC), 61, 136
Chicago Military Academy, 58
Chicago Public Schools (CPS). *See also
  specific elementary schools*
  accountability in, 39–40, 68
  administration appointed for, 36, 66
  African American social movements
    in, 32–34
  bilingual education policies of,
    105–106, 113–114, 119–124
  centralization of, 36, 38–39
  closing, 67
  Daley's, Richard M., control of, 36, 38
  decentralized management of, 9, 68
  demographics of, 3
  differentiated programs for, 48–57

district division of, 49–50, 51–52
dropout rates in, 34, 57
funding crisis for, 5, 34, 36
"good" schools of, 54–55, 103
"good sense" in, 39–40
IBs in, 56
income gap in, 25–26, 50, 108, 160,
  198n3, 200n13
Latino/a social movements in, 32–33,
  34–35
military schools in, 57–60
as national model, 2–3
opposition to, 154–157
parent report cards from, 47
Quality Review of, 125–127
reform in, xii, 2, 32–39
remediation in, 47
researching, 193–195, 202nn1–6
retained students in, 45, 64–65, 68
state policy for, 9
stratified schooling in, 61–63
test preparation in, 42–45
tracking in, 1, 57, 173–174
post-Vallas, 66–68
workforce, new urban, policies of,
  61–65
Chicago School Reform Act, 35–36
Chicago Tribune, 66, 73
Chicagoans United to Reform Education.
  See CURE
Chico, Gery, 36, 39, 58, 66
chief executive officers. *See* CEOs
Chubb, J. M., 202n1
Citizen Schools Project, 183–185
Civil Rights movement, 33–34
class size, 163
Clemens, Ms. (Farley Elementary
  teacher), 151–152
Clinton, Bill, 2, 9
Coalition to Save Public Housing, 73
college prep programs. *See* differentiated
  schooling
colonialism, 177, 197n1
Commercial Club of Chicago (CCC)
  education as priority of, 65–66
  redevelopment plans of, 28
  workforce reports from, 61–62
corporate power
  funding, 27–28, 29
  globalization increasing, 6, 7
  grassroots coalitions *v.*, 32
  racial diversity and, 132

CPS. *See* Chicago Public Schools
Crain's Chicago Business, 24
criminalization
   of African Americans, 73
   military schools and, 58, 60, 64
   probation associated with, 96–98
critical literacy
   defined, 109, 112
   education policy for, 17
   Farley Elementary's approach to, 139,
      143–150, 164–165
   goals for, 112–113, 164–165
   individual worth for, 145–147
   Latinos/as developing, 109–118
   for math, 114–118
   test preparation *v.,* 110–112, 131, 151
critical policy scholarship, 13
critical race theory, 17–18
cultural assimilation, 105–106, 118–124.
      See also bilingual education
cultural politics, 5–11, 17, 132–135,
      164–165
Cummins, J., 123
CURE (Chicagoans United to Reform
      Education), 35
"The Curie 12," 100, 191
curriculum
   BCS, 75, 83
   bilingual, 120–124
   Bridge, 47
   Citizen Schools Project, 184
   inquiry-based, 91–92, 109, 125
   ITBS, 4, 36, 47, 78–81, 90–92, 152–153
   math, 89, 91, 109
   meaning of, redefining, 79–81
   NCTM Standards based, 109, 114–118,
      145, 201n5
   performance standards for, 48
   professional development for, 88–92
   racial exclusion by, 62, 64
   reading, 75, 143–145
   resistance to, 92–95
   scripted, 36–37, 40, 44, 199n3
   test-based, 41, 42–45, 77–81, 88–92
Curriculum Framework Statements
      (CFS)
   developing, 48
   purpose of, 85, 199n8
   racial exclusion masked by, 87

Daley, Richard J.
   administration appointed by, 36, 66

   African Americans relocated by, 31
   anti-gang loitering law enforced by, 59
   Chicago development headed by,
      27–28
   CPS reform headed by, 36, 38
   military schooling viewed by, 64
Daley, Richard M., 2, 24–25, 28–29,
      198n1
Danns, D., 33
Darder, A., 124
Davis, M., 136–137
Day of the Dead holidays, 134
decentralization
   of CPS, 9, 68
   of cultural identities, 123–124
   of ITBS prep, 152–153
Delpit, L., 147, 187
"democratic localism," 2, 38–39
DI. *See* direct instruction
"didactic instruction," 43, 199n7
differentiated schooling, 48–57, 62–63
   African Americans in, 50–53, 64
   capitalism and, 63–64
   choices for, illusion of, 56–57
   demographics of, 53
   district division for, 49–50, 51–52
   economic impact of, 62–63
   equity of, 56–57
   "good" schools in, 54–55
   identities produced from, 63–65
   Latinos/as in, 50, 64
   minus category of, 49
   neoliberalist views on, 57
   plus category of, 49, 199n9
   after reform, 50, 52
   workforce preparation in, 62–65
DIR. *See Dive into Reading*
direct instruction (DI)
   categorization of, 49, 199n9
   demographics of, 52, 54
discipline
   as accountability, 46
   of African Americans, 64, 74, 159–161
   at Farley Elementary School, 141–142,
      146–147, 159–161
   at Grover Elementary School, 74
   military school code of, 58–59
   for personal property, 169
   self-regulation as, 141–142, 146–147
   Zero Tolerance policy for, 58, 59–60
discourses
   changing, 172–173

defined, 15, 63, 87
discussion groups, student, 145–146
displacement
    of African Americans, 24, 28, 30, 31, 72–74, 198n1
    of Latinos/as, 24, 30, 107
Dive into Reading (DIR), 144, 201n1
Dodge school, 67
double entry teaching, 92
dropout rates
    in CPS, 34, 57
    in Texas public schools, 199n6
"dual America," 11
"dual city," 23–32, 198n7
"dual language" requirement, 129, 201n9
Duncan, Arne, 44–45, 66–68

Eason-Watkins, Barbara, 66
Ebonics, 187
economy
    of Chicago, 24–25, 26–27
    differentiated schooling and, 62–63
    education policy for restructuring, 9–11, 164–165, 172
    informal, 10, 137
    state policy for pressures of, 12
    transnational movements changing, 6
    of urban districts, xi–xii, 5–11
Educating the "Right" Way (Apple), ix
education
    accessibility to, 11
    African American liberation in, 186–187
    redefining, 79–81, 181
    for social control, 175–177
education policy
    for agency, 17
    alternative, 180–183
    authoritarianism in, 188–190
    colonialist, 177
    for critical literacy, 17
    cultural politics of, 5–11, 17, 132–135, 164–165
    for economic restructuring, 9–11, 164–165, 172
    for equity, 16–17
    function of, 15–16
    for globalization, 178–180
    "good sense" in, 4, 16, 39–40
    ideology, 11–12, 129–131
    neoliberalism affect on, 9, 181
    after 9/11, 188–190

racial exclusion by, 177–178
reform, xi, 2–3
Education-to-Career Academies (ETCs)
    categorization of, 49
    goals of, 62, 173
English as a Second Language. *See* ESL
English as a Second Language Goals and Standards (CPS), 121
equity
    defined, 172
    of differentiated schooling, 56–57
    education policy for, 16–17
ESL (English as a Second Language), 120. *See also* bilingual education
ETCs. *See* Education-to-Career Academies
ethnicity, marketing, 134–135
Every Child, Every School (CPS), 67–68
expulsion, racial exclusion by, 59

failing students
    blame cultivated by, 113–114
    boycott by, 99–100
    demographics of, 45
    example of, ix–x
    globalization impeded by, 61
    labor and, 61
    pressure on, 95–96, 101–103
    probation for, 36, 39
    racial exclusion of, 178
    remediation for, 47
    teacher observation of, 102
Farley Elementary School
    accountability at, 139–140
    Board opposition by, 154–155
    challenges for, 139–140
    critical literacy taught at, 139, 143–150, 164–165
    demographics of, 140, 142–143
    discipline at, 141–142, 146–147, 159–161
    educational goals at, 147–150, 164–165
    facilities of, 141, 162–163
    improvement plans for, 155, 162–163
    mathematics approach at, 145
    neighborhoods of, 142–143
    parent activists for, 154–155, 156–157
    racism at, 158–162
    reading approach at, 143–145
    researching, 195, 202n6
    teachers at, 140–167
    testing approach of, 149–150, 152–154

favella community, 183–184
Feagin, J. R., 6, 26, 32
Ferguson, Ann Arnett, 160
Flecha, R., 11
food service jobs, 197n4
Foucault, M., 15, 46, 97, 178
Freire, P., 17, 109, 112
Friedman, Milton, 202n1
funding
    accountability rewarded by, 68
    crisis for CPS, 5, 34, 36
    development, corporate, 27–28, 29
    Latinos/as cut from, 67
    magnet schools, 51–52, 55, 56
    prioritizing, 181–182
    PTA as source of, 163
    school facility, 162–163, 181–182

games in school, allowing, 146–147
Gandin, Luís Armando, 183–185
gang loitering, ordinance against, 59
GED (General Education Degree),
    199n6
Gee, J. P., 164, 166–167, 174, 179
Generation Y, 53, 59
gentrification
    Chicago's strategy for, 27–30, 179–180
    globalization linked to, 29, 179
    "good" schools for, 54–55
    marketing ethnicity with, 134–135
    neighborhood, 50, 54–55,
        199nn12–13
    schools closed for, 67
Gill, S., 197n1
Giroux, H., 122
global cities
    defined, 7
    development of, 8
    dichotomy of, 23–24
    labor in, 25–26, 132
    real estate in, 8
globalization
    benefits of, 6
    contesting, 12
    corporate power and, 6, 7
    current phase of, 6
    education policy for, 178–180
    examples of, 4–5
    failing students impeding, 61
    gentrification linked to, 29, 179
    immigration and, 6–7

    labor restructuring caused by, 9–11
    origins of, 197n1
    real estate importance with, 29–30
    social class division caused by, xi, 6–8
    state policy affected by, 183
    in urban districts, 5–9
    World Social Forum model for, 183,
        191
Goals 2000, 9
Goldberg, D. T., 133
"good"
    schools, 54–55, 103, 172
    sense, 4, 16, 39–40
    teachers, 172
Grace, G., 12
graduation
    Chicago's rate of, 62
    importance of, 113
    Texas' rate of, 199n6
Gramsci, A., 4, 39, 99
grassroots coalitions
    corporate power v., 32
    for neighborhood preservation, 32
    for school facility improvement, 67
    for school reform, 34, 35–36
Grimes, Ms. (Westview Elementary
    principal), 76
Grover Elementary School
    administration of, 100–103, 156
    BCS monitoring of, 75, 83, 96, 97
    CAS at, use of, 85–88
    demographics of, 72
    discipline at, 74
    educational success defined by, 80
    facilities of, 74–75
    ITBS scoring of, 75
    neighborhoods of, 72–74
    oversight agencies for, 75, 83, 96
    on probation, 74–75, 80, 96–98
    professional development at, 88–92
    researching, 194–195, 202n6
    resistance at, 93–94
    social control at, 96–98, 175
    students sorted out at, 82
    surveillance at, 88–90, 96–98
    teachers at, 74–75, 77–84, 93–94,
        95–103
    test pressure at, 95–96
    test taking approach of, 77–78,
        98–100
Gutstein, Eric, 19, 194–195

Haney, W., 45
Haymes, Stephen, 31
hegemony
    of accountability, 99
    countering, models for, 183–188, 191
    theory of, 14
high schools
    converted, 54–55
    military, 58
    transition, 43–44, 47
    workforce training in, 62
High Stakes Education, ix, x, xii, 3
Hispanic Drop-out Task Force, 34
Hispanics. *See* Latinos/as
HUD (U.S. Department of Housing
    and Urban Development), 73,
    198n9
Hull, G., 164, 166–167, 174, 179

IB programs. *See* International
    Baccalaureate (IB) programs
identities
    bilingual education assimilating,
        120–124
    differentiated, producing, 63–65
    expressing, 108, 186–187
    language defining, 119, 122, 123, 187
    transnational, 106–107
ideology
    curriculum resistance, 92–95
    education policy, 11–12, 129–131
    racially coded basic skills, 64
Illinois State Achievement Test (ISAT),
    43, 68, 91, 152
immigrants
    campaign against, 120
    globalization and, 6–7
    labor for, 25–26
    Latino/a, 106, 132–134
    mutual assistance for, 133
imperialism, 197n1
income gaps, 25–26, 50, 108, 160, 198n3,
    200n13
industrial nations
    unemployment in, 7
    unions in, 10
informal economy, 10, 137
information industries
    magnet schools for, 57
    manufacturing and, 198n4
    qualifications in, 11

inquiry-based curriculum
    at Brewer Elementary School, 109, 125
    at Westview Elementary School, 91–92
Integrated Mathematics Program, 57
International Baccalaureate (IB)
    programs
    attendance at, 53
    categorization of, 49, 64
    purpose of, 56, 61
International Monetary Fund, 6
Iowa State Achievement Test (ISAT), 43
Iowa Test of Basic Skills (ITBS)
    bilingual education overlooked on,
        113–114, 119, 124
    boycotting, 99–100, 153–154
    curriculum, 36, 41, 47, 78–81, 90–92,
        152–153
    decentralization of, 152–153
    education redefined by, 79–81
    failing, 45, 47, 110–111, 113
    Grover Elementary scores on, 75
    NCTM Standards *v.*, 116–118
    remediation based on, 47, 82, 200n6
    replacement of, 68
    science portion of, 118
    score requirements for, 200–201n3
    speed of, 111
    third grade benchmark for, 201n5
Iraq war, boycotting, 191
ISAT. *See* Illinois State Achievement Test;
    Iowa State Achievement Test
ITBS. *See* Iowa Test of Basic Skills

Jamal, Mumia Abu, 98, 200n9
"Judgment Day for Racism in West Side
    Schools," 33–34, 191

Kahne, J., 198n13
Katz, Michael, xi
King, Joyce, 161

labor. *See also* wages
    African American, 10
    basic skills for, 61–62
    contingent, 10, 197n3
    demographics of, 10, 197n4
    division of, new, 6–7
    failing students and, 61
    in global cities, 25–26, 132
    high-paid, 7, 8, 25
    immigrant, 25

labor *(cont.)*
    Latino/a, 10, 107–108, 136–137
    low-paid, 25–26, 61–62, 107–108, 136
    reorganization of, 6, 9–11
    social class division by, 10–11, 197n5
    statistics, 61, 197n4
    unions, 10
    up-skilling, 26, 198n4
Ladson-Billings, G., 100, 161, 177, 187
language. *See also* bilingual education
    community cohesion by, 133
    dual, requirement for, 123
    identity defined by, 119, 122, 123, 187
Lankshear, C., 164, 166–167, 174, 179
Latinos/as. *See also* Brewer Elementary
    School
    college prep percentage of, 53
    critical literacy development for,
        109–118
    cultural suppression of, 122–123
    in differentiated schools, 50, 64
    discipline for, 64
    displacement of, 24, 30, 107
    dropout rates for, 34
    funding cuts for, 67
    graduation rate of, in Texas, 199n6
    immigration of, 106, 132–134
    income for, 108
    labor for, 10, 107–108, 136–137
    marketing culture of, 134–135
    in military schools, 58
    in MSTAs, 54
    neighborhoods of, 24, 30, 106–107,
        132–135
    political power of, 136–137
    population in Chicago, 136
    as principals, 105–106, 124–125
    in probation schools, 43–44, 199n2
    protests held by, 32–33, 34–35,
        99–100
    racial exclusion of, 1, 4, 132–135
    schools closed to, 67
    social movements by, 32–33, 34–35,
        136–137, 192
    as "surplus people," 60
    as teachers, 105–137
    tests failed by, 45, 113, 178
    transnational identities of, 106–107
    wages for, 27
Leadership for Quality Education,
    199n15
Lee, V. E., 43

Lewis, D. A., 37
Lingard, B., 197n1
Lipinski, Ms. (Grover Elementary
    principal), 74–75, 83
Lipman, Pauline, ix, xii, 20–21
literacy. *See* critical literacy
local school councils (LSCs)
    creation of, 35
    dominance over, 36, 38–39, 182
    PTA as, 155
lockers, availability of, 169–170
Logan, J. R., 27
LSCs. *See* local school councils

Macedo, D., 119
magnet schools
    accessibility of, 53–54
    categorization of, 49
    funding, 51–52, 55, 56
    for information industries, 57
    neighborhoods for, 50–52, 52, 54–55
    origination of, 50
    test exemption for, 201n4
*Make No Little Plans: Jobs for
    Metropolitan Chicago* (CCC), 61
manufacturing jobs
    availability of, 198n6
    decrease in, 26–27
    information industries and, 198n4
    skill requirements for, 62
Mastery Learning program, 154–155,
    201n3
Math, Science, Technology Academies.
    See MSTAs
Math Works, 89, 91
McNeil, L. M., 92, 156
Meaningful Mathematics (MM)
    basis of, 109
    elimination of, 117–118
    techniques, 115–116, 201nn6–7
    test preparation *v.*, 116–118
Mexican-Americans. *See* Latinos/as
Mickelson, R. A., 197n3
Midwest Center for Labor Research, 27
military schools
    African Americans enrolled in, 58
    criminalization and, 58, 60, 64
    demographics of, 54, 58
    discipline code for, 58–59
    Latinos/as enrolled in, 58
    NCLB and, 190
    purpose of, 64

racial exclusion by, 57–60, 179–180
Zero Tolerance policy and, 58, 59–60, 190
Mills, Charles, xi–xii
Mirel, J., 35
MM. *See Meaningful Mathematics*
Moe, T. E., 202n1
Molotch, H. L., 27
Morenoff, J. D., 198n7
Morrow, R. A., 9
MSTAs (Math, Science, Technology Academies), 49, 54, 56, 66–67

NAACP (National Association for the Advancement of Colored People), segregation reported by, 33
Nagaoka, J. K., 43, 199n1
Nakagawa, K., 37
A Nation At Risk, 202n1
National Association for the Advancement of Colored People. *See* NAACP
National Council of Teachers of Mathematics. *See* NCTM
National Research Council (NRC), 41, 42
NCLB. *See* No Child Left Behind Act
NCTM (National Council of Teachers of Mathematics), 109, 114–118, 145, 201n5
neighborhoods
African American, 24, 28, 30, 31, 72–74, 198n1
of Brewer Elementary School, 106–108
of Farley Elementary School, 142–143
gentrification of, 50, 54–55, 200nn12–13
grassroots coalitions for preservation of, 32
of Grover Elementary School, 72–74
"hot," 30, 55, 66, 134
Latino/a, 24, 30, 106–107, 132–135
of magnet schools, 50–52, 52, 54–55
tourism in, 134–135
of Westview Elementary School, 72–74
white, 50, 199n12
"yuppie," 198n7
neoliberalism
contesting, 12
democracy and, 185
differentiated schooling viewed by, 57
education policy changed by, 9, 181
social policy changed by, 9, 197n2

Newmann, F. M., 43, 199n1
9/11, education policy after, 188–190
No Child Left Behind Act (NCLB)
fulfillment of, 67–68, 170
inadequacy of, x–xi, xii, 9, 170
model for, 2
provisions of, 120, 190
NRC. *See* National Research Council

Orfield, Gary, 34

Ortiz, Ms. (Brewer elementary teacher), 107, 108, 125, 133

overcrowding
class size and, 163
lockers and, 169–170
protest against, 33–34
Ozga, J., 16, 63

parent teachers association. *See* PTA
Parenti, Christian, 60
parents
Board opposition by, 154–155, 156–157
conferences with, 163
cultural pride of, 108
discrimination fought by, 45
hunger strike by, 67
reform supported by, 34, 35–36, 199n16
report cards for, 47
teachers as, 127–128
testing viewed by, 153–154
Parents United for Responsible Education (PURE). *See* PURE
People's Coalition for Educational Reform, 34
performance standards, developing, 48
Perry, Teresa, 186–187
policy. *See also* education policy; social policy; state policy
analysis, 12–18
borrowing, 183
as common interest, 14
defined, 14–15
discourses, 15
hegemony theory and, 14
power centrality of making, 13
scholarship, critical, 12–13
social justice framework for, 16–18
World Social Forum model for, 183, 191

Popkewitz, T. S., 158, 164
Porto Alegre. *See* Brazil
power
  corporate, 6, 7, 24–25
  of Ebonics, 187
  of Latinos/as, political, 136–137
  in policy making, centrality of, 13
  of racialization, 17–18
  of real estate development, 29–30
  of social control, 176
  of teacher journals, 185–186
  testing as, 178, 189
pressure, test, 95–96, 101–103, 153
probation schools
  conditions of first wave, 74–75
  criminalization associated with,
    96–98
  demographics of, 43–44, 199n2
  Grover Elementary as, 74–75, 80,
    96–98
  teachers' views on, 96–98
professional development, 88–92
projects. *See* public housing
Proposition 227 (California), 120, 122
protests
  overcrowding, 33–34
  racial exclusion, 32–35
  test failure, 99–100
PTA (parent teachers association)
  funding by, 163
LSC function of, 155
public housing
  demolition of, 30, 72–74, 198n9
  dilapidation of, 72–73
  real estate values of, 73
PURE (Parents United for Responsible
  Education), 34, 45

Quality Review process, 125–127

racial exclusion. *See also* African
    American(s); Latinos/as
  by anti-gang ordinance, 59
  by basic skills curricula, 62, 64
  in Brazil, 184, 202n3
  CAS and CFS masking, 87
  Chicago development and, 31, 198n1
  Civil Rights movement against, 33–34
  community based on, 133
  by criminalization, 58, 60
  by education policy, 177–178

by expulsion, 59
of failing students, 178
at Farley Elementary, 158–162
for math curricula, 115
by military schools, 57–60, 179–180
normalization of, 17
power of, 17–18
protests against, 32–35
by teachers, 160
in workforce, 64–65
Zero Tolerance targeting, 59–60
Rast, J., 28, 32, 198n6
Ray, C. A., 197n3
reading, cultivating interest in, 143–145,
  151–152. *See also* critical literacy
Reading Recovery program, 75
Reading, Writing, and Rising Up
  (Christensen), 186
real estate
  abandoned, 30
  in global cities, 8
  with globalization, power of, 29–30
  "good" schools and, 54–55
  "hot," 30, 55, 66, 134
  public housing values in, 73
  social class division by, 8
reform
  for capitalism, 174
  Citizen Schools Project for, 185
  Clinton's support for, 2, 9
  CPS, xii, 2, 32–39
  by Daley, Richard M., 36
  differentiated schooling after, 50, 52
  grassroots coalitions for, 34, 35–36
  parent participation in, 34, 35–36,
    199n16
remediation, 47, 82, 200n6
"Renaissance Schools," 67
retention policy, 45, 64–65, 68
Rethinking Columbus, 185
Rethinking Globalization, 186
Rethinking Our Classrooms, 185
Rethinking Schools, 185
Rethinking Schools project, 185–186
Rizvi, E., 197n1
Rodríguez, Mr. (Brewer Elementary
    principal)
  community weakening noted by, 135
  educational vision of, 105–106
  inquiry-based teaching supported by,
    114–115, 124–125

mathematics curriculum decided by, 117–118
racism noted by, 136
self-evaluation of Brewer supported by, 125–127
test prep importance stated by, 129
Roll of Thunder, Hear My Cry (Taylor), 94
Rosenbaum, J. E., 61–62
Rosenkranz, T., 200n13

Safe Schools, 58, 59
Sanjek, R., 9, 197n4, 198n2
Sassen, Saskia, 7, 8
scholarship, critical policy, 12–13
school councils, local, 35–36, 38–39, 155, 182
school facilities
    boycotting, 33–34
    Brewer Elementary, 108, 141
    closing, 67
    dilapidated, ix, 33
    Farley Elementary, 141, 161–162
    funding, 162–163, 181–182
    Grover Elementary, 74–75
    improving, 65–67, 75, 162–163, 181–182
    Westview Elementary, 75–76
School Improvement Plan (SIP), 155
School Reform Law, ratification of, 2
school-to-work programs, 8
Scott, J., 57
Scott, Michael, 66, 67–68
scripted curriculum
    demographics of, 40, 44, 199n4
    implementation of, 36–37
    teachers learning, 47
Secret, Carrie, 187
segregation. *See* racial exclusion
servant class, xi
service jobs, 10
Shipps, D., 198n13
SIP. *See* School Improvement Plan
Slayton, J., 57
Smiley, M. A., 198n13
Smith, J. B., 43
Smith, M. P., 26
Smith, Neal, 29, 179
social classes
    accountability affect on, 45–47
    African American, 158–159
    globalization affect on, xi, 6–8

intraracial, 5
labor dividing, 10–11, 197n5
new, xi
real estate affect on, 8
in urban districts, xi–xii, 5
social control
    education for, 175–177
    of Grover Elementary School, 96–98, 175
    by surveillance, 96–98
social policy
    African American movements for, 32–34, 190–191
    for discipline, 46
    informal economy and, 137
    justice in, framework for, 16–18
    Latino/a movements for, 32–33, 34–35, 136–137, 192
    neoliberalism affects on, 9, 197n2
    probation as control of, 96–98
    Workers Party actions for, 12
standardization. *See* Chicago Academic Standards; testing, high stakes
state policy
    borrowing, 183
    for CPS, 9
    dual roles of, 88
    economic pressures dealt with by, 12
    formation of, 13–14
    globalization affects on, 183
    after 9–11, 189–190
stratified schooling, 61–63
striking
    African Americans, 137
    prohibition on, 36
    teachers, 34
summer school, 47, 82, 200n6
superintendents, 66, 68
"surplus people," 60
surveillance, 88–90, 96–98
sweatshops. *See* informal economy

TAP (Test of Academic Proficiency), failing, 36
Tax Increment Financing zones (TIFs), 29–30
teachers
    accountability for, 82–84, 92–95, 128, 150–154
    African American, 100–101, 140.151, 186

teachers *(cont.)*
  AIO prep for, 68
  "bad," 82–84
  bilingual education qualifications of,
    201n4
  Brewer Elementary, 109–134
  CAS, use of, 85–88
  categorization of, 93
  cheating and, 45
  development of, 88–92
  expectations from, raising, 40
  family stress noted by, 74
  Farley Elementary, 140–167
  "good," 172
  Grover Elementary, 74–75, 77–88,
    93–94, 95–103
  interviewing, 193–195, 202nn1–6
  journals for, 185–186
  Latino/a, 105–137
  new, ix–x
  as parents, 127–128
  probation viewed by, 96–98
  professional judgment of, 147–150
  racist, 160
  resignation of, 100–103, 112, 177
  resistance of, 92–95, 130, 152–154, 191
  scripting, 36–37, 40, 44, 47
  on strike, 34
  surveillance of, 88–90, 96–98
  testing viewed by, 41, 77–82, 110–111,
    130–131, 150–154
  unorthodox, 147–150
  Westview Elementary, 76, 77–86, 93,
    98, 102–103
Teachers for Social Justice, 169, 199n5
Test Best, 78, 89, 92
Test of Academic Proficiency. *See* TAP
Test Ready, 78
testing, high stakes. *See also* Iowa Test of
    Basic Skills
  accountability by, 42–45, 112, 129–131,
    150–154
  bilingual education and, 113–114, 119,
    124
  boycotting, 99–100
  Brewer approach to, 110–112,
    116–117, 127–129
  cheating on, 44–45, 148
  critical literacy *v.*, 110–112, 131, 151
  curriculum based on, 41, 42–45,
    77–81, 88–92
  exemption from, 157, 201n4

  failure, 36, 45, 99–100, 110, 113, 178
  Farley's approach to, 149–150,
    152–154
  Grover's approach to, 77–78, 98–100
  at magnet schools, 201n4
  parents' views on, 153–154
  pep rallies for, 43, 80
  power of, 178, 189
  preparation for, 42–45, 77–81,
    110–111, 116–117, 129–131,
    150–154
  pressure of, 95–96, 101–103, 153
  professional development for, 89
  raising scores on, 40, 42, 76, 129,
    199n4
  resistance to teaching for, 92–95, 130
  surveillance, 46
  teachers' views on, 41, 77–82, 110–111,
    130–131, 150–154
  Westview's approach to, 76–77, 78–79
  white students, 45, 113–114
  work ethic and, 151
Texas Assessment of Academic Skills,
    199n6
*Third International Mathematics and
    Science Study* (Schmidt, McKnight,
    & Raizen), 201n6
Thomas, Dr. (Grover Elementary
    principal), 74, 75, 83, 89
Tienda, M., 198n7
TIFs. *See* Tax Increment Financing zones
Torres, C. A., 9, 197n1
tourism, in Chicago, 134–135
tracking, 1, 57, 173–74
transnational movements
  economic changes from, 6
  of Latino/a identities, 106–107

Underwood, Mr. (Farley Elementary
    principal)
  accountability regime opposed by, 153
  qualification of, 141
  teacher support from, 148
  testing approach of, 152–154
unemployment, 7, 72
up-skilling labor, 26, 198n4
urban schools, xi–xii, 3–11, 181–183. *See
    also* Chicago Public Schools
U.S. Department of Housing and Urban
    Development. *See* HUD

Vallas, Paul, 36–37, 39–40, 58, 66, 99

Wacquant, L. J. D., 198n5
wages
  for African Americans, 27, 198n5
  gap in, 25–26, 50, 108, 160, 198n3,
    200n13
  for Latinos/as, 27, 137
  livable, 26–27
  poverty, xi–xii
  reduction in, 10
Washington, Harold, 32, 35, 37
Wells, A. S., 57
Westview Elementary School
  CAS at, use of, 85–86
  demographics of, 72
  educational success defined by, 80–81
  enrollment at, 74, 75
  facilities of, 75–76
  inquiry-based curriculum at, 91–92
  neighborhoods of, 72–74
  professional development at, 88–92
  researching, 194, 202n6
  resistance at, 93
  students sorted out at, 82
  surveillance of, 98
  teachers at, 76, 77–86, 93, 98, 102–103
  test taking approach of, 76–77, 78–79
white students
  at Brewer Elementary School, 108
  college prep percentage of, 53
  magnet school attendance by, 53

neighborhoods of, 50, 199n12
  in probation schools, 43
  testing, 45, 113–114
white supremacy, 31, 60, 120–121
Williams school, 67
Willis, Benjamin, 33
Wilson, W. J., 198n5
Workers Party, 12, 183–188
workforce. *See also* labor
  CCC reports on, 61–62
  CPS policies for new urban, 61–65
  differentiated identity development
    for, 63–65
  differentiated schooling prep for,
    62–63
  high school training for, 62
  racialization of, 64–65
  statistics predicted for, 61
World Bank, power of, increasing, 6
World Social Forum, globalization policy
  model of, 183, 191
World Trade Organization, power of,
  increasing, 6

Youth First Campaign, 191, 192
Youth Summit, 191
"yuppies," neighborhoods for, 198n7

Zero Tolerance discipline policy, 58,
  59–60, 190